Lecture Notes in Computer Science 10547

Commenced Publication in 1973
Founding and Former Series Editors:
Gerhard Goos, Juris Hartmanis, and Jan van Leeuwen

More information about this series at http://www.springer.com/series/7410

Giovanni Livraga · Chris Mitchell (Eds.)

Security and Trust Management

13th International Workshop, STM 2017
Oslo, Norway, September 14–15, 2017
Proceedings

 Springer

Editors
Giovanni Livraga (iD)
Università degli Studi di Milano
Crema
Italy

Chris Mitchell
University of London
Egham
UK

ISSN 0302-9743   ISSN 1611-3349   (electronic)
Lecture Notes in Computer Science
ISBN 978-3-319-68062-0   ISBN 978-3-319-68063-7   (eBook)
DOI 10.1007/978-3-319-68063-7

Library of Congress Control Number: 2017953412

LNCS Sublibrary: SL4 – Security and Cryptology

Printed on acid-free paper

This Springer imprint is published by Springer Nature
The registered company is Springer International Publishing AG
The registered company address is: Gewerbestrasse 11, 6330 Cham, Switzerland

Preface

This volume contains the papers selected for presentation at the 13th International Workshop on Security and Trust Management (STM 2017), held in Oslo, Norway, on September 14–15, 2017, in conjunction with the 22th European Symposium On Research In Computer Security (ESORICS 2017).

In response to the call for papers, 33 papers were submitted, and all submissions were evaluated on the basis of their significance, novelty, and technical quality. The Program Committee, comprising 30 members, performed an excellent task and with the help of additional reviewers all submissions went through a careful anonymous review process (three or more reviews per submission). As in previous years, reviewing was double-blind, that is, the identities of reviewers were not revealed to the authors of the papers and identities of authors were not revealed to the reviewers. The Program Committee's work was carried out electronically, yielding intensive discussions over a period of one week. Of the submitted papers, the Program Committee accepted ten full papers and six short papers for presentation at the workshop. Besides the technical program including the papers collated in these proceedings, the workshop featured an invited talk by the winner of the ERCIM STM WG 2017 Award for the best PhD thesis on security and trust management.

The credit for the success of STM 2017 belongs to a number of people, who devoted their time and energy to put together the workshop and deserve acknowledgment. We would like to thank all the members of the Program Committee and all the external reviewers, for their hard work in evaluating all the papers in a short time window, and for their active participation in the discussion and selection process. We are very grateful to everyone who gave assistance and ensured a smooth organization process: the ERCIM STM Steering Committee, and in particular its chair, Pierangela Samarati, for their guidance and support in the organization of the workshop; Angelo Genovese, for taking care of publicity; Sokratis Katsikas (ESORICS Workshop Chair), Einar Snekkenes (ESORICS General Chair), and Laura Georg (ESORICS Organization Chair), for their support in the workshop organization and logistics.

Last but certainly not least, thanks to all the authors who submitted papers and to all the workshop attendees. We hope you find the proceedings of STM 2017 interesting and an inspiration for your future research.

August 2017

Giovanni Livraga
Chris Mitchell

Organization

Program Chairs

Giovanni Livraga   Università degli Studi di Milano, Italy
Chris Mitchell   Royal Holloway, University of London, UK

Publicity Chair

Angelo Genovese   Università degli Studi di Milano, Italy

STM Steering Committee

Theo Dimitrakos   University of Kent, UK
Javier Lopez   University of Malaga, Spain
Fabio Martinelli   CNR, Italy
Sjouke Mauw   Université of Luxembourg, Luxembourg
Stig F. Mjølsnes   NTNU, Norway
Pierangela Samarati (Chair)   Università degli Studi di Milano, Italy
Ulrich Ultes-Nitsche   University of Fribourg, Switzerland

Program Committee

Ken Barker   University of Calgary, Canada
Colin Boyd   NTNU, Norway
David Chadwick   University of Kent, UK
Liqun Chen   University of Surrey, UK
Jorge Cuéllar   Siemens AG, Germany
Sabrina De Capitani   Università degli Studi di Milano, Italy
  di Vimercati
Josep Domingo-Ferrer   Universitat Rovira i Virgili, Spain
Sara Foresti   Università degli Studi di Milano, Italy
Joaquin Garcia-Alfaro   Telecom SudParis, France
Ehud Gudes   Ben-Gurion University, Israel
Michael Huth   Imperial College, UK
Costas Lambrinoudakis   University of Piraeus, Greece
Javier Lopez   University of Malaga, Spain
Fabio Martinelli   CNR, Italy
Sjouke Mauw   University of Luxembourg, Luxembourg
Catherine Meadows   NRL, USA
Stig F. Mjølsnes   NTNU, Norway
Charles Morisset   Newcastle University, UK
Siani Pearson   HP, UK

Günther Pernul	University of Regensburg, Germany
Marinella Petrocchi	CNR, Italy
Benoit Poletti	INCERT GIE, Luxembourg
Silvio Ranise	FBK, Italy
Ralf Sasse	ETH Zurich, Switzerland
Daniele Sgandurra	Royal Holloway, University of London, UK
Vicenç Torra	University of Skövde, Sweden
Fabian Van Den Broek	Radboud University of Nijmegen, The Netherlands
Vijay Varadharajan	University of Newcastle, Australia
Damien Vergnaud	ENS, France
Cong Wang	City University of Hong Kong, Hong Kong, SAR China

Additional Reviewers

Alexey Rabin	Andrea Saracino
Michael Hitchens	Luis Del Vasto
Sietse Ringers	Udaya Tupakula
Michael Kunz	Sergio Martinez
Florian Menges	Imad Mahaini
Patrick Ah-Fat	Sean Simpson
Fabian Böhm	Andrea Callia D'Iddio
Francesco Mercaldo	Carmen Fernandez
Rolando Trujillo	Brinda Hampiholi

Contents

Secure Systems

Cryptosystems and Applied Cryptography

Key Management for Versatile Pay-TV Services

Kazuto Ogawa[1]([✉]), Sakurako Tamura[2], and Goichiro Hanaoka[3]

[1] Japan Broadcasting Corporation, Tokyo, Japan
ogawa.k-cm@nhk.or.jp
[2] NTT Secure Platform Laboratories, Tokyo, Japan
tamura.sakurako@lab.ntt.co.jp
[3] National Institute of Advanced Industrial Science and Technology, Tokyo, Japan
hanaoka-goichiro@aist.go.jp

Abstract. The content of pay-TV services is encrypted and each subscriber has a security module that holds a decryption key. When subscribers want to receive the same pay-TV services that they receive at home outside their homes, they have to bring the security module with them. However, it is not easy to take the module out of the TV set. To enrich current and conventional pay-TV services and to make it easier for subscribers to obtain pay-TV services outside their homes, we propose a key management system using a temporary key, an attribute-based encryption (ABE) scheme, and a mobile terminal. The temporary key is not a conventional key, but has a backward compatibility. The ABE is used to restrict the time and location when and where the temporary key can be used. The mobile terminal has a role to take secret data related to the temporary key and ABE. In this system, a certain decryption key sk_t is stored in the mobile terminal. sk_t is used to decrypt a content key. Since sk_t is stored in a mobile terminal, it is vulnerable to being leaked. To protect services from such key leakage, we add a function to control when and where sk_t can be used. To introduce such a restriction, we employ an ABE scheme. The system uses ABE to exchange certain secret data between broadcasters and subscribers through communication networks. This key management system is secure against key leakage and enables subscribers obtain pay-TV services their homes.

Keywords: Pay-TV services · Functional encryption · Attribute · Valid period · Mobile terminal

1 Introduction

1.1 Background

Broadcasting and cable TV services encrypt their content before distributing it to subscribers for the purpose of copyright protection. Each subscriber needs a decoder with a security module for decrypting the content. In Japan, a smart card is used as a security module in broadcasting, and a decryption key is generated in the card [27]. Pay-TV services use the card to control the subscriber's

© Springer International Publishing AG 2017
G. Livraga and C. Mitchell (Eds.): STM 2017, LNCS 10547, pp. 3–18, 2017.
DOI: 10.1007/978-3-319-68063-7_1

access to their content. In particular, the card holds the subscriber's contract information, and decryption keys are generated from the information in the card.

If the card can be taken out of the TV receiver or set-top box, in principle, subscribers can get services outside the home. However, it is not easy to take the card out of receiver; in fact, breakage of cards is a concern.

On the other hand, if the decryption key(s) could be stored in mobile devices such as mobile phones and tablet PCs, subscribers would not need to take the card out or bring it with them. In this way, quality of service would be improved.

Nowadays, people can use hybrid systems, such as youview [32], HbbTV [30], Hulu [31], and Hybridcast [29], to obtain both broadcasting services through the air and network services through the Internet. In these systems, TV receivers and mobile terminals cooperate. This means that it becomes easy to transmit data from a receiver to a mobile terminal. However, when a third party can use the data transmitted into the mobile terminal, illegal use becomes a potential problem; particularly, copyrights may be infringed. Hence, when the data can be transmitted into the mobile terminal, countermeasures against illegal use of that data should be taken. Ogawa, Hanaoka, and Imai (OHI07) [20] proposed a method in which a decryption key is updated periodically and a temporary decryption key can be carried outside in order to enrich the current and conventional services. That is, the subscriber can obtain the same service outside as he or she would receive at home only during a limited period. Thus, even if the decryption key is leaked, the damage it causes would not extend beyond the valid period of the key.

1.2   Contributions

OHI07 controls a time during which a decryption key can be used. We extend this control and propose a key management system that can control when and where the key can be used. OHI07 cannot control the location of use and it is difficult to add a control function to it for this purpose.

First, we consider a situation in which a subscriber carries decryption keys and obtains the same services outside that they receive at home, e.g., someone travelling on business or sightseeing. In such a situation, where the subscriber stays during the period is likely decided before leaving home. Here, let us suppose that the subscriber would want to obtain services while staying at a hotel. Furthermore, the time during which the subscriber obtains the services at the hotel is limited. Then, generating a decryption key that can be used at the hotel and at the time and storing the key in the mobile terminal electronically makes it possible to obtain the expected services at the time and location the subscriber wants.

In the proposed system, we introduce a temporary work key k_{w_t} and a functional encryption scheme (FE) [1,3,7,18,21], and use a mobile terminal. Particularly, FE is an efficient tool to restrict the time and location. More concretely, we use an attribute-based encryption scheme (ABE) [4,6,12,15] that is a kind of FE and that can control each subscriber's access to content (data) according to the subscriber's attribute.

We will use the following travel situation as an example:

- travel destination (hotel location): XYZ hotel in Oslo, Norway
- travel duration: 9/11–15.

These data are used as attributes in the ABE scheme. However, it is impossible to substitute the current encryption schemes with the ABE scheme, since there are a lot of subscribers who have receivers that only work the current encryption scheme. To have backward compatibility, we need to add functions to the current systems. That is, the new system should not supersede the current system. It should use ABE to encrypt certain personal data of the subscriber. Hence, the ABE-encrypted data should not be transmitted through the air, because the capacity of broadcasting channels is not so large. Here, we introduce a temporary work key k_{w_t}, which plays a similar role as the current work key k_w and which has a valid period. A function to encrypt a content key k_s by using k_{w_t} is added to the current system. k_s is encrypted by using k_w and k_{w_t} simultaneously, and two versions of the ciphertext of k_s are transmitted simultaneously.

A function to encrypt k_{w_t} by using ABE is added to the current system. Before a subscriber gets k_{w_t}, the decryption key sk_t of ABE is generated under conditions of the above attributes. The subscriber obtains it through the communication networks, stores sk_t in the mobile terminal, and brings it to the travel destination. The data stored in the mobile terminal is sk_t, not a ciphertext of k_{w_t}, because the broadcasters mind that the k_{w_t} is extracted from the ciphertext and sk_t does not include any information on k_{w_t}. A ciphertext of k_{w_t} is necessary at the hotel; in this case, it is transmitted through communication networks to the mobile terminal just before it receives the services. The capacity of the broadcasting channel is not large, and using the communication networks enables the real-time property to be kept.

The proposed system uses two time and location data: data collected when the subscriber is at home and data when the subscriber measures at the hotel. Naturally, there are errors in these data, and then, we chose an ABE scheme that can specify the range of attributes carefully among a lot of ABE schemes.

By these techniques, the subscriber uses sk_t and the ciphertext of k_{w_t} to enjoy the enriched services.

1.3 Related Work

Our key management system uses time and location data as attributes of the key to control the access to the content. As far as we know, there has not been any related proposal except for OHI07 regarding access control to Pay-TV services and OHI07 cannot control the location where the decryption key is used.

However, a position based cryptography scheme (PBC) [9,11,14,23], which controls the decryption of a ciphertext according to the location the message sender specifies, and time released encryption scheme (TRE) [5,13,16,17, 19,22,26], which controls the decryption of a ciphertext according to the time the message sender specifies, can be used for the same purpose. That is, by considering position data as an attribute, PBC can be viewed as a kind of ABE, and because the time data be considered an attribute, TRE can also be viewed as a kind of ABE.

For PBC, a correct and unmodified position should be used, or else the security of the ciphertext cannot be guaranteed. For this reason, position authentication has been studied [9,23]. The basic idea involves a measurement of the response. That is, the speed of the response depends on the distance between the sender and receiver, and hence, the measurement of the response speed is an effective method against spoofing of the position. The concept was first proposed by Brands and Chaum [8]. Chandran et al. used a query challenge for this measurement [10]. Dziembowski and Zdanowicz's scheme [14] assumes a noisy measurement channel. Chandran et al. later proposed a scheme using a bounded storage model [11].

By considering position data as an attribute, PBC can be viewed as a kind of ABE. Although studies on PBC schemes are on the decline for this reason, a lot of protocols that control something using position data, including ones for RFIDs, car security, applications using GPS, etc., have been developed.

May proposed the first TRE [19]. Hwang et al. scheme [16] decrypts the ciphertext before the appointed time by using an additional release key. Baek, Safavi-Naini, and Susilo proposed a scheme [5] that generates a decryption key by using a token published periodically by a trusted third party (TTP). Yoshida et al. [26] improved Baek et al.'s scheme; their scheme can generate a decryption key at a later time than the appointed one. Dent and Tang [13] revised the security model of Hwang et al.'s scheme and proposed a new approach using KEM-DEM frameworks. Paterson and Quaglia' scheme can specify a certain time range [22]. Kasamatsu et al. proposed a scheme [17] whose computational cost and data sizes are small and that has forward security.

Because the time data can be considered an attribute, TRE can also be viewed as a kind of ABE. Currently, the studies are included in that on ABE.

A combination of PBC and TRE can realize the access control to the content, which allows the subscribers obtain outside the home identical services to those inside the home. However, two distinct encryption schemes would have to be used in both encryption and decryption, and this is inefficient.

2   Preliminaries

2.1   Current Broadcasting System

There are a lot of pay-TV services in North America, Europe, and Asia. The systems in North America and Europe are various from broadcaster to broadcaster, and their details are not disclosed. Although the Common Descrambling System of Digital Video Broadcasting (DVB-CSA) [28] is standardized in Europe, non-disclosure agreement is necessary to see its details, and naturally, the details cannot be disclosed. On the other hand, Japanese broadcasting system is disclosed. Figure 1 shows the current broadcasting system used in Japan [27].

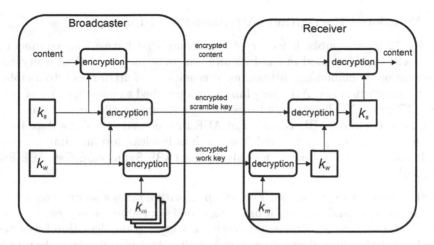

Fig. 1. Current broadcasting system: k_s is a content (scramble) key, k_w is a work key, and k_m is a master key.

The broadcaster encrypts the content M by using a scramble key k_s. It broadcasts the encrypted content $C_M = Enc(k_s, M)$. $Enc(k, M)$ denotes that the plaintext M is encrypted by using a key k. k_s is encrypted by using a work key k_w, and the broadcaster generates an encrypted scramble key $C_{k_s} = Enc(k_w, k_s)$. In addition, k_w is encrypted by using a master key k_m, and the broadcaster generates an encrypted work key $C_{k_w} = Enc(k_m, k_w)$. C_M, C'_{k_s}, and C'_{k_w} are multiplexed and transmitted to the subscribers.

There are multiple symmetric encryption schemes in the Japanese system. That is, the scrambling scheme used for content encryption is different from the encryption scheme used for k_s and k_w encryption. This difference does not affect the proposed system. Hence, we use the same notation $Enc(\cdot, \cdot)$ as in symmetric encryption.

Each receiver needs a smart card as a security module that holds a k_m. It should be noted that each smart card has a distinct k_m and the broadcasters can transmit private contract information to each subscriber (receiver) by using this k_m. C_M, C_{k_s}, and C_{k_w}, which are transmitted through the air, are demultiplexed in the receiver. k_w is decrypted by using k_m in the smart card as follows: $k_w = Dec(k_m, C_{k_w})$. $Dec(k, C)$ denotes that a ciphertext C is decrypted by using a key k. k_s is decrypted by using k_w: $k_s = Dec(k_w, C_{k_s})$. k_s is sent to the receiver, and M is decrypted (descrambled) by using k_s: $M = Dec(k_s, C_M)$ in the receiver.

Since all the encryption schemes are symmetric, their encryption and decryption keys are identical. Regarding decryption, the descrambling scheme used for content decryption is different from that of k_w and k_s decryption in the actual Japanese broadcasting system, but this difference does not affect the proposed system. Hence, we use the same notation $Dec(\cdot, \cdot)$.

2.2 Functional Encryption (Attribute-Based Encryption)

FEs [4,6,12,15] are public key encryption schemes that have advanced functionalities. ABEs are included in the FEs and can prescribe the logic of encryption or decryption by embedding attributes or conditions of attributes into a ciphertext or a decryption key. Arbitrary functions, described as combinations of AND gates, OR gates, NOT gates, and threshold gates, are possible conditions.

Ciphertext-policy ABE is a kind of ABE that embeds attribute data into a decryption key and a policy (condition), such as Boolean formula, into a ciphertext. It consists of the following four algorithms (ABE_Setup, ABE_Gen, ABE_Enc, ABE_Dec).

- ABE_Setup(1^λ) $\rightarrow$ (msk, pk): The set-up algorithm takes a security parameter 1^λ as an input and outputs a master key msk and a public key pk.
- ABE_Gen(msk, S) $\rightarrow$ sk: The decryption key generation algorithm takes msk and attributes of a decryption key S as inputs and outputs a decryption key sk.
- ABE_Enc(pk, β, M) $\rightarrow$ C: The encryption algorithm takes pk, attributes and its condition β, such as a Boolean function, and a message M as inputs and outputs a ciphertext C.
- ABE_Dec(sk, C, β) $\rightarrow$ M: The decryption algorithm takes sk, C, and β as inputs and outputs M.

The proposed system uses the above ciphertext-policy ABE, more specifically, one in [4] that can assign an attribute with a range. The range is included in β.

3 Proposal: Key Management System

There are two kinds of broadcasting service: through the air (via the broadcasting satellite, communication satellite, or terrestrial station) and through communication cable networks. The ones through the air provide the same services to subscribers in a wide area, while the ones through cables provide services in a limited area.

In this paper, we consider a situation in which a subscriber travels to a certain destination and wants to obtain services there that are identical to ones he or she receives at home. That means wider service area is preferable. Hence, we will focus on services through the air. In addition, we assume that the subscriber signed a contract with a certain broadcaster and can obtain services at home. In the proposed system, this services are extended and the subscribers can obtain services outside the home.

Below, we explain how to apply the system to the Japanese broadcasting system as an example.

3.1 Discussion: Bringing Current Keys

The simplest way to obtain the same services outside the home is to bring a security module from the home to the destination. However, it is difficult to dismount the security module even if it is a smart card.

Let us consider the way to take out the keys, k_s, k_w, and k_m, used in the current system. If the subscriber takes them out from the security module electronically, stores it in his/her mobile terminal, and transmits the key from the mobile terminal to the receiver at the hotel electronically, he or she can easily obtain the desired services outside the home.

k_s is updated every two seconds and it is not practical to bring all k_s's used during travel, as the number of keys would be enormous.

k_w's update period varies from channel to channel and broadcaster to broadcaster, but the key is not updated as frequently as the change of on-air programs. That is, an update of k_w leads to an update of the subscriber's contract, and from the viewpoint of the service continuity, it is impossible for the contract to change as frequently as an on-air program. If the subscriber has a long-term contract, such as several months, with a broadcaster, it is easy for the broadcaster to continue to use the same k_w for several months. However, such long-term use leads to risk of key exposure and is not preferable from the viewpoint of security. Even if there is a long-term contract, k_w should be updated periodically; in practice, it is updated almost every month. Although it is possible to take out k_w and this might be practical in the sense that the number of keys that the subscriber should carry is small, its valid period is too long considering the potential damage caused by its exposure. Broadcasters would thus prefer shorter term keys.

k_m is used only when contract between a broadcaster and a subscriber is changed or updated or when k_w is updated. Hence, it is not appropriate to take out k_m to obtain services outside the home without any contract change.

From the above discussion, there is no adequate key among the three that can be taken out. Instead, what is required is a key that acts as a work key and that has a moderately long valid time.

3.2   Discussion: Key Transmission Through the Air

In the previous section, k_s should not be taken outside from the viewpoint of the number of keys and k_w should not be taken outside from the viewpoint of the valid term of keys. In this section, we show that an encrypted k_s or k_w should not be transmitted through the air for the private use of this extended service, either.

When the encrypted k_s is transmitted, a distinct encryption key must be used for each subscriber. When the number of subscribers is small, the broadcaster can transmit the encrypted k_s's through the air, but when the number is large, the limited transmission capacity of broadcasting makes this difficult. That is, the amount of additional transmitted data increases in proportion to the number of subscribers, since every encrypted k_s is different from that for the other subscribers. For example, it would take about one hour for the data to be sent to every security module in Japan. Although the number of people who spend time outside the home during the golden week, silver week, summer, and New Years holidays in Japan is smaller than the number of all security modules, it is still a huge number. Assuming that almost all vacationers would want to use the proposed system, it would take too long a time to transmit the encrypted k_s's; k_s changes every two seconds, so it would be impossible to transmit all encrypted k_s in real-time. As one of the strong points of broadcasting is that it provides identical services simultaneously to all subscribers, but the loss of the real-time property would eliminate it. Hence, it is not practical to transmit encrypted k_s's through the air.

Now let us consider transmitting an encrypted k_w through the air for the private use of the extended service. k_w is a long-term key, and it is not necessary to transmit an encrypted k_w or decrypt it in real-time. That is, although the subscriber has to wait until the encrypted k_w to be transmitted for the service to start, after it is decrypted, he or she can seamlessly obtain services in real-time. In this sense, k_w is more adequate than k_s. However, k_w is common for all subscribers. That is, once k_w is decrypted, it can be used at any time (sometimes for several months) and at any location even when and where the subscribers assigned before the travel. The damage caused by the leakage of k_w would thus be unacceptably large from the viewpoint of content copyright protection. Finer control of the time and location is required.

3.3   Discussion: Use of Mobile Terminal and Attribute-Based Encryption Scheme

If the mobile terminal of a subscriber stores a key, there is a risk that the key may be leaked unintentionally or intentionally. The leaked data can be easily copied, and a broadcaster cannot use a system that does not have any countermeasure against such leakage. It is difficult to sweep the anxious away, but it is important to take a measure not to extend the damage caused by the key leakage.

We need finer control of the key. In Sect. 3.1, we described that it is not preferable to take out k_s, k_w, and k_m because of their roles, importance to maintaining security, and number. The discussion in Sect. 3.2 indicates that it is not preferable to transmit k_s and k_w through the air for the private extended service to the subscriber because of the lack of transmission capacity and security. In addition, it was pointed out that keys that act together a work key and that have a moderately long valid time and fine control of when and where the subscriber receives services are required. We thus introduce a temporary work key k_{w_t} and the ABE scheme. In the following, we discuss how k_{w_t} can be used to realize a secure key management system.

The system we propose minimizes the damage caused by leak of data stored in the mobile terminal and can control when and where the data can be used. We employ an FE, especially an ABE. We use the location of the hotel, and the travel date as attributes of ABE. The attributes make it possible to control when and where a leaked key can be used and to lessen the value of the key to other people.

The easy way to use ABE is that a broadcaster encrypts k_w by using ABE and transmits the encrypted k_w. In this case, a subscriber carries a decryption key and decrypts k_w at the hotel. However, as described in Sect. 3.1, it is not preferable to have subscribers bring k_w with them, so this issue remains even if ABE is used.

To deal with this issue, we use a temporary work key k_{w_t} that has a valid period and is updated frequently. k_w is used to encrypt k_s, and k_{w_t} is used for the same purpose. However, the update period of k_{w_t} is shorter than that of k_w. The shorter update period makes finer control of the key possible. In this paper, we set the update period to one day. k_{w_t} is changed every day, so the damage caused by a leak of k_{w_t} is limited to one day.

If k_{w_t} cannot be used except for the assigned time period, security level of the system holds high. We thus need a way how for the subscriber to carry k_{w_t} securely and efficiently outside the home.

If the plaintext of k_{w_t} is stored in the mobile terminal, it is vulnerable, and thus, copyright of the content may be violated. While it is possible to encrypt k_{w_t} by using k_m, it is impossible to control the location at which k_{w_t} is used. ABE can be used to control the time and location, but as mentioned in Sect. 3.2, it takes time until k_{w_t} is obtained, and this threatens the real-time property. To deal with this problem, we modify the system that has real-time property. The modified system uses both communication networks and broadcasting channels, so that broadcasters can respond to each subscriber's request almost in real-time. Such real-time service cannot be realized without communication networks.

In addition, mobile terminals work effectively to respond each subscriber's request. People merely lend their mobile terminal and the terminal can be used for the owner's authentication.

There are three key management methods for ABE schemes. The first is that the subscriber carries both an ABE-encrypted temporary work key $C_{k_{w_t}} =$ ABE_Enc(pk, β, k_{m_t}) and sk_t stored in the mobile terminal. The second is that the subscriber carries only $C_{k_{w_t}}$ in the mobile terminal. The third is that the subscriber carries only sk_t in the mobile terminal.

In the first method, the subscriber has both a ciphertext and its corresponding decryption key, and he/she can decrypt the ciphertext and obtain k_{w_t} when desired. Hence, the method is as same as one in which the subscriber carries a plaintext k_{w_t}; that means it is vulnerable to key leakage. In the second method, the data the subscriber gets before its travel is deeply related to k_{w_t}. Compared with the third method, it has more chance of k_{w_t} being extracted from the data of the subscriber. That is, broadcasters would find the third method preferable to the second.

In addition, the operation related to k_{w_t} should be the same as that of k_w, since the broadcaster does not want any special operation. Hence, the broadcaster can generate k_{w_t} whenever it wants. If the broadcaster generates k_{w_t} just before k_{w_t} becomes valid, the subscriber may not obtain k_{w_t} before beginning the journey. That is, considering the timing at which the broadcaster generates k_{w_t}, the third method is preferable, because the subscriber carries only sk_t in the mobile terminal. In the following, we will assume that only sk_t is stored in the mobile terminal.

We show more details. The subscriber needs to obtain a decryption key $sk_t =$ ABE_Gen(msk, S) before beginning to travel, where S is the set of attributes and it includes the location data of the hotel (latitude, longitude) $= (p_{px}, p_{py})$ and travel period t_p. To obtain sk_t, the subscriber sends (p_{px}, p_{py}) and t_p to the key issuance center through communication networks. The key issuance center generates sk_t and returns it to the subscriber. The subscriber gets sk_t, stores it in the mobile terminal, and takes it with him/her.

For the subscriber to obtain services at the hotel, the key issuance center has to generate an ABE-encrypted k_{w_t} by using the subscriber's current location and current time. That is, when the mobile terminal requests k_{w_t} to the key issuance center, it sends its GPS data. This GPS data contains the current location data (p_{cx}, p_{cy}) and the current time t_c. The key issuance center generates an ABE-encrypted temporary work key $C_{k_{w_t}} = \mathsf{ABE\_Enc}(pk, \beta, k_{w_t})$ by using the data as attributes and the policy β. Errors are naturally contained in the GPS data. In addition, there would be differences between (p_{px}, p_{py}) and (p_{cx}, p_{cy}) and between t_p and t_c in principle. For this reason, we chose the ABE scheme, which can specify a range of attributes [4]. Concretely, the policy of ABE is as follows: $\beta = (p_{px} \in \{p_{cxl}, p_{cxu}\}) \wedge (p_{py} \in \{p_{cyl}, p_{cyu}\}) \wedge (t_p = t_c)$, where $p_{cxl} = p_{cx} - \epsilon_x$, $p_{cxu} = p_{cx} + \epsilon_x$, $p_{cyl} = p_{cy} - \epsilon_y$, $p_{cyu} = p_{cy} + \epsilon_y$, where ϵ_x, ϵ_y are acceptable error values with regard to latitude and longitude, and where $\wedge$ denotes an AND gate.

At the hotel, the subscriber obtains an ABE-encrypted temporary work key $C_{k_{w_t}}$ from Key issuance center through communication networks, decrypts a temporary work key $k_{w_t} = \mathsf{ABE\_Dec}(sk_t, C_{k_{w_t}})$ by using sk_t brought from the home, and obtains services at the hotel.

There is a limit to the transmission capacity if $C_{k_{w_t}}$ and sk_t are sent through the air, and the subscribers may have to wait a half an hour or more. However, in the above method, the subscriber can get services without having to wait a long time. That is, he or she can get k_{w_t} at the desired time, and the quality of services improves.

The key point of this key management system is the use of a temporary work key k_{w_t}. k_{w_t}'s role is different from that of k_w, so the new functions associated with k_{w_t} should be added to the conventional system. New data signal(s) must be transmitted from the broadcasting station. In particular, the operation of k_{w_t} should be the same as that of k_w; hence, the broadcaster encrypts k_s by using k_w and k_{w_t} simultaneously, generates $C_{ks} = Enc(k_w, k_s)$ and $C_{ks_t} = Enc(k_{w_t}, k_s)$, and transmits C_{ks} and C_{ks_t} simultaneously to all subscribers through the air. After receiving the signal, receivers at home decrypt C_{ks} by using k_w and generate $k_s = Dec(k_w, C_{ks})$. On the other hand, the receivers at the hotels decrypt C_{ks_t} by using k_{w_t} and generate $k_s = Dec(k_{w_t}, C_{ks_t})$. Subsequently, receivers at both locations obtain the same services.

The roles of valid time of k_{w_t} and the time attribute of ABE are slightly different. The valid time of k_{w_t} is a countermeasure against work key leakage and meets the requirements of broadcasters. On the other hand, the time attribute of ABE is a restriction on the decryption time.

3.4 Proposed System

Figure 2 illustrates the system on which the above service is offered. The entities in the system are as follows:

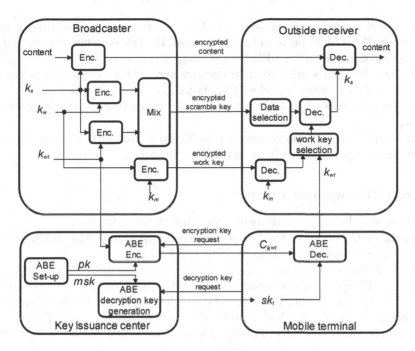

Fig. 2. Proposed system: Enc. and Dec. denote encryption and decryption blocks, respectively.

- Mobile terminal: A subscriber that has a contract with a broadcaster.
- Broadcaster: It encrypts content and transmits it to all subscribers.
- Key issuance center: It generates the keys regarding to ABE.
- Outside receiver: Receiver at a hotel.

New functions associated with k_{w_t} have to be added to each entity. In particular, the broadcaster has to have a new function to generate k_{w_t} and a function to encrypt k_s by using k_{w_t}. The similar function is standardized as an extension of the system (Part 3, Chap. 3 in [27]) and the impact on the broadcaster is light. The mobile terminal is a new entity, which is not used in conventional broadcasting services. It collaborates with receivers, which receive k_{w_t} from it, and decrypts k_s by using k_{w_t}. Here, we assume that the outside receivers do not have any contract with broadcasters, and hence, that the outside receivers cannot get any k_w. However, in reality, some outside receivers may actually have contracts, so a function to select one among k_w and k_{w_t} and a function to select one among C_{ks} and C_{ks_t} are necessary. The functions required by each entity are as follows.

The key issuance center is a new entity. It has, at least, the following four functions: (1) a function to obtain k_{w_t} from the broadcaster, (2) a function to set up an ABE scheme, (3) a function to generate a decryption key sk_t, and (4) a function to encrypt k_{w_t} and generate $C_{k_{w_t}} = \mathsf{ABE\_Enc}(pk, \beta, k_{w_t})$.

The mobile terminals need at least three functions: (1) a function to store sk_t securely, (2) a function to obtain $C_{k_{w_t}}$ from the key issuance center, and (3) a function to decrypt $k_{w_t} = \mathsf{ABE\_Dec}(sk_t, C_{k_{w_t}})$.

Two new functions are added to the receivers: (1) a function to select k_{w_t} not k_w and (2) a function to select C_{kst} not C_{ks}.

The broadcasters have a new function: (1) a function that encrypts k_s by using k_{w_t}.

These additional functions make it possible for subscribers to obtain the same services that they receive at home outside their homes.

3.5   Key Management Procedure

Figure 3 shows the key management procedure in the system.

To prepare the services, the key issuance center performs $\mathsf{ABE\_Setup}(1^\lambda)$ and generates master and public keys of ABE (msk, pk).

As Fig. 2 shows, two versions of an encrypted scramble key $C_{ks} = Enc(k_w, k_s)$ and $C_{kst} = Enc(k_{w_t}, k_s)$ are transmitted by the broadcaster, and the outside receiver selects one version. Precisely, the security module in the receiver selects one version. Generally, the hotel does not have a contract for pay-TV services, and it does not have any k_w of the pay-TV services. When the subscriber brings

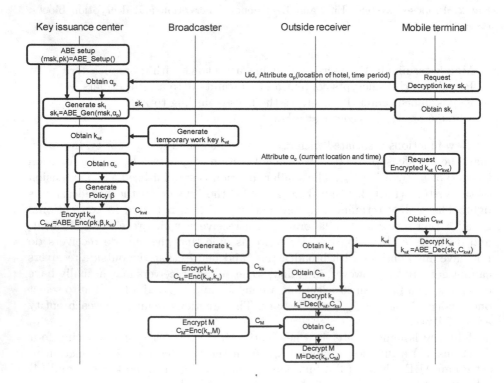

Fig. 3. Key management procedure of the system

the key k_{w_t} in its mobile terminal, k_{w_t} is transmitted to the outside receiver. The receiver selects C_{ks_t} and decrypts it by using k_{w_t}. If the subscriber does not bring the key k_{w_t}, he or she cannot obtain the services.

In addition, when and where the subscriber uses the services must be specified before travel. If the actual time or location is different from the specified time or location, he or she cannot obtain the service. These two controls are enabled by the following procedure.

When the key issuance center generates a decryption key sk_t, the attributes of the subscriber are sent to the key issuance center and the sk_t associated with the attributes is generated. When the key issuance center generates an encrypted k_{w_t}, a ciphertext $C_{k_{w_t}}$ associated with the policy regarding the attributes and their error range is generated. When the mobile terminal decrypts k_{w_t}, k_{w_t} can be decrypted if the set of attributes of sk_t matches the policy of $C'_{k_{w_t}}$.

k_{w_t} is decrypted in the mobile terminal and is transmitted to the security module in the outside receiver after communication between the mobile terminal and the outside receiver is established. k_{w_t} is then used to decrypt $k_s = Dec(k_{w_t}, C_{ks})$ by using $C_{ks} = Enc(k_{w_t}, k_s)$, and finally, content M is decrypted $M = Dec(k_s, C_M)$ by using k_s and $C_M = Enc(k_s, M)$. The details of the procedure are as follows:

(1) The key issuance center performs ABE_Setup(a^λ) to prepare the services and generates (msk, pk).
(2) A subscriber sends its identifier (Uid) and its attributes (time when staying at the hotel and location of the hotel $\alpha_p := ((p_{px}, p_{py}), t_p)$) to the key issuance center by using his/her mobile terminal.
(3) The key issuance center checks the Uid and the subscriber's contract, generates a decryption key $sk_t = $ ABE_Gen(msk, α_p) and returns sk_t to the subscriber.
(4) The subscriber stores sk_t in the mobile terminal.
(5) A broadcaster generates a temporary work key k_{w_t} and sends it to the key issuance center.
(6) The subscriber obtains his/her current location (p_{cx}, p_{cy}) by using the GPS function of the mobile terminal.
(7) The subscriber sends a decryption key request including the subscriber's attributes $\alpha_c := ((p_{cx}, p_{cy}), t_c)$ to the key issuance center.
(8) The key issuance center extracts $p_c = (p_{cx}, p_{cy})$ from α_c, and calculates the range of attributes $p_{cxl} \sim p_{cxu}$ $p_{cyl} \sim p_{cyu}$, where (ϵ_x, ϵ_y) are errors of latitude and longitude and they are decided previously, and where $p_{cxl} = p_{cx} - \epsilon_x$, $p_{cxu} = p_{cx} + \epsilon_x$, $p_{cyl} = p_{cy} - \epsilon_y$, $p_{cyu} = p_{cy} + \epsilon_y$ are upper and lower bounds of latitude and longitude.
(9) The key issuance center generates an encrypted temporary work key $C_{kwt} = $ ABE_Enc(pk, β, k_{w_t}) by using a public key pk and a policy $\beta = (p_{px} \in \{p_{cxl}, p_{cxu}\}) \wedge (p_{py} \in \{p_{cyl}, p_{cyu}\}) \wedge (t_p = t_c)$ and transmits C_{kwt} to the mobile terminal through communication networks.
(10) The mobile terminal decrypts the temporary work key $k_{w_t} = $ ABE_Dec(sk_t, C_{kwt}) from an encrypted temporary work key C_{kwt} transmitted through communication networks.

(11) The subscriber establishes a link between his/her mobile terminal and the receiver at the outside receiver (at the hotel) and sends k_{w_t} from the mobile terminal to the outside receiver.

(12) The outside receiver decrypts the scramble key $k_s = Dec(k_{w_t}, C_{k_s})$ by using k_{w_t}.

(13) Finally, the outside receiver decrypts content $M = Dec(k_s, C_M)$ by using k_s.

The acceptable error range (ϵ_x, ϵ_y) between location data $p_p = (p_{px}, p_{py})$ obtained from the hotel's address and the location data $p_c = (p_{cx}, p_{cy})$ obtained by using the GPS function of mobile terminal should be adequately determined according to the services to be provided.

4   Conclusion

We proposed a key management system that allows subscribers enjoy versatile broadcasting services. The subscribers can obtain services identical to those they normally receive at home outside their homes. The system uses a temporary key that has compatibility with the conventional key, an ABE scheme that can assign a range of attributes [4], and a mobile terminal. Although the system needs a key issuance center, it does not impact the conventional broadcasting system in a big way and has backward compatibility.

The current location data comes from the GPS function of a mobile terminal. The terminal is the subscriber's and there are a lot of reports on modifying GPS data. If the mobile terminal has a secure memory and can store a signing key in the memory, and if the mobile terminal has a high-performance CPU, the terminal can sign its GPS data electronically and the signature would be an effective countermeasure against modification attacks on GPS data. If the terminal does not have a high-performance CPU, the nearest mobile station or edge router should be used as a TTP, and the TTP should issue the current location and time instead of the mobile terminal. However, mobile stations and edge routers are not densely allocated, and in many cases, the nearest station or router would be far away from, say, the hotel where the subscriber is staying, and the distance between the mobile terminal and the nearest station or router depends on the station or router allocation plan of the communications provider. Subsequently, such stations and routers are impractical. Recently, a lot of researches has gone into mobile edge computing (MEC) [2, 24, 25, 33] and edge computers on the mobile networks handling loads instead of mobile terminals. An edge computer could be used as a TTP, but it has yet to be decided where and how many computers are to be assigned.

An actual system must be trustworthy. A digital signature scheme or TTP should be considered for this purpose. Efficiency is also important in practice. The ABE schemes used in our system have a heavier load than that of conventional encryption schemes, such as RSA, but the number of processes involving them in the mobile terminal during travel is only one and the load only lasts a number of seconds. Therefore, a subscriber would not likely find the load of the ABE process to be unacceptable. On the other hand, the load of the key issuance center would be much heavier, especially if the number of subscribers is large. That means we have to construct a system with a lighter load.

Acknowledgment. A part of this work is supported by JST CREST grant number JPMJCR1688.

References

1. Agrawal, S., Freeman, D.M., Vaikuntanathan, V.: Functional encryption for inner product predicates from learning with errors. In: Lee, D.H., Wang, X. (eds.) ASIACRYPT 2011. LNCS, vol. 7073, pp. 21–40. Springer, Heidelberg (2011). doi:10.1007/978-3-642-25385-0_2
2. Ahmed, A., Ahmed, E.: A survey on mobile edge computing. In: Proceedings of IEEE ISCO 2016. IEEE (2016)
3. Attrapadung, N., Libert, B.: Functional encryption for public-attribute inner products: achieving constant-size ciphertexts with adaptive security or support for negation. J. Math. Cryptol. 5(2), 115–158 (2012)
4. Attrapadung, N., Hanaoka, G., Ogawa, K., Ohtake, G., Watanabe, H., Yamada, S.: Attribute-based encryption for range attributes. In: Zikas, V., De Prisco, R. (eds.) SCN 2016. LNCS, vol. 9841, pp. 42–61. Springer, Cham (2016). doi:10.1007/978-3-319-44618-9_3
5. Baek, J., Safavi-Naini, R., Susilo, W.: Token-controlled public key encryption. In: Deng, R.H., Bao, F., Pang, H.H., Zhou, J. (eds.) ISPEC 2005. LNCS, vol. 3439, pp. 386–397. Springer, Heidelberg (2005). doi:10.1007/978-3-540-31979-5_33
6. Bethencourt, J., Sahai, A., Waters, B.: Ciphertext-policy attribute-based encryption. In: Proceedings of IEEE S&P 2007, pp. 321–334. IEEE (2007)
7. Boneh, D., Sahai, A., Waters, B.: Functional encryption: definitions and challenges. In: Ishai, Y. (ed.) TCC 2011. LNCS, vol. 6597, pp. 253–273. Springer, Heidelberg (2011). doi:10.1007/978-3-642-19571-6_16
8. Brands, S., Chaum, D.: Distance-bounding protocols. In: Helleseth, T. (ed.) EUROCRYPT 1993. LNCS, vol. 765, pp. 344–359. Springer, Heidelberg (1994). doi:10.1007/3-540-48285-7_30
9. Capkun, S., Hubaux, J.: Secure positioning of wireless devices with application to sensor networks. In: Proceedings of IEEE Infocom 2005, pp. 1917–1928. IEEE (2005)
10. Chandran, N., Goyal, V., Moriarty, R., Ostrovsky, R.: Position based cryptography. In: Halevi, S. (ed.) CRYPTO 2009. LNCS, vol. 5677, pp. 391–407. Springer, Heidelberg (2009). doi:10.1007/978-3-642-03356-8_23
11. Chandran, N., Goyal, V., Moriarty, R., Ostrovsky, R.: Position-based cryptography. SIAM J. Comput. 43(4), 1291–1341 (2014). SIAM
12. Chen, J., Wee, H.: Semi-adaptive attribute-based encryption and improved delegation for Boolean formula. In: Abdalla, M., De Prisco, R. (eds.) SCN 2014. LNCS, vol. 8642, pp. 277–297. Springer, Cham (2014). doi:10.1007/978-3-319-10879-7_16
13. Dent, A.W., Tang, Q.: Revisiting the security model for timed-release encryption with pre-open capability. In: Garay, J.A., Lenstra, A.K., Mambo, M., Peralta, R. (eds.) ISC 2007. LNCS, vol. 4779, pp. 158–174. Springer, Heidelberg (2007). doi:10.1007/978-3-540-75496-1_11

14. Dziembowski, S., Zdanowicz, M.: Position-based cryptography from noisy channels. In: Pointcheval, D., Vergnaud, D. (eds.) AFRICACRYPT 2014. LNCS, vol. 8469, pp. 300–317. Springer, Cham (2014). doi:10.1007/978-3-319-06734-6_19
15. Goyal, V., Pandey, O., Sahai, A., Waters, B.: Attribute-based encryption for fine-grained access control of encrypted data. In: Proceedings of ACM CCS 2006, pp. 89–98. ACM (2006)
16. Hwang, Y.H., Yum, D.H., Lee, P.J.: Timed-release encryption with pre-open capability and its application to certified e-mail system. In: Zhou, J., Lopez, J., Deng, R.H., Bao, F. (eds.) ISC 2005. LNCS, vol. 3650, pp. 344–358. Springer, Heidelberg (2005). doi:10.1007/11556992_25
17. Kasamatsu, K., Matsuda, T., Emura, K., Attrapadung, N., Hanaoka, G., Imai, H.: Time-specific encryption from forward-secure encryption: generic and direct constructions. Int. J. Inf. Secur. 15(5), 549–57 (2016)
18. Lewko, A., Okamoto, T., Sahai, A., Takashima, K., Waters, B.: Fully secure functional encryption: attribute-based encryption and (hierarchical) inner product encryption. In: Gilbert, H. (ed.) EUROCRYPT 2010. LNCS, vol. 6110, pp. 62–91. Springer, Heidelberg (2010). doi:10.1007/978-3-642-13190-5_4
19. May, T.: Time-release crypto (1993). http://www.cyphernet.org/cyphernomicon/chapter14/14.5.html
20. Ogawa, K., Hanaoka, G., Imai, H.: Traitor tracing scheme secure against key exposure and its application to anywhere TV service. IEICE Trans. Fundam. Electron. Commun. Comput. Sci. E90–A(5), 1000–1011 (2007). IEICE
21. Okamoto, T., Takashima, K.: Fully secure functional encryption with general relations from the decisional linear assumption. In: Rabin, T. (ed.) CRYPTO 2010. LNCS, vol. 6223, pp. 191–208. Springer, Heidelberg (2010). doi:10.1007/978-3-642-14623-7_11
22. Paterson, K.G., Quaglia, E.A.: Time-specific encryption. In: Garay, J.A., De Prisco, R. (eds.) SCN 2010. LNCS, vol. 6280, pp. 1–16. Springer, Heidelberg (2010). doi:10.1007/978-3-642-15317-4_1
23. Sastry, N., Shankar, U., Wagner, D.: Secure vefirication of location claims. In: Proceedings of ACM Wireless Security 2003, pp. 1–10. ACM (2003)
24. Takahashi, N., Tanaka, H., Kawamura, R.: Analysis of process assignment in multi-tier mobile cloud computing and application to edge accelerated web browsing. In: Proceedings of IEEE Mobile Cloud 2015, pp. 233–234. IEEE (2015)
25. Tran, T.X., Pnadey, P., Hajisami, A., Pompili, D.: Collaborative multi-bitrate video caching and processing in mobile-edge computing networks. In: Proceedings of IEEE WONS 2017, pp. 165–172. IEEE (2017)
26. Yoshida, M., Mitsunari, S., Fujiwara, T.: A timed-release key management scheme for backward recovery. In: Won, D.H., Kim, S. (eds.) ICISC 2005. LNCS, vol. 3935, pp. 3–14. Springer, Heidelberg (2006). doi:10.1007/11734727_3
27. ARIB: Conditional Access System Specifications for Digital Broadcasting. ARIB STD-B25 (2007)
28. ETSI: DVB Common Scrambling Algorithm-Distribution Agreements. Technical report (2013)
29. http://www.nhk.or.jp/hybridcast/online/
30. http://www.hbbtv.org/
31. http://www.hulu.com/
32. http://www.youview.com/
33. ETSI: Mobile Edge Computing (MEC); Framework and Reference Architecture. http://www.etsi.org/deliver/etsi_gs/MEC/001_099/003/01.01.01_60/gs_MEC003v010101p.pdf

Dynamic Similarity Search over Encrypted Data with Low Leakage

Daniel Homann[(✉)], Christian Göge, and Lena Wiese

Institut für Informatik, Universität Göttingen,
Goldschmidtstraße 7, 37077 Göttingen, Germany
{homann,christian.goege,wiese}@cs.uni-goettingen.de

Abstract. Though cloud databases offer advantages in terms of maintenance cost, they require encryption in order to protect confidential records. Specialized searchable encryption schemes are needed to provide the functionality of privacy preserving search on encrypted data. In many use cases, a search which also returns the correct documents when the search term was misspelled is very desirable. Therefore, we present a novel similarity searchable encryption scheme. Our scheme uses symmetric encryption primitives, is dynamic, i.e. allows the efficient addition and deletion of search terms and has sub-linear search cost. We prove that the leakage of our scheme is low and that it provides forward security. Our scheme is built by employing a new construction technique for similarity searchable encryption schemes. In this construction a searchable encryption scheme is used as storage layer for a similarity searchable encryption scheme.

Keywords: Similarity search · Fuzzy search · Searchable encryption · Symmetric encryption · Cloud databases

1 Introduction

Outsourcing data to cloud providers is becoming more and more common. While this offers great advantages in terms of maintenance cost, the confidentiality of the data is in peril. One solution to this problem is the use of encryption. While standard symmetric encryption algorithms like e.g. AES offer good security by encrypting all records, the cloud data store loses any search functionality and degrades to just a bunch of encrypted files. However, among the desirable functionality of a database is the ability to efficiently perform full-text search.

This paper deals with the problem of efficient searching in encrypted cloud databases. Efficiency means to perform the searches in less than linear time in the number of document-keyword pairs. For searching encrypted data several algorithms have been proposed. They can be divided in symmetric and public-key solutions. Public-key searchable encryption schemes offer multi-user capabilities but they require computationally costly public-key operations. Therefore, it appears to be more practical to pursue symmetric key searchable encryption.

© Springer International Publishing AG 2017
G. Livraga and C. Mitchell (Eds.): STM 2017, LNCS 10547, pp. 19–35, 2017.
DOI: 10.1007/978-3-319-68063-7_2

Users sometimes misspell search terms. However, in many use cases it is very desirable that small spelling errors still lead to the correct results. One solution for this is checking the keyword in a dictionary before searching. This makes the search more expensive on the client-side and adds additional complexity by requiring the client to decide between several correct words which are within a certain distance of the entered term. Furthermore, the client might want to search for a keyword that is not contained in the dictionary, like a specialist term or a name.

To overcome these problems, we propose a new similarity searchable encryption scheme. Our scheme has the following key properties:

1. It is dynamic, i.e. it allows to add new documents and keywords efficiently. The amortized runtime of adding a document with m keywords to an index of size N is $\mathcal{O}(m \cdot \lambda \cdot N \cdot \log^2 N)$. Here λ is an encoding dependent constant.
2. It has a small leakage and provides forward security, i.e. when adding a new document it does not reveal which of the old documents contains similar words to the new document.
3. The search takes sub-linear time in the number of document-keyword pairs. Its runtime is $\mathcal{O}(\lambda \min \{\beta + \log N, \gamma \log^3 N\})$, where γ is the number of documents which are similar to the search term and β is the number of historically added, but perhaps deleted, documents similar to the search term.
4. It supports similarity search (also known as: fuzzy search). This means it also finds documents containing slightly misspelled keywords.

To the best of our knowledge no other existing searchable encryption scheme provides this desirable combination of properties. Furthermore our scheme is defined in such a way, that it is not restricted to the problem domain of fuzzy text search. By specifying an appropriate family of locality sensitive hash functions it could be applied to other domains e.g. biometric data.

Our scheme achieves these properties by combining two existing searchable encryption schemes. The first scheme is a secure and dynamic searchable encryption scheme without similarity search capabilities [19], while the second scheme is a non-dynamic similarity search scheme [14]. They are combined in such a way that the former acts as a storage layer for the latter. This technique of combining a non-fuzzy and a fuzzy searchable encryption scheme, seems very powerful to us, as it allows to build very good similarity searchable encryption schemes from existing searchable encryption schemes.

In the next section, we will describe the state of the art regarding symmetric searchable encryption. In Sect. 3, we will give a formal security definition for our scheme. Our scheme for general similarity search is described in Sect. 4. In Sect. 5 we explain how to apply this general scheme towards similarity search for text. We prove that our scheme fulfils the security definition in Sect. 6. In the following sections, we will give an experimental analysis of our scheme (Sect. 7) and draw a conclusion (Sect. 8).

2   Background

2.1   Symmetric Searchable Encryption (SSE)

For symmetric searchable encryption there is a wide range of proposed algorithms (for an overview see [2]). They all consist of at least two different protocols. The first protocol generates a secure index structure from a set of *documents*. Each of these documents contains a set of *features* (e.g. words). When searching for a feature, the server returns the *identifiers* of all documents containing this feature.

The first searchable symmetric encryption schemes were given by [4,6,8,18]. Most of the early schemes were not dynamic, i.e. when adding a new document-keyword pair the complete index had to be rebuilt from scratch. The runtime of this rebuild operation is at least linear in the number of document-keyword pairs, since every document-keyword pair has to be processed at least once. As a result, index changes in such schemes might be possible but incur large performance penalties. Furthermore, during the rebuild the index is usually stored on the client meaning that the index may not become larger than the client's storage. In typical Big Data applications, the amount of data stored on the server is much larger than the storage of a single client. As a result, in such use cases a rebuild would not only be inefficient but simply impossible.

The security of searchable encryption schemes is usually evaluated in a client-server setting with a honest-but-curious server as adversary. Its security is then quantified by the amount of information that is *leaked* to the server, i.e. that the server could compute in polynomial-time from its observation of the protocol execution. The common security definitions were first given by [6]

Dynamic schemes allow for the addition of new document-keyword pairs at runtime with lower rebuilding cost. In the following, we will consider schemes to be dynamic if the amortized rebuilding cost is sub-linear in the number of document-keyword pairs. Of the proposed dynamic SSE schemes [3,10,12, 13,18,19], the best security properties are offered by the scheme of [19], as it provides forward security. Dynamic schemes are called *forward secure* if they do not leak to an attacker if an added document contains a keyword which was previously searched for. A dynamic scheme is called *backward secure* if an already deleted document containing feature w is not contained in the leakage of a search for feature w. To our knowledge, no existing SSE scheme achieves backward security.

Recent research highlights the importance of forward security [26]. They showed in a modified threat model, that SSE schemes without forward security are more vulnerable to attacks. In their threat model the server is able to inject files in the index, but otherwise behaves in an honest-but-curious manner.

2.2   Similarity Searchable Symmetric Encryption (SSSE)

Often spelling errors occur while typing search queries. Nevertheless, the correct result set should be found. To achieve this, the notion of searchable symmetric encryption was extended to similarity searchable symmetric encryption.

Similarity search can be understood in two ways. In the following, we will use the term similarity search as the search for a single feature (e.g. word), which may be slightly altered (e.g. misspelled) but nevertheless should be found. In the literature, a search returning documents which contain a subset of a given feature set is also called similarity search [17,20,21,24].

In the following, we will only consider the first meaning of similarity search. Known SSSE schemes in this sense are given by [1,5,11,14–16,22,23]. While searching misspelled words in larger bodies of text is the most important application, similarity search can also be applied to other problem domains, e.g. similarity of biometric data [1]. An important property for the classification of SSSE schemes is their generality: They can either be focused on a single problem domain (e.g. text search) or be of general use. In the latter case, they can be adopted to a specific domain by a problem specific similarity mapping.

Very specific to the problem domain of searching text are schemes using wild cards letters [11,15,16,23]. Such schemes were first sketched in [15] and described in more detail in [23]. Several modifications of this approach were proposed [11,16]. The disadvantage of all these SSSE is that they do not allow dynamic updates of the index.

The scheme of [14] is of much greater generality. It encodes features in Bloom filters. Afterwards, it employs locality sensitive hashing (LSH) on the Bloom filter and stores the generated *subfeatures* in an index structure. By specifying an encoding to Bloom filters and choosing a suitable LSH family, any kind of data, i.e. not just text, can be subject to similarity search. However, the main disadvantage of this scheme is that data cannot be added dynamically.

In [5] the authors also encode words in Bloom filters but store the index in a tree-based structure. Their scheme is dynamic but has a very high leakage, as the similarity between all documents is leaked even if no search operations have been performed. Another scheme given by [22] also uses Bloom filters. Searches are not efficient in this scheme, as the runtime of search operations is linear in the number of stored documents.

The authors of [1] provide a definition of SSSE which is very strict with regard to result quality and permissible leakage. They show that no space-efficient scheme satisfying their definition can exist. For a slightly relaxed version of their definition they give a SSSE scheme for fingerprint data which is still quite space-inefficient.

In the introduction of [25] which addresses similarity of entire documents, a similar scheme to the one we describe here is briefly considered but dismissed because it "does not achieve practical efficiency" for their use case. However, for our use case our scheme achieves a competitive asymptotic search and update runtime. This will be shown in Sect. 4.3.

3   Security Definition

Our scheme is a set of protocols executed between a client (user) and a server. The server stores the index structure of the scheme and is queried by the client.

The client is a trusted computing device while the server is untrustworthy. As in the standard security model of SSE, we consider the server to be honest-but-curious. Thus, the server might inspect the request and the stored data and try to deduce information from it but otherwise follows the prescribed protocol. This section adapts previous work [6,14,19] to our setting. In order to give a formal security definition we first define our understanding of a dynamic similarity searchable encryption scheme.

Definition 1 (DSSSE). *A dynamic similarity searchable symmetric encryption (DSSSE) is given by a set of three protocols executed between a client and a server:*

- *Setup(1^κ): Create an empty data structure with security parameter κ on the server.*
- *Search(w, k): Based on feature w, the client calculates a matrix of trapdoors T and sends them to the server. The server executes the search and returns an encrypted result vector. The client decrypts the vector and returns the identifiers of the top-k results.*
- *Update(D, id, op): If $op = add$, then the server adds the features of document D with identifier id to the index, otherwise ($op = del$) it deletes the keywords of document D with identifier id from the index.*

In contrast to non-dynamic searchable encryption schemes, our scheme does not need a protocol that builds an index from a document collection as the index can be build step-by-step by adding documents with the update protocol.

The concept of the history captures the operation of the scheme from the client's point of view. The definition of the history from [6] has to be changed to account for the possible dynamic addition of documents.

Definition 2 (History). *Between a client and a server a DSSSE is initialized via the setup protocol. After a total number of n executions of the search and update protocols the history $\mathcal{H}_n$ is given by:*

$$\mathcal{H}_n = (h_1, \ldots, h_n).$$

Let S_i be a data structure describing which feature is associated to which document identifier after the execution of the i-th step. The h_i are defined depending on the type of protocol executed in the i-th step. If the i-th operation was a search operation, then $h_i = (S_i, w_i)$, where w_i is the feature that was searched for. Otherwise $h_i = (S_i, (D_i, id_i, op_i))$ where (D_i, id_i, op_i) are the parameters of the executed update protocol.

Next we want to define which of this information is leaked to the server. The different types of leakage to the server are given by the following five definitions.

Definition 3 (Protocol Pattern). *For a history $\mathcal{H}_n$ the protocol pattern $\mathcal{P}_i$ is a vector given by:*

$$\mathcal{P}_i = \begin{cases} 1 & \text{if the } i\text{-th step is a search operation} \\ 0 & \text{else} \end{cases} \qquad \forall 1 \leq i \leq n$$

Definition 4 (Search Pattern). *For every search protocol execution h_i the search pattern is given by a vector $\mathcal{F}$:*

$$\mathcal{F}_j = \begin{cases} 1 & \text{if } \mathcal{P}_j = 1 \text{ and } w_j = w_i \\ 0 & \text{else} \end{cases} \quad \forall 1 \leq j < i$$

Definition 5 (Access Pattern). *Let h_i be a search protocol execution. Let $w_i^1, \ldots w_i^\lambda$ be the subfeatures of w_i. Then the access pattern is given by:*

$$\mathcal{A} = (\mathcal{A}_1, \ldots, \mathcal{A}_\lambda)$$

where $\mathcal{A}_j$ are the identifiers of documents added or removed in the past containing the subfeature w_i^j.

Definition 6 (Similarity Pattern). *Let h_i be a search protocol execution. Let $w_i^1, \ldots w_i^\lambda$ be the subfeatures of w_i. Then the similarity pattern $\mathcal{S}$ is given by:*

$$\mathcal{S}_{a,j,b} = \begin{cases} 1 & \text{if } \mathcal{P}_j = 1 \text{ and } w_i^a = w_j^b \\ 0 & \text{else} \end{cases} \quad \forall 1 \leq j < i, \forall 1 \leq a, b \leq \lambda$$

Definition 7 (Update Pattern). *For every update operation h_i the update pattern $\mathcal{U}$ is given by:*

$$\mathcal{U} = (op_i, id_i, |D_i|)$$

where $|D_i|$ is the number of subfeatures in D_i.

With these patterns we could now define the trace which is the maximal amount of information the adversary (server) should be able to compute from the leaked information.

Definition 8 (Trace). *The trace $\mathcal{T}(\mathcal{H}_n)$ for a history $\mathcal{H}_n$ consists of the protocol pattern $\mathcal{P}$ and for each search operation the search pattern $\mathcal{F}$, access pattern $\mathcal{A}$ and similarity pattern $\mathcal{S}$ and for each update operation the update pattern $\mathcal{U}$.*

Our definition of the update pattern does not leak whether a feature of the updated document D was searched for previously. Therefore, a scheme with a trace as given above provides forward security. Since deleted documents which match the search term are still included in the access pattern, this definition of the trace does not provide backward security.

For a given history $\mathcal{H}_n$, the information that is leaked to the server is called the view and denoted by $\mathcal{V}(\mathcal{H}_n)$. We want that the server in our scheme cannot deduce more information than the trace $\mathcal{T}(\mathcal{H}_n)$ from this view. Therefore, the following security definition should hold for our scheme. We will prove that it indeed satisfies this security definition in Sect. 6.

Definition 9 (Adaptive Semantic Security for DSSSE). *A scheme provides adaptive semantic security if one can define a simulator S such that for all polynomial size distinguishers D and for all polynomials p and a large r holds:*

$$\mathsf{P}[D(\mathcal{V}(\mathcal{H}_n)) = 1] - \mathsf{P}[D(S(\mathcal{T}(\mathcal{H}_n)) = 1] < \frac{1}{p(r)}$$

with probabilities taken over $\mathcal{H}_n$ and the coins of the scheme's key generation and encryption.

4   Our Scheme

Our scheme combines the dynamic SSE of Stefanov et al. [19] with the similarity search of Kuzu et al. [14]. This way, the scheme achieves very good security (see Sect. 3) and an efficient similarity search at the same time. In this section we will describe our scheme in detail.

4.1   Preliminaries

Our construction is based on the following primitives. Oblivious sorting and the LSH family are described below in more detail.

- A function keygen(κ) which generates a new, random symmetric encryption key, the length of which is determined by the security parameter κ.
- Symmetric (probabilistic) encryption and decryption functions Encrypt and Decrypt.
- Symmetric, deterministic encryption and decryption functions DetEncrypt and DetDecrypt.
- A keyed hash function H_{key}.
- A random oracle H_{key}^*. For the security proof we need this keyed hash function to be modelled as random oracle (see Sect. 6).
- A hash function h.
- An oblivious sorting protocol o-sort.
- A metric space embedding ρ which maps features w into a metric space F.
- A (r_1, r_2, p_1, p_2)-sensitive LSH family $G = (g_i)_{1 \leq i \leq \lambda}$.

Oblivious Sorting. With the oblivious sorting protocol, the client sorts the data stored on the server in such a way that the server remains oblivious about the order of the items. In each step of this protocol the client downloads a chunk of $\mathcal{O}(N^\alpha)$ entries from the server, decrypts them for sorting and afterwards uploads them in encrypted form to the server. The parameter $0 < \alpha \leq 1$ can be chosen so that the chunk still fits in the client's memory. We used the oblivious k-way mergesort algorithm from [9] as this algorithm was specifically created for external oblivious sorting.

LSH Family. Let dist be a metric on a metric space F. Then a family of hash functions G is called (r_1, r_2, p_1, p_2)-sensitive if for any features $x, y \in F$ and for any $g \in G$ holds:

- if $\text{dist}(x, y) \leq r_1$ then $\mathsf{P}[g(x) = g(y)] \geq p_1$
- if $\text{dist}(x, y) \geq r_2$ then $\mathsf{P}[g(x) = g(y)] \leq p_2$.

An LSH family of a desired sensitivity can be constructed from another LSH family with a different sensitivity as a result of an AND- and OR-construction of this existing family. For further details see [14]. How to choose the metric space embedding ρ and the LSH family G for text search is given in Sect. 5.

The following parameters of our scheme can be chosen by a user to customize it to a certain setting:

κ Security parameter defining the length of the symmetric encryption keys.
α This value is used to adapt the scheme to available storage on the client.
ρ Mapping of the features to a metric space depending on the problem's domain.
G A family of LSH functions. The value of $\lambda = |G|$ is very critical for the scheme's performance as well as storage demand.

4.2 Detailed Construction

The index structure of our scheme consists of $L = \lceil \log_2 N \rceil + 1$ hash maps $\mathbb{H}_i$ of size 2^i for $0 \leq i \leq L$ which are stored on a server. Here i denoted the level of an entry in the data structure. Added or deleted document-subfeature pairs will always be added to the first empty hash map. For each hash map $\mathbb{H}_i$ the client possesses a symmetric encryption key k_i.

The scheme consists of the three protocols Setup (Protocol 1), Update (Protocol 2) and Search (Protocol 4). While the Update protocol sometimes requires several roundtrips between the client and the server, the Setup and Search protocols are non-interactive (1-round protocol). Furthermore, there are two helper functions for encoding (Algorithm 5) and searching (Algorithm 6) entries in the hash map structure. During updates an additional Rebuild protocol (Protocol 3) is used to partially rebuild the hash map structure.

Protocol 1. Setup(Security parameter κ)

$\mathrm{esk} \leftarrow \mathbf{keygen}(\kappa)$
$L \leftarrow 0$
$\mathbb{H}_0 \leftarrow \emptyset$

Protocol 2. Update(document D, identifier id, operation op)

$V \leftarrow \emptyset$
for all features $w \in D$ **do**
$\quad \overrightarrow{w} \leftarrow \rho(w)$
$\quad$ **for all** $g \in G$ **do**
$\quad\quad V \leftarrow V \cup \{g(\overrightarrow{w})\}$
for all $v \in V$ in random order **do**
$\quad$ **if** $\mathbb{H}_0$ is empty **then**
$\quad\quad k_0 \leftarrow \mathbf{keygen}(\kappa)$
$\quad\quad \mathbb{H}_0 \leftarrow \mathbf{encodeEntry}(v, \mathrm{id}, \mathrm{op}, 0, \mathrm{esk}, k_0)$
$\quad$ **else**
$\quad\quad$ Execute protocol: $\mathbf{Rebuild}(v, \mathrm{id}, \mathrm{op})$

Setup (Protocol 1). The Setup algorithm generates a encryption key esk, initializes the number of levels L with 0 and creates an empty hash map $\mathbb{H}_0$ for level 0.

Protocol 3. Rebuild(subfeature v, identifier id, operation op)

$l_{new} \leftarrow$ Smallest l for which $\mathbb{H}_l$ is empty

Set $e^* \leftarrow$ encodeEntry$(v, \text{id}, \text{op}, 0, \text{esk}, k_0)$ and store e^* on the server

Let B denote $\{e^*\} \cup \bigcup_{i=0}^{l-1} \mathbb{H}_i$

for all $e = (\text{hkey}, c_1, c_2) \in B$ on server **do**
    $(v, \text{id}, \text{op}, \text{cnt}) \leftarrow$ Decrypt$_{\text{esk}}(c_2)$
    Replace e on server with Encrypt$_{\text{esk}}(v, \text{id}, \text{op}, \text{cnt})$

$B \leftarrow$ o-sort(B) according to sorting key $(v, \text{id}, \text{op})$

for all $e =$ Encrypt$_{\text{esk}}(v, \text{op}, \text{id}, \text{cnt}) \in B$ on server **do**
    if e is the start of a new feature v for operation op **then**
        $\text{cnt}_{\text{op},v} \leftarrow 0$
        Replace e on server with Encrypt$_{\text{esk}}(v, \text{id}, \text{op}, 0)$

    if e and next entry in B arc add and del operations for the same word **then**
        Replace each of them by Encrypt$(\perp)$ on the server
    else
        $\text{cnt}_{\text{op},v} \leftarrow \text{cnt}_{\text{op},v} + 1$
        Replace e on server with Encrypt$_{\text{esk}}(v, \text{id}, \text{op}, \text{cnt}_{\text{op},v})$

Permute B randomly by $B \leftarrow$ o-sort(B) according to sorting key hkey

$k_l \leftarrow$ keygen(κ)

for all $e \in B$ on the server **do**
    $(v, \text{id}, \text{op}, \text{cnt}) \leftarrow$ Decrypt$_{\text{esk}}(e)$
    Add encodeEntry$(v, \text{id}, \text{op}, \text{cnt})$ to $\mathbb{H}_l$ on server

Remove all entries from $\mathbb{H}_i$ for $i = 0, \ldots, l - 1$

Update (Protocol 2). The Update algorithm is used to add or delete documents to the search scheme. An addition operation is specified by op = add and a deletion operation by op = del. The algorithm processes all features w of the document. These features are embedded in a metric space where the LSH family G is applied. The set of all these hash values is then shuffled randomly and inserted in the data structure on the server. During this process two cases have to be distinguished. If the hash map on the first level ($\mathbb{H}_0$) is empty, the current hash will be inserted in this level. Otherwise a rebuild (see Protocol 3) of the data structure is required. This works as follows: First the first completely empty level l is determined. The rebuild will operate on the entries of the hash maps $\mathbb{H}_i$ with $i < l$ and the new entry e^*. For better readability we denote this set of entries by B. At the end of the protocols all the entries of B will be inserted in $\mathbb{H}_l$ and the levels $\mathbb{H}_i$ with $i < l$ will be empty. In a for loop the encoding of the elements of B is changed for easier subsequent processing. This loop as well as the later for loop only requires constant storage on the client, as the entry, after processing, is stored again on the server. Now, all entries of $\mathbb{H}_l$ are sorted according to $(v, \text{id}, \text{op})$. The sorting employs oblivious sorting to not leak any information about the entries to the server. In Subsect. 4.1 we describe how this can be achieved using only sublinear client's storage. Then the cnt values of entries belonging to the same (v, id) tuple are enumerated in the sorted order.

Protocol 4. Search(feature w, number of results k)

Client:
  $\vec{w} \leftarrow \rho(w)$
  $t \leftarrow (g_i(\vec{w}))_{1 \leq i \leq \lambda}$
  $T \leftarrow \left(H_{k_j}(h(t_i)) \right)_{1 \leq i \leq \lambda, 0 \leq j \leq L}$
  Send T to server
Server:
  $C \leftarrow \emptyset$
  for all $1 \leq i \leq \lambda$ **do**
      for all $l \in \{L, L-1, \ldots, 0\}$ **do**
          cnt $\leftarrow 0$
          eid $\leftarrow$ **Lookup**$(T_{i,l}, \text{add}, \text{cnt})$
          while eid $\neq \bot$ **do**
              $C \leftarrow C \cup \{\text{eid}\}$
              cnt $\leftarrow$ cnt $+ 1$
              eid $\leftarrow$ **Lookup**$(T_{i,l}, \text{add}, \text{cnt})$
          cnt $\leftarrow 0$
          eid $\leftarrow$ **Lookup**$(T_{i,l}, \text{del}, \text{cnt})$
          while eid $\neq \bot$ **do**
              $C \leftarrow C \setminus \{\text{eid}\}$
              cnt $\leftarrow$ cnt $+ 1$
              eid $\leftarrow$ **Lookup**$(T_{i,l}, \text{del}, \text{cnt})$
  return C to client
Client:
  $D \leftarrow$ empty dictionary
  for all eid $\in C$ **do**
      $v, \text{id} \leftarrow$ **DetDecrypt**(c)
      if id not in C **then**
          $D[\text{id}] \leftarrow 0$
      $D[\text{id}] \leftarrow D[\text{id}] + 1$
  return the identifiers from C with top-k values

To remove complementary operations pairs of add and del operations belonging to the same (v, id) tuple both of them are replaced with $\bot$. Afterwards, a new level key k_l is chosen to re-encode the entries.

When the client possesses enough storage to hold all the entries in B a simpler rebuild is possible by transferring all the entries of B to the client, decrypting them, performing a processing similar to line 8–16 in Protocol 3 locally and storing them in $\mathbb{H}_l$ on the server again. (see [19] for details).

Search (Protocol 4). For the execution of the Search algorithm as described in Protocol 4 only a single round of interaction between the client and server suffices. In a first step the client embeds the search term in a metric space and applies the locality sensitive hash functions on this vector. Based on these hash values trapdoor values T are generated and sent to the server. The server starts with initializing an empty dictionary C where the found encrypted ids of possible

Algorithm 5. Algorithm for the generation of the hash map entries

procedure ENCODEENTRY(v, id, op, cnt, esk, k_l)
    token $\leftarrow H_{k_l}(h(v))$
    hkey $\leftarrow H^*_{\text{token}}(0||\text{op}||\text{cnt})$
    $c_1 \leftarrow$ DetEncrypt$_{\text{esk}}(v||\text{id}) \oplus H^*_{\text{token}}(1||\text{op}||\text{cnt})$
    $c_2 \leftarrow$ Encrypt$_{\text{esk}}(v||\text{id}||\text{op}||\text{cnt})$
    return (hkey, c_1, c_2)

Algorithm 6. Algorithm for the lookup of a certain entry in the hash maps

procedure LOOKUP(token, op, cnt))
    hkey $\leftarrow H^*_{\text{token}}(0||\text{op}||\text{cnt})$
    if hkey $\in \mathbb{H}_l$ **then**
        return $\mathbb{H}_l[\text{hkey}].c_1 \oplus H^*_{\text{token}}(1||\text{op}||\text{cnt})$
    else
        return $\perp$

hits are stored. Now the server iterates over all hash values. Starting in the last one, it searches the hash maps for documents containing an add operation for the considered subfeature. In order to execute this search operation the trapdoor T is required. When successful the identifier is added to a list of search results C. Afterwards, the server searches for del-operations for the same subfeature. The corresponding identifiers are removed from C as this document-subfeature pair was deleted from the index. Concluding its operation, the server sends C to the client. The client decrypts the values of C with the key esk. Then the contained identifiers are ranked according to their number of occurrence in C. Finally, the client returns the identifiers with top-k scores.

4.3 Analysis

Runtime Update. The rebuild of level l requires $\mathcal{O}(2^l \cdot l)$ operations as this level contains at most 2^l entries. A rebuild of level l is always required after 2^l update operations. Therefore, for a total number of N inserted subfeatures we get an amortized update cost of $\mathcal{O}(N \cdot \log^2 N)$ per update. As a result, the amortized update cost of inserting a document with m features is given by: $\mathcal{O}(m \cdot \lambda \cdot N \cdot \log^2 N)$, where λ is the size of the used LSH family.

Runtime Search. In the worst case the protocol described here does not achieve sub-linear search time. This can be seen when adding a subfeature multiple times to the index and then deleting all of them except one. However, the authors of [19] describe how to slightly modify their scheme to achieve a sub-linear search time. This is achieved by storing the level of the corresponding add entry in del entries. As the algorithm works exactly as described in their paper, we decided to leave it out here. With these additions our scheme achieves a runtime for searching a single feature of $\mathcal{O}(\lambda \min\{\beta + \log N, \gamma \log^3 N\})$, where γ is the number of documents having a subfeature in common with the search query and β is the number of added (but maybe in the meantime deleted) documents containing one of the searched subfeatures.

Roundtrips. As stated before, the Setup and Search protocols consist of a single round of communication between the client and the server. The number of roundtrips for the Update Protocol is determined by the Rebuild Protocol. As most rebuilds concern the upper levels of the hash maps, the data of the concerned levels will fit into the client's memory of size $\mathcal{O}(N^\alpha)$ and hence only a single round of communication is required. In the worst case, the whole data structure has to be rebuild. A result of [9] on his oblivious sorting algorithm gives us the number of $\mathcal{O}(N^{1-\alpha} \log^2 N^{1-\alpha})$ roundtrips in this case. Although such large rebuilds happen only very occasionally the high number of roundtrips favour fast RAM over disk storage as storage location for the hash maps.

Required Storage. For every subfeature, the three values hkey, c_1 and c_2 are stored in a hash map. When using AES-256 for encryption and an SHA-256 based keyed hash function, hkey and c_1 will require 32 Bytes, while c_2 requires 48 Bytes of storage. Thus, $112\,\lambda m$ Bytes are necessary for storing a document with m features.

5   Parameters for Text Search

In the last section our scheme was presented in great generality so that it is applicable to a large range of problem domains. However, in order to apply the scheme to fuzzy text search, we have to specify a metric space embedding and a LSH family. Their parameters are chosen as in [14].

Metric Space Embedding ρ. We will define the metric space embedding as function $\rho : w \mapsto \{0,1\}^{500}$. This is accomplished by considering the word w as a set of bigrams. All the bigrams of a word are then encoded in a common Bloom filter of length 500 by using 15 hash functions per bigram. The bits of the Bloom filter hit by a hash function then give $\rho(w)$.

LSH Family. We use the following LSH family $G = (g_i)_{1 \le i \le \lambda}$ with $\lambda = 37$. We define:

$$g_i(x) = h_{i,1}(x) || \cdots || h_{i,k}(x)$$

with $k = 5$. For all $1 \le i \le \lambda$ and for all $1 \le j \le k$ we set:

$$h_{i,j} : \{0,1\}^{500} \to \{0,1,\ldots,499\}, \quad x \mapsto \min\left\{y \mid 0 \le y \le 499 \text{ and } x_{\pi_{i,j}(y)} = 1\right\},$$

where $\pi_{i,j}$ is a random permutation on $\{0,\ldots,499\}$. The parameters given here will be used in the Implementation in Sect. 7.

6 Security Proof

In this chapter we will prove that our proposed protocol indeed provides Adaptive Semantic Security for DSSE. For this purpose we will adopt the security proof of [19].

Theorem 1. *The DSSE given in Sect. 4 provides Adaptive Semantic Security for DSSE (Definition 9) in the random oracle model.*

Proof. We will show that there exists a polynomial-size simulator S, such that the simulated view $S(T(\mathcal{H}_n))$ and the real view $\mathcal{V}(\mathcal{H}_n)$ are computationally indistinguishable. To show the existence of such a simulator S we will state how it constructs the different elements of the view from the available trace $T(\mathcal{H}_n)$. The number of executed protocol steps is available to the simulator via the trace. Furthermore, it can access via the protocol pattern whether a protocol step was an update or a search operation. We can therefore consider update and search operations separately:

Update. We describe the behaviour of S separately for every subfeature $v \in V$ in the update protocol. The update pattern of previous updates contains the number of subfeatures which have been inserted in the data structure. As the entries are inserted deterministically into the hash maps $\mathbb{H}_i$, the simulator can calculate the level l in which the new subfeature v will be stored by the number of already inserted entries. The simulator S can also calculate the number of entries in $\mathbb{H}$. During the oblivious sorting protocol chunks of size $\mathcal{O}(N^\alpha)$ are transferred to the client, sorted in its memory and uploaded back to the adversary. The simulator S simulates this step by generating correctly sized chunks of encoded entries $e = (\text{hkey}, c_1, c_2)$ and uploading them to the adversary. The values of hkey and c_1 are chosen at random, while c_2 as semantically-secure ciphertext is chosen as the value of $\text{Encrypt}(0)$. Due to the obliviousness of the sorting algorithm this successfully simulates the rebuild protocol.

Search. In the case of search operation, the simulator knows the access pattern $\mathcal{A}$, the search pattern $\mathcal{F}$ and the similarity pattern $\mathcal{S}$. By the update patterns of all the previous update operations, the simulator knows the size of the data structure N. Furthermore it can deduce by the update and access pattern the levels in which the subfeatures v of the query are stored. The client generates the following trapdoor T. If the subfeature has not been searched before or its level l has been rebuilt meanwhile, the trapdoor token$_l$ for this subfeature and level l consists of random values. Otherwise, it resends the old trapdoor token$_l$. Due to the pseudorandomness of the keyed hash function H, the adversary cannot distinguish between these pseudorandom values and the output of H. Furthermore, due to this pseudorandomness the probability that this same token has already been sent to the adversary is also negligible.

We now want to program the random oracle H^* in the right way, i.e. such that $H^*_{\text{token}_l}(0||\text{op}||\text{cnt})$ and $H^*_{\text{token}_l}(1||\text{op}||\text{cnt})$ return the "right" values, when queried by the adversary. If the oracle $H^*_{\text{token}_l}$ is queried for $(0||\text{op}||\text{cnt})$ or $(1||\text{op}||\text{cnt})$ where cnt is greater than $\text{cnt}_{\text{op},v}$ it returns random values. In all other cases it should return a valid pair of $(\text{hkey}, \text{id} \oplus c_1)$ values when queried for $(0||\text{op}||\text{cnt})$ and $(1||\text{op}||\text{cnt})$.

Now two cases can be considered. It could be the case that all items $(v, \text{id}, \text{op})$ belonging to the same (v, id) are in the same level. In this case, the random oracle chooses a random, unused entry from this level and returns it when queried for the values mentioned above. If these items are not in the same level, the simulator randomly chooses a level according to the distribution of the entries. As the insertion order of entries belonging to the same document is random, this return values are indistinguishable from real values for the adversary. Since by this construction all elements of $S(\mathcal{T}(\mathcal{H}_n))$ and $\mathcal{V}(\mathcal{H}_n)$ are computationally indistinguishable, our scheme fulfils the security definition. □

By slightly changing the protocol, the assumption of the random oracle is not necessary [19]. As this change increases the amount of computation performed on the client as well as the communication bandwith between client and server, we will not describe it here.

7   Experimental Results

We implemented the proposed scheme in Java to evaluate its performance. The encryption and decryption is implemented as AES-256. For the hash function we used SHA-256, and for the keyed hash function H as well as the random oracle H^* we used HMAC-SHA-256. Within the rebuild algorithm we used a 8-way mergesort and assumed a client storage of 1024 entries, which is significantly lower than in [19]. Our implementation is single-threaded and does not contain the optimizations described in Sect. 4.3 to achieve the asymptotic search runtime also in the worst case. In our opinion, this worst case occurs too seldom to justify the overhead introduced by improving its asymptotic runtime. For our benchmark the client as well as the server code was deployed on the same machine.

For measuring the update and search runtime we used the bodies of the mails in the Enron e-mail data set [7]. This dataset contains 517 401 mails with a total of 688 270 unique keywords. The total number of document-keyword pairs in this dataset is 60 920 970, i.e. each mail contains an average number of about 118 unique keywords. We generated the keywords by changing all letters to lower case and thereafter considering all strings of a length greater than one character. The large number of unique keywords can be explained by the fact that the mails sometimes contain misspelled words or e-mail addresses.

In order to test the update operations, we inserted part of the mail dataset in a random order. For 100 000 document-keywords pairs, we achieved an insertion performance of about 26 document-keyword pairs per second on our test system (Intel i7-3770 @ 3.40 GHz, 16 GB RAM, Ubuntu 14.04, Oracle Java 8).

The search operation was benchmarked by queries chosen at random from the set of unique keywords. The probability of choosing a certain keyword was given by its relative frequency in the whole dataset. When executing search operations over an index containing 100 000 document-keyword pairs, we achieved a average performance of 20 queries per second. Since all identifiers have to be ranked, this figure is independent of the number k of returned identifiers. We did not benchmark the quality of our search results as the results of [14] regarding precision and recall remain unchanged.

8   Conclusion

Our SSSE scheme is dynamic, provides sub-linear search time and has low leakage. This is accomplished by combining a fuzzy and a non-fuzzy searchable encryption scheme. In our opinion, this technique of combining fuzzy and non-fuzzy schemes is interesting in its own right. It allows to consider searchable encryption and similarity search separately. By combining such schemes, very promising candidates for feature-rich similarity search schemes could be created.

Our scheme could be easily extended to a multi-keyword search by slightly changing the Search Protocol. To achieve this the client would send the trapdoors belonging to several words to the server. When the client ranks the results, identifiers of documents containing all search terms (conjunctive search) then are ranked higher than documents containing only a subset of the search terms.

To apply our scheme to a specific problem domain a appropriate metric space embedding has to be used. In Sect. 5 we showed how this embedding can be chosen in the case of text search. It would be an interesting task to find such mappings for other problem domains, e.g. different types of biometric date as fingerprints or iris images.

The (amortized) asymptotic runtime of search and update operations of our scheme is good compared to other fuzzy search schemes. However, as our implementation shows, the involved constants are high. Although a further optimisation of the scheme might achieve better runtime, the most compelling aspect of our scheme is something different: By achieving good asymptotic runtimes with low leakage, our work complements the theoretical work of [1]. They investigated how much performance in terms of asymptotic runtime, low leakage and storage efficiency an SSSE scheme can achieve. On the one hand, their impossibility result for a certain combination of these properties can be seen as an upper bound for the performance of any DSSE scheme. On the other hand, our construction of a good scheme with regard to this performance characteristics can be understood as lower bound for an optimal DSSE scheme. Further research is necessary in order to find the "optimal" scheme.

Acknowledgment. This work was funded by the DFG under grant number Wi 4086/2-2.

References

1. Boldyreva, A., Chenette, N.: Efficient fuzzy search on encrypted data. In: Cid, C., Rechberger, C. (eds.) FSE 2014. LNCS, vol. 8540, pp. 613–633. Springer, Heidelberg (2015). doi:10.1007/978-3-662-46706-0_1

2. Bösch, C., Hartel, P.H., Jonker, W., Peter, A.: A survey of provably secure searchable encryption. ACM CSUR. **47**(2), 18:1–18:51 (2014)
3. Cash, D., Jaeger, J., Jarecki, S., Jutla, C.S., Krawczyk, H., Rosu, M., Steiner, M.: Dynamic searchable encryption in very-large databases: data structures and implementation. In: NDSS 2014 (2014)
4. Chang, Y.-C., Mitzenmacher, M.: Privacy preserving keyword searches on remote encrypted data. In: Ioannidis, J., Keromytis, A., Yung, M. (eds.) ACNS 2005. LNCS, vol. 3531, pp. 442–455. Springer, Heidelberg (2005). doi:10.1007/11496137_30
5. Chuah, M., Hu, W.: Privacy-aware bedtree based solution for fuzzy multi-keyword search over encrypted data. In: IEEE ICDCS 2011, pp. 273–281 (2011)
6. Curtmola, R., Garay, J.A., Kamara, S., Ostrovsky, R.: Searchable symmetric encryption: improved definitions and efficient constructions. In: CCS 2006, pp. 79–88 (2006)
7. Enron email dataset (2015). www.cs.cmu.edu/~./enron/
8. Goh, E.: Secure indexes. IACR Cryptology ePrint Archive (2003)
9. Goodrich, M.T., Mitzenmacher, M.: Privacy-preserving access of outsourced data via oblivious RAM simulation. In: Aceto, L., Henzinger, M., Sgall, J. (eds.) ICALP 2011. LNCS, vol. 6756, pp. 576–587. Springer, Heidelberg (2011). doi:10.1007/978-3-642-22012-8_46
10. Hahn, F., Kerschbaum, F.: Searchable encryption with secure and efficient updates. In: ACM SIGSAC, pp. 310–320 (2014)
11. Hu, C., Han, L.: Efficient wildcard search over encrypted data. Int. J. Inf. Sec. **15**(5), 539–547 (2016)
12. Kamara, S., Papamanthou, C.: Parallel and dynamic searchable symmetric encryption. In: Sadeghi, A.-R. (ed.) FC 2013. LNCS, vol. 7859, pp. 258–274. Springer, Heidelberg (2013). doi:10.1007/978-3-642-39884-1_22
13. Kamara, S., Papamanthou, C., Roeder, T.: Dynamic searchable symmetric encryption. In: CCS, pp. 965–976 (2012)
14. Kuzu, M., Islam, M.S., Kantarcioglu, M.: Efficient similarity search over encrypted data. In: IEEE ICDE, pp. 1156–1167 (2012)
15. Li, J., Wang, Q., Wang, C., Cao, N., Ren, K., Lou, W.: Fuzzy keyword search over encrypted data in cloud computing. In: INFOCOM, pp. 441–445 (2010)
16. Liu, C., Zhu, L., Li, L., Tan, Y.: Fuzzy keyword search on encrypted cloud storage data with small index. In: IEEE CCIS, pp. 269–273 (2011)
17. Örencik, C., Kantarcioglu, M., Savas, E.: A practical and secure multi-keyword search method over encrypted cloud data. In: IEEE CLOUD, pp. 390–397 (2013)
18. Song, D.X., Wagner, D., Perrig, A.: Practical techniques for searches on encrypted data. In: IEEE S&P, pp. 44–55 (2000)
19. Stefanov, E., Papamanthou, C., Shi, E.: Practical dynamic searchable encryption with small leakage. In: NDSS (2014)
20. Strizhov, M., Ray, I.: Secure multi-keyword similarity search over encrypted cloud data supporting efficient multi-user setup. TDP **9**(2), 131–159 (2016)
21. Sun, W., Wang, B., Cao, N., Li, M., Lou, W., Hou, Y.T., Li, H.: Privacy-preserving multi-keyword text search in the cloud supporting similarity-based ranking. In: ACM ASIA CCS, pp. 71–82 (2013)
22. Wang, B., Yu, S., Lou, W., Hou, Y.T.: Privacy-preserving multi-keyword fuzzy search over encrypted data in the cloud. In: INFOCOM, pp. 2112–2120 (2014)
23. Wang, C., Ren, K., Yu, S., Urs, K.M.R.: Achieving usable and privacy-assured similarity search over outsourced cloud data. In: INFOCOM, pp. 451–459 (2012)

24. Xia, Z., Wang, X., Sun, X., Wang, Q.: A secure and dynamic multi-keyword ranked search scheme over encrypted cloud data. IEEE TPDS **27**(2), 340–352 (2016)
25. Yuan, X., Cui, H., Wang, X., Wang, C.: Enabling privacy-assured similarity retrieval over millions of encrypted records. In: Pernul, G., Ryan, P.Y.A., Weippl, E. (eds.) ESORICS 2015. LNCS, vol. 9327, pp. 40–60. Springer, Cham (2015). doi:10.1007/978-3-319-24177-7_3
26. Zhang, Y., Katz, J., Papamanthou, C.: All your queries are belong to us: the power of file-injection attacks on searchable encryption. In: USENIX, pp. 707–720 (2016)

Enhanced Modelling of Authenticated Key Exchange Security

Papa B. Seye and Augustin P. Sarr$^{(\boxtimes)}$

Laboratoire ACCA, Université Gaston Berger de Saint-Louis,
Saint Louis, Senegal
aug.sarr@gmail.com

Abstract. The security models for Authenticated Key Exchange do not consider leakages on pre-computed ephemeral data before their use in sessions. We investigate the consequences of such leakages and point out damaging consequences. As an illustration, we show the HMQV-C protocol vulnerable to a Bilateral Unknown Key Share (BUKS) and an Unilateral Unknown Key Share (UUKS) Attack, when precomputed ephemeral *public* keys are leaked. We point out some shades in the seCK model in multi-certification authorities setting. We propose an enhancement of the seCK model, which uses a liberal instantiation of the certification systems model from the ASICS framework, and allows reveal queries on precomputed ephemeral (public and private) keys. We propose a new protocol, termed eFHMQV, which in addition to provide the same efficiency as MQV, is particularly suited for implementations wherein a trusted device is used together with untrusted host machine. In such settings, the non-idle time computational effort of the device safely reduces to one digest computation, one integer multiplication, and one integer addition. The eFHMQV protocol meets our security definition, under the Random Oracle Model and the Gap Diffie-Hellman assumption.

Keywords: Unknown Key Share · seCK^{cs} · ASICS · HMQV-C · eFHMQV

1 Introduction

A large body of works on the modelling of Authenticated Key Exchange (AKE) security have been proposed since this approach was pioneered by Bellare and Rogaway [3]. The recent security models, CK [7], eCK [21], CK$_{HMQV}$ [17] and seCK [25, 28] for instance, consider finely grained information leakages, including leakages on static and ephemeral private keys, session keys, and intermediate results. Working in another direction, Boyd *et al.* propose the ASICS framework [5] which provides a finely grained model of multi-certification systems and related attacks.

P.B. Seye—Supported by the CEA-MITIC of UGB.

G. Livraga and C. Mitchell (Eds.): STM 2017, LNCS 10547, pp. 36–52, 2017.
DOI: 10.1007/978-3-319-68063-7_3

In implementations of AKE protocols, ephemeral data are often pre-computed to boost implementations performance. The pre-computed data may then leak to an adversary. To take this into account, the recent models, such as CK [7], eCK [21], CK_{HMQV} [17] and seCK [25,28] among others, consider adversaries which may gain access to ephemeral secrets. Unfortunately, while leakages on precomputed ephemeral secrets may occur before their use in sessions, these models consider such leakages only while the keys are in use in a session (*i.e.* *after* the session owner knows his peer), *not before*.

The works [5,6] provide a generic framework termed ASICS, which considers not only leakages on the randomness used for ephemeral key generation, but also various attacks related to Certification Authorities (CAs) corruptions. Instantiations of the framework lead, depending on the allowed queries, to the eCK [21], the eCK^w [9], eCK-PFS [9], and to the CK_{HMQV} [17] models.

By considering an adversary which may learn the intermediate results in a session, the seCK model [25,28] aims at a better capture of information leakages. In this model, it is assumed at each party that a trusted computation area (a trusted platform module, a smart card, a hardware security module, etc.) is used together with an untrusted one (an untrusted host machine). It is assumed also that AKE implementations may differ from one party to another. Two implementations approaches are considered depending on the area wherein the ephemeral keys are computed. And, reveal queries are defined to allow an adversary to learn any information which is computed or used in the untrusted area.

Albeit the seCK model seems to provide a better capture of information leakages than the CK, eCK or ASICS models, the seCK definition considers only one honest CA and assumes that each party registers only one public key. The attacks that may occur in the multi-CA settings, wherein a party may have many certificates, and some of the CAs may be adversary controlled are not captured. Moreover, similar to the ASICS, eCK, and CK models, the seCK definition unnaturally omits leakages of ephemeral public and private keys, *before* their use in sessions. We investigate, in the multi-CA setting, the consequences of leakages on precomputed ephemeral keys. We show that even leakages on *ephemeral public keys* may have damaging consequences. As an illustration, we point out Unknown Key Share (UKS) attacks against the HMQV-C protocol [17], which was designed to provably provide explicit mutual key authentication. We propose an enhancement of the seCK model which uses a liberal instantiation of the ASICS certification systems model. Contrary to the previous models, the $seCK^{cs}$ definition considers leakages on precomputed ephemeral public and private keys before their use in sessions, and captures various kind of UKS "related" attacks. We propose also an efficient protocol, termed eFHMQV, which is $seCK^{cs}$-secure under the Random Oracle model and the Gap Diffie-Hellman assumption.

This paper is organized as follows. In Sect. 2, we point out some limitations in the security models for AKE, we illustrate with UKS attacks against HMQV-C. In Sect. 3 we present the $seCK^{cs}$ model. In Sect. 4 we propose the eFHMQV protocol.

We use the following notations. H is λ bits hash function, where λ is the security parameter, $\bar{H}$ is a $l = \lambda/2$ bits hash function. $\mathcal{G} = \langle G \rangle$ is a multiplicatively written group of prime order p, $\mathcal{G}^*$ is the set non-identity elements in $\mathcal{G}$. If n is an integer, $|n|$ denotes its bit-length and $[n]$ denotes the set $\{1, \cdots, n\}$. The symbol $\in_R$ stands for "chosen uniformly at random in". For two bit strings m_1 and $m_2, m_1 \| m_2$ denotes their concatenation. If $x_1, x_2, \cdots, x_k$ are objects belonging to different structures (group, bit-string, etc.) $(x_1, x_2, \cdots, x_k)$ denotes the concatenation of their representations as bit-strings.

2   Some Limitations in Existing Security Models

In this section we point out some limitations in the security models used for the analysis of Authenticated Key Exchange (AKE) protocols. We show that even leakages on pre-computed ephemeral *public* keys, may have damaging consequences. Such leakages are not considered in any of the security definitions for AKE we are aware of.

There are many arguments in favour of considering leakages on ephemeral keys (both public and private) *before* their use in sessions (*i.e.* before the peer in the session wherein the key is used is known). First, ephemeral keys pairs may be precomputed and stored in an untrusted memory; this matches, for instance, the implementation approach 1 in the seCK model [25,28] (see Fig. 1), and motivates the HMQV analysis in [17, Sect. 7]. Second, even in the seCK's implementation approach 2, wherein ephemeral keys are computed in a trusted area, there may be a limited storage space in a this area (a smart card, for instance). The ephemeral *public* keys may then be stored unencrypted[1] in the untrusted area, as when encrypted, the advantages of pre-computing may be (partially) lost, because of the time required for deciphering. It seems then realistic to consider leakages on precomputed ephemeral public keys before their use in sessions.

2.1   (Bilateral) Unknown Key Share Attacks

Key authentication is a fundamental AKE security attribute which guarantees that, besides a session owner, a session key is (possibly) known only by the peer. A key authentication is said to be *implicit* from a party $\hat{A}$ to another party $\hat{B}$, if when $\hat{B}$ completes a session with intended peer $\hat{A}$, then he has some assurance that $\hat{A}$ is the only other entity that can be in possession of the session key. *Explicit* key authentication from $\hat{A}$ to $\hat{B}$ is achieved if at the completion of the session at $\hat{B}$, he has some assurance that $\hat{A}$ is the only other entity in possession of the session key. A protocol is said to provide *mutual* key authentication (either explicit or implicit) when it provides key authentication both from $\hat{A}$ to $\hat{B}$ and from $\hat{B}$ to $\hat{A}$.

Unknown Key Share (UKS) attacks, also termed *identity misbinding* [16], seem to have been identified for the first time in [10]. Different formulations of

---

[1] However, digests of the public keys are stored in the tamper proof device, so that it is possible to verify that the keys were not altered.

an UKS attack can be found in the literature [4,15,16,23], although they convey essentially the same idea. The definition from [15], requires that an attacker, say $\hat{E}$, coerces two entities $\hat{A}$ and $\hat{B}$ into sharing a session key while *at least* one of them does not know that the session key is shared with the other; vulnerability to UKS attacks is then a failure in key authentication. A protocol is said to be vulnerable to an Unilateral UKS (UUKS), if an attacker can succeed in making two parties, say $\hat{A}$ and $\hat{B}$ share a session key, while *exactly* one of the parties, say $\hat{A}$ believes having shared the key with a party $\hat{C} \neq \hat{B}$. A protocol is said to be vulnerable to a BUKS attack if an attacker is able to make two entities, say $\hat{A}$ and $\hat{B}$, share a session key, while $\hat{A}$ believes having shared the key with some party $\hat{E}_1 \neq \hat{B}$ and $\hat{B}$ believes having shared the key with $\hat{E}_2 \neq \hat{A}$, the parties $\hat{E}_1$ and $\hat{E}_2$ may be different or not. BUKS attacks are then a specific case of UKS attacks (see [8] for a further discussion about UUKS and BUKS attacks).

Usually, in an (B, U)UKS attack, the attacker does not know the shared session key, he cannot then decipher or inject messages in the communications between the parties sharing the key. However, he may take advantage from the "unknown key share(s)", as shown in [4, Sect. 5.1.2] for UUKS attacks. For BUKS attacks, suppose that $\hat{A}$ is renowned chess player, $\hat{B}$ is a famous Artificial Intelligence (AI) creator, who claims having created an AI program that can win against $\hat{A}$, and the attacker $\hat{E}$ is an AI program creator who wants to take advantage from the reputations of $\hat{A}$ or $\hat{B}$. If the game parties between $\hat{A}$ and $\hat{B}$'s program are played online, using some AKE protocol Π which is vulnerable to a BUKS, $\hat{E}$ may claim having created an AI program that he expects to win against both $\hat{A}$ and the program from $\hat{B}$. Then $\hat{E}$ interferes in the session between $\hat{A}$ and $\hat{B}$ such that $\hat{A}$ (resp. $\hat{B}$) believes having shared the session key with $\hat{E}$, while it is shared with $\hat{B}$ (resp. $\hat{A}$). If $\hat{A}$ wins the game, $\hat{E}$ claims that his program won against the one from $\hat{B}$. Otherwise, he claims the converse. In any case, $\hat{E}$ takes advantage from the reputation of either $\hat{A}$ or $\hat{B}$. Such attacks may be damaging in any setting wherein the attacker can get some *credit* from a BUKS attack.

2.2 BUKS and UUKS Attacks Against HMQV-C

The HMQV protocol is a "hashed variant" of the MQV protocol [22], designed to provably overcome the "analytical shortcomings" in the MQV design [17,18]. In particular, HMQV is claimed to be provably resilient to UKS attacks. The three pass variant of HMQV, termed HMQV-C (the 'C' stands for key *confirmation*) is designed to provide, besides the HMQV security attributes, *explicit mutual key confirmation* and perfect forward secrecy. It is then a major design goal in HMQV-C that when a session key is shared between two honest parties, say $\hat{A}$ and $\hat{B}, \hat{A}$ (resp. $\hat{B}$) gets assurance that, besides himself, the session key is known only to $\hat{B}$ (resp. $\hat{A}$). Let $\hat{A}$ and $\hat{B}$ are two parties with respective static key pairs $(a, A = G^a)$ and $(b, B = G^b)$, with $A, B \in \mathcal{G}^*$. An execution of the HMQV-C protocol between them is as in Protocol 1; the execution aborts if any verification fails.

Protocol 1. The HMQV-C Protocol

(I) The initiator $\hat{A}$ does the following:
    (a) Choose $x \in_R [p-1]$ and compute $X = G^x$.
    (b) Send $(\hat{A}, \hat{B}, X)$ to $\hat{B}$.

(II) At receipt of $(\hat{A}, \hat{B}, X)$, $\hat{B}$ does the following:
    (a) Choose $y \in_R [p-1]$ and compute $Y = G^y$.
    (b) Compute $d = \bar{H}(X, \hat{B})$, $e = \bar{H}(Y, \hat{A})$, $s_B = y + eb \bmod p$, $\sigma_B = (XA^d)^{s_B}$,
        $K = H(\sigma_B, 1)$, and $K_m = H(\sigma_B, 0)$.
    (c) Send $(\hat{B}, \hat{A}, Y, \mathrm{MAC}_{K_m}(\text{``1''}))$ to $\hat{A}$.

(III) At receipt of $(\hat{B}, \hat{A}, Y, \mathrm{MAC}_{K_m}(\text{``1''}))$, $\hat{A}$ does the following:
    (a) Compute $d = \bar{H}(X, \hat{B})$, $e = \bar{H}(Y, \hat{A})$, $s_A = x + da \bmod p$, $\sigma_A = (YB^e)^{s_A}$,
        $K = H(\sigma_A, 1)$, and $K_m = H(\sigma_A, 0)$.
    (b) Validate $\mathrm{MAC}_{K_m}(\text{``1''})$.
    (c) Send $(\hat{A}, \hat{B}, X, \mathrm{MAC}_{K_m}(\text{``0''}))$ to $\hat{B}$.

(IV) At receipt of $(\hat{A}, \hat{B}, X, \mathrm{MAC}_{K_m}(\text{``0''}))$, $\hat{B}$ validates $\mathrm{MAC}_{K_m}(\text{``0''})$.

(V) The shared session key is K.

A BUKS Against HMQV-C. Suppose an attacker, with identity $\hat{E}$ (X509 Distinguished Name in [19]), which learns $\hat{A}$ and $\hat{B}$'s pre-computed ephemeral *public* keys X and Y, respectively, before their use. Proceeding as in Attack 2, $\hat{E}$ interferes such that $\hat{A}$ and $\hat{B}$ share a session key, while each of them believes having shared the key with $\hat{E}$.

Attack 2. BUKS Attack against HMQV-C

---

(1) Compute $d = \bar{H}(X, \hat{E})$, $X' = XA^dG$, $u = \bar{H}(X', \hat{B})$, and $E_1 = G^{-u^{-1} \bmod p}$.
(2) Register the key E_1 using the identity $\hat{E}$ to get a certificate crt_1.
(3) Compute $e = \bar{H}(Y, \hat{E})$, $Y' = YB^eG$, $v = \bar{H}(Y', \hat{A})$, and $E_2 = G^{-v^{-1} \bmod p}$.
(4) Register the key E_2 using the identity $\hat{E}$ to get a certificate crt_2.
(5) Induce $\hat{A}$ to initiate a session with peer $\hat{E}$ (using crt_2), and receive $(\hat{A}, \hat{E}, X)$ from $\hat{A}$.
(6) Initiate a session with peer $\hat{B}$ (using crt_1) by sending $(\hat{E}, \hat{B}, X')$.
(7) Receive $(\hat{B}, \hat{E}, Y, t_B = \mathrm{MAC}_{K_m}(\text{``1''}))$ from $\hat{B}$.
(8) Send $(\hat{E}, \hat{A}, Y', t_B)$ to $\hat{A}$.
(9) Receive $(\hat{A}, \hat{E}, X, t_A = \mathrm{MAC}_{K_m}(\text{``0''}))$ from $\hat{A}$.
(10) Send $(\hat{E}, \hat{B}, X', t_A)$ to $\hat{B}$.

As the attacker knows the static private keys corresponding to the keys he registers using his own identity, the registrations succeed even if a proof of knowledge of the private keys is required; he may register the keys at different CAs, in the case CAs do not register one identifier for many keys. Furthermore, the dual signature $\hat{A}$ derives is $\sigma_A = \mathrm{CDH}(XA^d, Y'E_2^v)$ wherein $d = \bar{H}(X, \hat{E})$ and $v = \bar{H}(Y', \hat{A})$. As $Y' = YB^eG$ where $e = \bar{H}(Y, \hat{E})$, and $E_2 = G^{-v^{-1}}$, we have $Y'E_2^v = YB^eG(G^{-v^{-1}})^v = YB^e$, and $\sigma_A = \text{CDH}(XA^d, YB^e)$. Similarly, the session signature at $\hat{B}$ is $\sigma_B = \text{CDH}(YB^e, X'E_1^u)$ where $u = \bar{H}(X', \hat{B})$. As $X' = XA^dG$, we have $X'E_1^u = XA^dG(G^{-u^{-1}})^u = XA^d$, and $\sigma_B = \text{CDH}(YB^e, XA^d) = \sigma_A$. Then $\hat{A}$ and $\hat{B}$ derive the same session signature, the same session key $K = H(\sigma_A, 1) = H(\sigma_B, 1)$, and also the same MACing key $K_m = H(\sigma_A, 0) = H(\sigma_B, 0)$. Hence the MAC validations succeed in the sessions at $\hat{A}$ and $\hat{B}$, which both accept. As a consequence, $\hat{A}$ and $\hat{B}$ share the same session key $(K = H(\sigma_A, 1) = H(\sigma_B, 1))$ while each of them believes having shared the key with $\hat{E}$ (who is not in possession of the session key).

Applicability of the Attack Against other Protocols. Variants of our BUKS attack can be launched against the MQV [22], HMQV [17], SIG-DH [7], $\mathcal{P}$ [24], and DIKE [34] protocols; similar attacks are already known, from [8], against the four DHKE [29], the modified STS [4], and the alternative Oakley [4] protocols. In the HMQV instantiations under consideration for P1363 standardization (see the current P1363 draft at tinyurl.com/jolno5n), it is not mandated that the protocols be executed in the pre-specified-peer model (see [24] for a further discussion about the pre- and post-specified peer models). When these protocol are executed in the *post-specified-peer* model, *i.e.* when a session initiator discovers his peer's identity after he receives a message from him, variants of the attack can be launched *without any leakage assumption*. Without *further assumptions* the attack fails against the MQV-C and FHMQV protocols. In MQV-C, $\hat{B}$ provides to $\hat{A}$ a MAC of $(2, \hat{B}, \hat{A}, Y, X)$ and receives from him a MAC of $(3, \hat{A}, \hat{B}, X, Y)$, so when the attack is launched, although the MACing keys at $\hat{A}$ and $\hat{B}$ are the same, due to changes in the MACed data they expect, the validations fail.

An UUKS Attack Against HMQV-C.

In [24], Menezes and Ustaoglu point out an UUKS against the *two-pass HMQV* in post-specified peer model. The attack can be launched if (i) a party can select its own identifier, and (ii) at key registration a proof of knowledge of the private key is *not* required. In a setting with 2^k honest parties, the attack requires roughly $2^{|p|/2-k}$ operations.

Assuming that the attacker may learn precomputed ephemeral *public* keys, we propose in Attack 3 an UUKS attack against HMQV-C. Our attack holds in the pre-specified peer model and seems to be more realistic than Menezes and Ustaoglu's attack. When Attack 3 is launched, $\hat{A}$ computes $\sigma_A = \text{CDH}(XA^d, Y'E^v)$ where $d = \bar{H}(X, \hat{E})$ and $v = \bar{H}(Y', \hat{A})$. As $Y'E^v = YB^eG(G^{-v^{-1}})^v$, it follows that $\sigma_A = \text{CDH}(XA^d, YB^e)$ where $e = \bar{H}(Y, \hat{A})$. The party $\hat{B}$, activated with peer $\hat{A}$, computes $\sigma_B = \text{CDH}(YB^e, XA^d)$ wherein $d = \bar{H}(X, \hat{B}) = \bar{H}(X, \hat{E})$. Then $\hat{A}$ and $\hat{B}$ share the same session dual signature, making the MAC validations succeed in the sessions at both $\hat{A}$ and $\hat{B}$. So, $\hat{A}$ and $\hat{B}$ derive the same session key, while $\hat{A}$ believes having shared the key with $\hat{E}$, and $\hat{B}$ believes having shared the key with $\hat{A}$.

Similar to the attack from [24], in a setting with 2^k parties, our attack requires roughly $2^{|p|/2-k}$ operations (the computations at step 3). For $|p| = 160$ and $k = 20$, the attack requires 2^{60} operations and is not then out of reach of our computational capabilities [13,20]. Moreover, contrary to the Attack from [24], in our attack (i) the computations at step 3 are performed offline (after the attacker learns X), and (ii) the attacker knows the private key corresponding to the static key he registers. Our UUKS attack (against HMQV-C) is then more practical than the one from [24].

Attack 3. UUKS Attack against HMQV-C

(1) Learn an ephemeral *public* key X from a part, say $\hat{A}$.

(2) Compute $\mathcal{D} = \left\{ (C, \bar{H}(X, \hat{C})) : \hat{C} \text{ is an honest party} \right\}$.

(3) Find an identifier $\hat{E}$ (which is different from honest parties identifiers) such that for some honest $\hat{B}$, $(\hat{B}, \bar{H}(X, \hat{E})) \in \mathcal{D}$.

(4) Learn an ephemeral *public* key Y at $\hat{B}$.

(5) Compute $e = \bar{H}(Y, \hat{A})$, $Y' = YB^e G$, $v = \bar{H}(Y', \hat{A})$, and $E = G^{-v^{-1} \mod p}$.

(6) Register the key E using the identifier $\hat{E}$.

(7) Induce $\hat{A}$ to initiate a session with peer $\hat{E}$, and receive $(\hat{A}, \hat{E}, X)$ from $\hat{A}$.

(8) Send $(\hat{A}, \hat{B}, X)$ to $\hat{B}$.

(9) Intercept $\hat{B}$'s response $(\hat{B}, \hat{A}, Y, t_B = \mathrm{MAC}_{K_m}(\text{"1"}))$.

(10) Send $(\hat{E}, \hat{A}, Y', t_B)$ to $\hat{A}$.

(11) Receive $(\hat{A}, \hat{E}, X, t_A = \mathrm{MAC}_{K_m}(\text{"0"}))$ from $\hat{A}$.

(12) Send $(\hat{A}, \hat{B}, X, t_A)$ to $\hat{B}$.

2.3   About the Capture of UKS Related Attacks in Security Models

By UKS *related* attacks we refer to the attacks wherein the attacker succeeds in making non matching sessions yield unhashed secrets (session signatures) such that given one of the secrets, the other can be efficiently computed. Our attacks occur in the specific case wherein the unhashed secrets are the same.

Two weaknesses in the $\mathrm{CK_{HMQV}}$ model explain the co-existence of our attack and the HMQV(-C) security reduction. First, although the settings wherein ephemeral keys are pre-computed motivate the analysis in [17, Sect. 7], leakages on ephemeral keys are considered *only* while they are in use (*i.e.* after the peer in the session is known), *not* before. Then, the attacks assuming leakages on ephemeral public keys before their use are not captured. Moreover, when in addition to considering leakages on precomputed ephemeral keys, an attacker may learn some intermediate secrets (as modelled in the seCK definition [26,28]), further attacks can be launched. We stress that leakages on intermediate results is a realistic assumption. For instance, the AKE implementations in TPM2.0 are divided into two phases. In the first phase an outgoing ephemeral key is generated, using the command TPM2_EC_Ephemeral() (see [31, Sect. 19.3]). In the second phase (the relevant command is TPM2_ZGen_2Phase() [31, Sect. 14.7]) the TPM computes (using the peer's public keys) the unhashed shared secret (σ in the case of MQV). The session key is computed on the host machine (which may be infected by a malware), using the unhashed shared secret. When leakages on the unhashed shared secrets are considered, variants of our attacks can be launched against (H, C)MQV-C, even if nonces or the peers identities are included in the final digest for session key derivation.

We found no variant of our attacks against the FHMQV or SMQV protocols [25,28], as long as the CAs are honest and each party has only one certificate. However, in a multi-CA setting, where a party may have many certificates, some shades occur. We stress that considering a multi-CA setting, as modelled in the ASICS framework [5] wherein some of the CAs may be adversarially controlled, seems to be realistic. Indeed, for most browsers, only few clicks are required to add a rogue CA certificate in the trust-store (the set of CA certificates the user trusts), and it may also occur that users do not change their systems default trust-stores passwords.

For a party, say $\hat{A}$, with two certificates (with different keys), say crt_1 and crt_2, the disclosure of the private key corresponding to crt_1 should have no adverse effects in the sessions wherein $\hat{A}$ uses crt_2. And, when an attacker registers a certificate crt^* using $\hat{A}$'s identity and a static key which is different from the one corresponding to crt_2, the existence of crt^* should have no adverse effect on the sessions wherein $\hat{A}$ uses crt_2. Hence, the notion of "corruption" should be about certificates, not on parties. As a shade in the seCK model, in multi-CA settings, consider two parties $\hat{A}$ and $\hat{B}$, with respective certificates crt and crt', executing the (C, F)HMQV protocol (see [32] and [25,28] for descriptions of CMQV and FHMQV respectively), and an attacker which performs as in Attack 4.

Attack 4. Attack against (C, F)HMQV in a multi-CA setting

(a) Register $E - GA$ where A is $\hat{A}$'s static public key using $\hat{A}$'s identifier to obtain a certificate crt^*.

(b) When $\hat{A}$ initiates a session with peer $\hat{B}$ intercept his message $(\mathsf{crt}, \mathsf{crt}', X)$ and send $(\mathsf{crt}^*, \mathsf{crt}', X)$ to $\hat{B}$.

(c) Intercept $\hat{B}$'s response $(\mathsf{crt}', \mathsf{crt}^*, Y)$ and send $(\mathsf{crt}', \mathsf{crt}, Y)$ to $\hat{A}$.

The session signatures $\hat{A}$ and $\hat{B}$ derive are respectively $\sigma_A = \mathrm{CDH}(XA^d, YB^e)$ and $\sigma_B = \mathrm{CDH}(X(GA)^d, YB^e) = \sigma_A YB^e$, where B is $\hat{B}$'s static key and d and e are the $\bar{H}$ digest values in (C, F)MQV. The sessions at $\hat{A}$ and $\hat{B}$ are non-matching and the session at $\hat{A}$ is seCK-fresh. When the attacker issues a session signature reveal query (to learn σ_B), he can compute the session key at $\hat{A}$ and succeed in a distinguishing game. An enhancement of the seCK security definition to clarify the shades and capture the consequences of leakages on precomputed ephemeral public keys is desirable. We propose such a model.

3   Enhancing the seCK Security Model

Broadly, in the seCK model [25,28], it is assumed two computation areas at each party, a trusted one (a smart card, a tamper proof device, etc.) and an untrusted one (a host machine), and that any information which is computed or used in the untrusted area can leak to an adversary. In addition, it is assumed that implementations may differ from one party to another; information leakages may then differ from one party to another. This seems to correspond to real word vulnerabilities [14,30,33]. Unfortunately, the seCK definition considers only one honest CA, and assumes that each party has only one honestly generated static key pair, and does not capture some attacks in a multi-CA setting.

In contrast, the ASICS framework considers a multi-CA setting, and captures a wide class of attacks based on adversarial key registration, including small subgroup attacks, UUKS attacks, and the attacks that may occur when a party can register many static keys. However, the ASICS model defines reveal queries only on static keys, randomness and session keys, leaving realistic leakages that may occur, through side-channel attacks for instance. As an example, in the CMQV variant, shown secure in [5,6], if an attacker learns a sufficiently large part of the ephemeral secret exponent at a part (s_A or s_B in Protocol 1), he can impersonate indefinitely the session owner to its peer [1,26].

We propose the seCK^{cs} (the 'cs' stands for certification systems) to enhance the seCK model [25,28] in the following ways: (i) seCK^{cs} provides a capture of the attacks exploiting leakages on pre-computed ephemeral public and private keys, (ii) it uses a liberal instantiation of the multi-CA model from [5], and (iii) captures various "kinds" of UKS related attacks.

3.1   The seCK^{cs} Security Model

We suppose m parties $M_1, \cdots, M_m$, and an adversary $\mathcal{A}$, modelled as PPT Turing machines, sharing a securely generated set domain parameters, we denote by dp. The adversary is supposed to be in total control of the communication links between parties. We assume also n identities $\mathsf{id}_1, \cdots, \mathsf{id}_n$, with $m \leqslant n \leqslant R(\lambda)$ for some polynomial R. And, we require that different honest parties have distinct identities; we allow however a party to have many identities.

Key Generation and Certificate Registration. We assume a liberal certification authority (CA) which *accepts all the queries from the adversary*, including queries with the key and identity of an honest party. We only require that two certificates issued at distinct registrations be different, even if they have the same key and identity. In other words, we assume that each certificate has some specific information, we denote by Unique Identifier (ui), which is unique and efficiently computable. When various certificate formats are used, assuming that a CA does not issue two certificates with the same serial number, the ui can be, for instance, the quadruple (date of issuance, serial number, issuer, subject).

The adversary can direct a party, say M_i, to *generate a static key pair* trough $\mathsf{GenSKP}(M_i)$ query. This query can be issued many times at each party. When it is issued, M_i generates (using dp) a key pair (a, A) and provides $\mathcal{A}$ with A. Once A generated, $\mathcal{A}$ is allowed to direct M_i to *honestly register* A by issuing $\mathsf{HReg}(M_i, A, \mathsf{id}_k)$. When this query is issued, M_i registers A with the identity id_k to obtain a certificate. We stress that the HReg query is for *honest* key registration, so for the query to succeed, we require that no $\mathsf{HReg}(M_{i'}, A', \mathsf{id}_k)$

with $i' \neq i$ have been successfully issued before; *i.e.* that when different parties *honestly* register static keys, they use different identities.

The attacker can *maliciously* register *any* (valid or invalid) key, including honest parties static keys, together with any string of its choice (including a honest party's identity) using the $\mathsf{MReg}(Q, \mathsf{id})$ query; this query *always* succeeds. For a certificate crt, we refer to the certificate's public key, identity, and ui respectively by $\mathsf{crt.pk}$, $\mathsf{crt.id}$, and $\mathsf{crt.ui}$.

Sessions. A session is an instance of a protocol run at a party; $\mathcal{A}$ decides about session activations. To activate a session, say at M_i with peer $M_{i'}$, $\mathcal{A}$ issues a Create query with parameters $(\mathsf{crt}, \mathsf{crt}')$ or $(\mathsf{crt}, \mathsf{crt}', m)$, where m is a message supposed to be from $M_{i'}$, and crt and crt' are certificates belonging to M_i and $M_{i'}$ respectively. If the creation parameter is $(\mathsf{crt}, \mathsf{crt}')$, M_i is said to be the initiator $(\mathcal{I})$, otherwise he is said to be the responder $(\mathcal{R})$. At session creation, the activated party may provide $\mathcal{A}$ with an outgoing message (sid', m') where sid' is a session identifier and m' is a message to be processed in sid'. Each session is identified with a tuple $(\mathsf{crt}, \mathsf{crt}', \mathsf{out}, \mathsf{in}, \mathsf{role})$, where crt is the owner's certificate, crt' is the peer's certificate (in the owner's view), out is the list of the outgoing messages, in is the list of the incoming messages, and $\mathsf{role} \in \{\mathcal{I}, \mathcal{R}\}$ is the owner's role. For an identifier $\mathsf{sid} = (\mathsf{crt}, \mathsf{crt}'\, \mathsf{out}, \mathsf{in}, \mathsf{role})$, we refer respectively to $\mathsf{crt}, \mathsf{crt}', \mathsf{out}, \mathsf{in}$, and role by $\mathsf{sid}_{\mathsf{oc}}, \mathsf{sid}_{\mathsf{pc}}, \mathsf{sid}_{\mathsf{in}}, \mathsf{sid}_{\mathsf{out}}$, and $\mathsf{sid}_{\mathsf{role}}$. For the two pass Diffie-Hellman protocols, we refer to the incoming and outgoing ephemeral keys by $\mathsf{sid}_{\mathsf{iEPK}}$ and $\mathsf{sid}_{\mathsf{oEPK}}$ respectively. Each session has a status we denote by $\mathsf{sid}_{\mathsf{status}} \in \{\mathsf{active}, \mathsf{accepted}, \mathsf{rejected}\}$. The status is accepted if the session has completed, *i.e.* the session key is computed and accepted. It is rejected if the session has aborted, it is active if it is neither accepted nor rejected. For an accepted session $\mathsf{sid}, \mathsf{sid}_{\mathsf{key}}$ denotes the derived key. The adversary can issue a $\mathsf{Sd}(\mathsf{sid}, m)$ query, where m is a message to be processed in sid. When this query is issued, the session owner is provided with m. He may update $\mathsf{sid}_{\mathsf{in}}$ to include m; he may also compute an outgoing message (sid', m') and update $\mathsf{sid}_{\mathsf{out}}$ and $\mathsf{sid}_{\mathsf{status}}$ accordingly. Two sessions sid and sid' are said to be *matching* if $\mathsf{sid}_{\mathsf{oc}} = \mathsf{sid}'_{\mathsf{pc}}, \mathsf{sid}_{\mathsf{pc}} = \mathsf{sid}'_{\mathsf{oc}}, \mathsf{sid}_{\mathsf{out}} = \mathsf{sid}'_{\mathsf{in}}, \mathsf{sid}_{\mathsf{in}} = \mathsf{sid}'_{\mathsf{out}}$, and $\mathsf{sid}_{\mathsf{role}} \neq \mathsf{sid}'_{\mathsf{role}}$.

Reveal Queries. Similar to the seCK model [25, 28], we assume two computation areas at each party, a trusted and an untrusted one. We suppose that implementations may be performed differently from one party to another, and define reveal queries to allow the adversary to learn any information that is computed or used in the untrusted area. Moreover, the adversary may bypass the tamper protection mechanisms and learn the long term secrets. We assume implementations performed using one of the seCK approaches. In Approach 1, the static key is computed and used in the trusted area, and the ephemeral keys are computed in the untrusted area. This implementation approach corresponds to reveal queries as defined in the eCK and ASICS models. In Approach 2, both static and ephemeral private keys are computed and used in the trusted area, and all the other intermediate results are used in the untrusted host-machine. This approach is similar but stronger than the way AKE implementations are performed in TPM2.0. In both approaches, the session key is used in the untrusted area.

These approaches are not the only possible, and the model can be enriched with other implementation approaches, however the two approaches we consider seem to be typical in real word settings.

The adversary is allowed to direct a certificate owner, say M_i, to generate an ephemeral public key pair using a GenEKP(crt) query. When it is issued, M_i generates a key pair (x, X) and provides the attacker with X. If M_i, follows the Approach 1, $\mathcal{A}$ can issue a RvEPK(X) query to learn the ephemeral private key x. We stress that this query may be issued before the public key X is used in a session. At a party using Approach 2, a reveal query is defined to allow $\mathcal{A}$ to learn *any* information that is computed of used in the untrusted area. In both approaches, the adversary can learn the private key corresponding to a static public key A, by issuing RvSPK(A). For a completed session sid, the attacker can issue a RvSesK(sid) query to learn $\mathrm{sid}_{\mathrm{key}}$. For the protocols of the MQV family, at a party using the Approach 2, $\mathcal{A}$ can issue RvSecExp(sid) to obtain the ephemeral secret exponent in sid (s_A or s_B in HMQV-C), and a RvSesSig(sid) query to obtain the dual signature (σ_A or σ_B) (Tables 1 and 2).

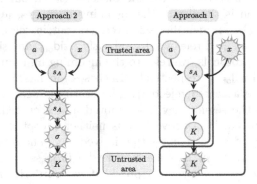

Fig. 1. (e)FHMQV implementation approaches in the seCK model [25,28]

Table 1. Summary of the queries

GenSKP, RvSPK	static key pair generation, static private key reveal query
HReg, MReg	*honest* key registration, *malicious* key registration
GenEKP, RvEPK	ephemeral key pair generation, ephemeral private key reveal query
Create, Sd	Session creation, message sending
RvSesK	session key reveal query
RvSecExp	ephemeral secret exponent reveal query (for the MQV family)
RvSesSig	session signature reveal query
Test	test session query

Table 2. Overview of the notations

dp	public domain parameters
crt, crt$_{x, x \in \{pk, id, ui\}}$	a certificate, the public key (pk), identity (id), or unique identifier (ui) in the certificate crt
sid, sid$_{x, x \in \{oc, pc, out, in, role\}}$	session identifier, the owner's certificate (oc), peer's certificate (pc), list of outgoing messages (out), list of incoming messages (in), or the owner's role in the session sid
sid$_{x, x \in \{iEPK, oEPK\}}$	incoming ephemeral public key (iEPK) or outgoing ephemeral public key (oEPK) in a session (for DH protocols)

Session Freshness. A completed session with identifier sid is said to be:

Locally exposed: if (a) $\mathcal{A}$ issued a RvSesK(sid) query, or (b) the session owner follows the Approach 1 and $\mathcal{A}$ issued both RvSPK(sid$_{oc}$.pk) and RvEPK(sid$_{oEPK}$), or (c) the session owner follows the Approach 2 and $\mathcal{A}$ issued a reveal query on an intermediate result which is computed or used in the untrusted area.

Remark 1. For the protocols of the MQV family, the condition (c) is "the session owner follows the Approach 2 and $\mathcal{A}$ issued RvSecExp(sid) or RvSesSig(sid)."

Exposed: if (a) it is locally exposed, or (b) its matching session exists and is locally exposed, or (c) its matching session does no exist and (c.i) sid$_{pc}$ was maliciously registered, or (c.ii) sid$_{pc}$ was honestly registered and $\mathcal{A}$ issued RvSPK(sid$_{pc}$.pk);
Fresh: if it is not exposed.

The security experiment is initialized with a securely generated public set of domain parameters dp for some security parameter λ. The adversary is allowed to issue all the queries defined above. At some point of the game he issues a Test(sid) query on a completed and fresh session sid. When the Test query is issued a bit $b \in_R \{0, 1\}$ is chosen, and $\mathcal{A}$ is provided with $k = \begin{cases} \text{sid}_{key} \text{ if } b = 1 \\ k' \in_R \{0, 1\}^{\lambda}, \text{otherwise.} \end{cases}$
After the Test query is issued, $\mathcal{A}$ can issue all the queries of its choice as long as sid remains fresh. Finally, he produces a bit b' and wins the game if $b = b'$.

Definition 1 (seCK^{cs} security). *A protocol Π is said to be seCK^{cs} secure if,*

- *except with negligible probability, two sessions yield the same session key if and only if they are matching, and*
- *for all efficient attacker playing the above game, $|2 \Pr(b = b') - 1|$ is negligible.*

3.2 Comparing the seCK^{cs} with the seCK and ASICS Models

The seCK^{cs} definition encompasses the seCK model [25,28] together with a liberal instantiation of the ASICS multi-CA setting [5,6]. The modelling of the

CAs is realistic, as illustrated with recent CA breaches [11,12]. And, as already pointed out in [5, p. 6], although we explicitly consider one CA, we implicitly capture multi-CA settings with independent CAs.

However, there are some differences between the key registration queries in the ASICS and seCK^{cs} models. The honest key registration query in the ASICS model, hregister, takes two parameters, a public key and an identity. The parties and their implementation approaches are modelled in seCK^{cs}, so the honest key registration, HReg, is enriched to include a parameter which indicates the party registering the key. Also, we do not differentiate *malicious* key registrations depending on the validity of the static key the adversary provides, as with the pkregister and npkregister in ASICS. We assume simply that any malicious registration query succeeds (*i.e.* the MReg query always succeeds). Moreover, there are less restrictions in the seCK^{cs} freshness definition than in the ASICS instantiations from [5, Sects. 3–4]. For a session sid without a matching session, both definitions require that no RvSPK(sid$_{pc}$.pk) was successfully issued. However, while [5,6, Theorem 1] requires that MReg(sid$_{pc}$.pk, sid$_{pc}$.id) was not issued, we require that sid$_{pc}$ was not registered by $\mathcal{A}$, meaning that sid remains fresh even if $\mathcal{A}$ issued MReg(sid$_{pc}$.pk, sid$_{pc}$.id), as long as sid$_{pc}$ was not registered by $\mathcal{A}$. Besides, the ASICS model considers only leakages on static keys, randomness and session keys, leaving realistic leakages that may occur, on unhashed shared secrets (in AKE implementations in TPM2.0 for instance); while seCK^{cs} considers reveal queries on precomputed ephemeral keys and any information which is computed or used in the untrusted area.

The seCK^{cs} definition is strictly stronger than seCK, which is already known to be strictly stronger than the eCK model [28]. To illustrate the separation between the seCK^{cs} and seCK models, we consider the Attack 4 against (C, F)HMQV, wherein $\hat{B}$ belong to the set of parties following the second implementation approach. We recall that FHMQV and CMQV are known respectively to be secure in the seCK and ASICS models. In Attack 4, the session at $\hat{A}$ is seCK^{cs}-fresh. Given the relation between the session signatures in the sessions at $\hat{A}$ and $\hat{B}$, $\mathcal{A}$ succeeds in the seCK^{cs} distinguishing game, with probability ≈ 1, as follows: (*i*) he chooses the session at $\hat{A}$ as a test session, (*ii*) issues a RvSesSig on the session at $\hat{B}$ to obtain σ_B, and (*iii*) compute the session signature and the session key $\hat{A}$ derives. The attacker's success follows from its ability to make non-matching sessions yield related session signatures, such that given one of the session signatures, the other can be efficiently computed. By requiring that non-matching sessions do not yield the same session key, seCK^{cs}-security captures classical (B, U)UKS attacks. Moreover, it ensures that non-matching session do not yield related session signatures. The seCK^{cs} model captures not only "classical" UKS attacks, but also the attacks related to unknown share of unhashed session secrets.

4 The enhanced FHMQV (eFHMQV) Protocol

A main improvement in FHMQV [25,26] compared to HMQV [17] is the use of the incoming and outgoing ephemeral keys in the computation of the digest values d and e; this design choice makes FHMQV resilient to leakages on ephemeral secret exponents (s_A and s_B). We use a similar idea in the eFH-MQV design. An execution of eFHMQV between two parties $\hat{A}$ and $\hat{B}$ with respective certificates crt and crt$'$ is as in Protocol 5.

Protocol 5. The eFHMQV Protocol

(I) The initiator $\hat{A}$ does the following:
    (a) Verify that crt$'$.pk $\in \mathcal{G}^*$, choose $x \in_R [p-1]$ and compute $X = G^x$.
    (b) Send (crt, crt$'$, X) to $\hat{B}$.
(II) At receipt of (crt, crt$'$, X), $\hat{B}$ does the following:
    (a) Verify that $X \in \mathcal{G}^*$ and crt.pk $\in \mathcal{G}^*$, choose $y \in_R [p-1]$ and compute $Y = G^y$.
    (b) Send (crt$'$, crt, X, Y) to $\hat{A}$.
    (c) Compute $d = \bar{H}(X, Y, \text{crt.pk}, \text{crt.id}, \text{crt.ui}, \text{crt}'.\text{pk}, \text{crt}'.\text{id}, \text{crt}'.\text{ui})$.
    (d) Compute $e = \bar{H}(Y, X, \text{crt.pk}, \text{crt.id}, \text{crt.ui}, \text{crt}'.\text{pk}, \text{crt}'.\text{id}, \text{crt}'.\text{ui})$.
    (e) Compute $s_B = y + eb$, where $b = \log_G \text{crt}'.\text{pk}$, and $\sigma_B = (X(\text{crt.pk})^d)^{s_B}$.
    (f) Compute $K = H(\sigma_B, \text{crt.pk}, \text{crt.id}, \text{crt.ui}, \text{crt}'.\text{pk}, \text{crt}'.\text{id}, \text{crt}'.\text{ui}, X, Y)$.
(III) At receipt of (crt$'$, crt, X, Y), $\hat{A}$ does the following:
    (a) Verify that $Y \in \mathcal{G}^*$.
    (b) Compute $d = \bar{H}(X, Y, \text{crt.pk}, \text{crt.id}, \text{crt.ui}, \text{crt}'.\text{pk}, \text{crt}'.\text{id}, \text{crt}'.\text{ui})$.
    (c) Compute $e = \bar{H}(Y, X, \text{crt.pk}, \text{crt.id}, \text{crt.ui}, \text{crt}'.\text{pk}, \text{crt}'.\text{id}, \text{crt}'.\text{ui})$.
    (d) Compute $s_A = x + da$, where $a = \log_G \text{crt.pk}$, and $\sigma_A = (Y(\text{crt}'.\text{pk})^e)^{s_A}$.
    (e) Compute $K = H(\sigma_A, \text{crt.pk}, \text{crt.id}, \text{crt.ui}, \text{crt}'.\text{pk}, \text{crt}'.\text{id}, \text{crt}'.\text{ui}, X, Y)$.
(IV) The shared session key is K.

In an eFHMQV session with identifier sid $= (\text{crt}, \text{crt}', X, Y, \mathcal{I})$ the digests d and e are computed as indicated in the steps (IIIb) and (IIIc). As a result, even if the step (a) of Attack 4 is modified to make $\mathcal{A}$ issues $\mathsf{MReg}(\text{crt.pk}, \text{crt.id})$, i.e. $\mathcal{A}$ *registers $\hat{A}$'s key using $\hat{A}$'s identity* to obtain crt*, the attack fails as long as different certificates have different unique identifiers. Indeed, as $\hat{B}$ computes $d' = \bar{H}(X, Y, \text{crt}^*.\text{pk}, \text{crt}^*.\text{id}, \text{crt}^*.\text{ui}, \text{crt}'.\text{pk}, \text{crt}'.\text{id}, \text{crt}'.\text{ui})$ and $e' = \bar{H}(Y, X, \text{crt}^*.\text{pk}, \text{crt}^*.\text{id}, \text{crt}^*.\text{ui}, \text{crt}'.\text{pk}, \text{crt}'.\text{id}, \text{crt}'.\text{ui})$ and crt*.ui $\neq$ crt.ui, except with negligible probability $d' \neq d$ and $e' \neq e$. Then, even if $\mathcal{A}$ issues $\mathsf{RvSecExp}(\text{crt}', \text{crt}_A, Y, X, \mathcal{R})$ in the distinguishing game and receives $s_B = y + e'b$, as $e' \neq e$, he cannot derive $\sigma_A = \text{CDH}(XA^d, YB^c)$ wherein $A = \text{crt.pk}$, $B = \text{crt}'.\text{pk}$. A direct proof of this claim can be obtained using the Knowledge of Exponent Assumption [2]. However, as we show in Theorem 1, this assumption is not necessary.

An execution of eFHMQV requires at most 2.5 times a single exponentiation; this equals the efficiency of the famous MQV protocol. In addition, in Approach 2, the ephemeral public keys can be computed in idle time on a trusted device (a smart card for instance) and stored *unencrypted* in an untrusted host machine. It is only necessary that a digest of the keys be stored on the device so that alterations can be detected. When eFHMQV is implemented in this way, the non-idle time computational effort on the device reduces to one digest computation, one integer addition, and one integer multiplication. We stress that the

(C,H)MQV protocols [17, 22, 32] cannot achieve such a performance, as they do not confine the adverse effects of leakages on secrets exponents (s_A and s_B). And, in the seCK^{cs} security definition, FHMQV and SMQV [26–28] are insecure, and cannot then provably achieve such a performance.

Theorem 1. *Under the Gap Diffie-Hellman assumption and the Random Oracle model, the eFHMQV protocol is seCK^{cs}-secure.*

The FXCR and FDCR schemes [25, 28] are the main ingredients in the proof of this theorem we do not provide here (for lack of space). A detailed proof is given in the extended version of this paper.

5 Concluding Remarks

We pointed out and illustrated some limitations in existing AKE security models. We showed that even leakages on precomputed ephemeral *public* keys may have damaging consequences, we illustrated with (B, U)UKS attacks against the HMQV-C protocol. We proposed the seCK^{cs} security definition which encompasses the seCK model, integrates a strong model of multi-CA settings, and considers leakages on precomputed ephemeral (public and private) keys.

We proposed the eFHMQV protocol, which is particularly suited for distributed implementation environments wherein an untrusted computer is used together with a tamper-resistant device. In such an environment, the non-idle time computational effort of the device reduces to one digest computation, one integer addition, and one integer multiplication. The eFHMQV protocol is seCK^{cs}-secure under the Random Oracle Model and the Gap Diffie-Hellman assumption.

In a forthcoming stage, we will be interested in Perfect Forward Secrecy in the seCK^{cs} model.

References

1. Basin, D., Cremers, C.: Modeling and analyzing security in the presence of compromising adversaries. In: Gritzalis, D., Preneel, B., Theoharidou, M. (eds.) ESORICS 2010. LNCS, vol. 6345, pp. 340–356. Springer, Heidelberg (2010). doi:10.1007/978-3-642-15497-3_21
2. Bellare, M., Palacio, A.: The knowledge-of-exponent assumptions and 3-round zero-knowledge protocols. In: Franklin, M. (ed.) CRYPTO 2004. LNCS, vol. 3152, pp. 273–289. Springer, Heidelberg (2004). doi:10.1007/978-3-540-28628-8_17
3. Bellare, M., Rogaway, P.: Entity authentication and key distribution. In: Stinson, D.R. (ed.) CRYPTO 1993. LNCS, vol. 773, pp. 232–249. Springer, Heidelberg (1994). doi:10.1007/3-540-48329-2_21
4. Boyd, C., Mathuria, A.: Protocols for Authentication and Key Establishment. Springer, Heidelberg (2003). doi:10.1007/978-3-662-09527-0
5. Boyd, C., Cremers, C., Feltz, M., Paterson, K.G., Poettering, B., Stebila, D.: ASICS: authenticated key exchange security incorporating certification systems. In: Crampton, J., Jajodia, S., Mayes, K. (eds.) ESORICS 2013. LNCS, vol. 8134, pp. 381–399. Springer, Heidelberg (2013). doi:10.1007/978-3-642-40203-6_22

6. Boyd, C., Cremers, C., Feltz, M., Paterson, K.G., Poettering, B., Stebila, D.: ASICS: Authenticated key exchange security incorporating certification systems. Cryptology ePrint Archive: Report 2013/398

7. Canetti, R., Krawczyk, H.: Analysis of key-exchange protocols and their use for building secure channels. In: Pfitzmann, B. (ed.) EUROCRYPT 2001. LNCS, vol. 2045, pp. 453–474. Springer, Heidelberg (2001). doi:10.1007/3-540-44987-6_28

8. Chen, L., Tang, Q.: Bilateral unknown key-share attacks in key agreement protocols. J. Univ. Comput. Sci. 14(3), 416–440 (2008)

9. Cremers, C., Feltz, M.: Beyond eCK: perfect forward secrecy under actor compromise and ephemeral-key reveal. Des. Codes Crypt. 74(1), 183–218 (2013). Springer

10. Diffie, W., Van Orschot, P.C., Wiener, M.J.: Authentication and authenticated key exchanges. Des. Codes Crypt. 2(2), 107–125 (1992). Springer

11. Ducklin, P.: Serious security: Google finds fake but trusted SSL certificates for its domains, made in France. http://tinyurl.com/hrmo8pa

12. FOX IT: Black Tulip: report of the investigation into the DigiNotar Certificate Authority breach. http://preview.tinyurl.com/lj6938c

13. Güneysu, T., Pfeiffer, G., Paar, C., Schimmler, M.: Three years of evolution: cryptanalysis with COPACOBANA. In: Workshop Record of "Special-Purpose Hardware for Attacking Cryptographic Systems"–SHARCS 2009 (2009)

14. Huq, N.: PoS RAM Scraper Malware: Past, Present, and Future. A Trend Micro Research Paper (2014). http://tinyurl.com/jcwc8wz

15. Kaliski, B.S.: An unknown key-share attack on the MQV key agreement protocol. ACM Trans. Inf. Syst. Secur. (TISSEC) 4(3), 275–288 (2001). ACM

16. Krawczyk, H.: SIGMA: the 'SIGn-and-MAc' approach to authenticated Diffie-Hellman and its use in the IKE protocols. In: Boneh, D. (ed.) CRYPTO 2003. LNCS, vol. 2729, pp. 400–425. Springer, Heidelberg (2003). doi:10.1007/978-3-540-45146-4_24

17. Krawczyk, H.: HMQV: a hight performance secure Diffie-Hellman protocol. Cryptology ePrint Archive, Report 2005/176 (2005)

18. Krawczyk, H.: HMQV: a high-performance secure Diffie-Hellman protocol. In: Shoup, V. (ed.) CRYPTO 2005. LNCS, vol. 3621, pp. 546–566. Springer, Heidelberg (2005). doi:10.1007/11535218_33

19. Krawczyk, H.: HMQV in IEEE P1363. Submission to the IEEE P1363 working group. http://tinyurl.com/opjqknd

20. Kumar, S., Paar, C., Pelzl, J., Pfeiffer, G., Rupp, A., Schimmler, M.: How to break DES for € 8,980. In: International Workshop on Special-Purpose Hardware for Attacking Cryptographic Systems – SHARCS'06, Cologne, Germany, April 2006

21. LaMacchia, B., Lauter, K., Mityagin, A.: Stronger security of authenticated key exchange. In: Susilo, W., Liu, J.K., Mu, Y. (eds.) ProvSec 2007. LNCS, vol. 4784, pp. 1–16. Springer, Heidelberg (2007). doi:10.1007/978-3-540-75670-5_1

22. Law, L., Menezes, A., Qu, M., Solinas, J., Vanstone, S.: An efficient protocol for authenticated key agreement. Des. Codes Crypt. 28, 119–134 (2003). Springer

23. Menezes, A., Van Oorschot, P.C., Vanstone, S.A.: Handbook of Applied Cryptography. CRC Press, Boca Raton (1996)

24. Menezes, A., Ustaoglu, B.: Comparing the pre- and post-specified peer models for key agreement. Int. J. Appl. Crypt. 1(3), 236–250 (2009). Inderscience

25. Sarr, A.P., Elbaz–Vincent, P.: On the security of the (F)HMQV protocol. In: Pointcheval, D., Nitaj, A., Rachidi, T. (eds.) AFRICACRYPT 2016. LNCS, vol. 9646, pp. 207–224. Springer, Cham (2016). doi:10.1007/978-3-319-31517-1_11

26. Sarr, A.P., Elbaz-Vincent, P., Bajard, J.-C.: A secure and efficient authenticated Diffie–Hellman protocol. In: Martinelli, F., Preneel, B. (eds.) EuroPKI 2009. LNCS, vol. 6391, pp. 83–98. Springer, Heidelberg (2010). doi:10.1007/978-3-642-16441-5_6

27. Sarr, A.P., Elbaz-Vincent, P., Bajard, J.C.: A secure and efficient authenticated Diffie-Hellman protocol. Cryptology ePrint Archive: Report 2009/408

28. Sarr, A.P., Elbaz-Vincent, P., Bajard, J.-C.: A new security model for authenticated key agreement. In: Garay, J.A., De Prisco, R. (eds.) SCN 2010. LNCS, vol. 6280, pp. 219–234. Springer, Heidelberg (2010). doi:10.1007/978-3-642-15317-4_15

29. Shoup, V.: On formal models for secure key exchange. Cryptology ePrint Archive, 1999/012 (1999)

30. Trend Labs Security Intelligence Blog: RawPOS Technical Brief. http://tinyurl.com/joyazja

31. TCG: Trusted Platform Module Library Part 3: Commands, Level 00 Revision 01.38 (2016)

32. Ustaoglu, B.: Obtaining a secure and efficient key agreement protocol from (H)MQV and NAXOS. Des. Codes Crypt. **46**(3), 329–342 (2008)

33. VISA Data Security Alert: Retail Merchants Targeted by Memory-Parsing Malware 2013. http://tinyurl.com/j3duvlg

34. Yao, A.C., Zhao, Y.: Deniable internet key exchange. In: Zhou, J., Yung, M. (eds.) ACNS 2010. LNCS, vol. 6123, pp. 329–348. Springer, Heidelberg (2010). doi:10.1007/978-3-642-13708-2_20

Software Security and Risk Management

Authentic Execution of Distributed Event-Driven Applications with a Small TCB

Job Noorman, Jan Tobias Mühlberg[✉], and Frank Piessens

imec-DistriNet, KU Leuven, Celestijnenlaan 200A, 3001 Leuven, Belgium
jantobias.muehlberg@cs.kuleuven.be

Abstract. This paper presents an approach to provide strong assurance of the secure execution of distributed event-driven applications on shared infrastructures, while relying on a small Trusted Computing Base. We build upon and extend security primitives provided by a Protected Module Architecture (PMA) to guarantee authenticity and integrity properties of applications, and to secure control of input and output devices used by these applications. More specifically, we want to guarantee that *if* an output is produced by the application, it was allowed to be produced by the application's source code. We present a prototype implementation as an extension of Sancus, a light-weight embedded PMA that extends the TI MSP430 CPU. Our evaluation of the security and performance aspects of our approach and the prototype show that PMAs together with our programming model form a basis for powerful security architectures for dependable systems in domains such as Industrial Control Systems, the Internet of Things or Wireless Sensor Networks.

1 Introduction

This paper studies the problem of securely executing distributed applications on a shared infrastructure with a small Trusted Computing Base (TCB). We want to provide the owner of such an application with strong assurance that their application is executing securely. We focus on (1) *authenticity* and *integrity* properties of (2) *event-driven* distributed applications, because for this security property and class of applications, it is relatively easy to specify the exact security guarantees offered by our approach. But we believe our approach to be valuable for any kind of distributed application (event-driven or not). In particular, our prototype supports arbitrary C code for building distributed applications.

The approach discussed here has been experimented with in previous work, where a secure smart metering infrastructure [12] is built, which we build upon, generalize and partly formalize. Roughly speaking, our notion of *authentic execution* is the following: if the application produces a physical output event (e.g., turns on an LED), then there must have happened a sequence of physical input events such that that sequence, when processed by the application (as specified in the high-level source code), produces that output event. Let us elaborate this.

First, it is clear that authentic execution gives *no* availability guarantees: if the execution never produces any output, then it is vacuously secure. Extending

© Springer International Publishing AG 2017
G. Livraga and C. Mitchell (Eds.): STM 2017, LNCS 10547, pp. 55–71, 2017.
DOI: 10.1007/978-3-319-68063-7_4

our approach with availability guarantees is a challenging direction for future work. Second, while our *implementation* does offer confidentiality, this is not the focus of this paper: We specify authentic execution *without* confidentiality guarantees, i.e., attackers can observe events in the system. Indeed, securing applications in domains such as safety-critical control systems requires authenticity while confidentiality is typically not desired so as to simplify system monitoring and forensics. Third, authentic execution *does* provide strong integrity guarantees: it rules out both spoofed events as well as tampering with the execution of the program. Informally, if the executing program produces an output event, it must also have produced that same event if no attacker was present. Any physical output event can be explained by means of the untampered code of the application, and the actual physical input events that have happened.

The main contributions of this paper are: (1) The design of an approach for authentic execution of event-driven programs under the assumption that the execution infrastructure offers specific security primitives – standard Protected Modules (PMs) [16] plus support for secure I/O (Sect. 3). (2) A novel technique for implementing such support for secure I/O by means of protected driver modules on small microprocessors such as the MSP430 (Sect. 4). (3) A prototype implementation of the approach for an MSP430 microprocessor where all security primitives are implemented in hardware, which results in a very small TCB (Sect. 4). (4) An evaluation of the performance and security aspects of that implementation (Sect. 5). Our complete implementation and all supplementary materials, including a formalization and proof sketch of our security guarantees, are available at https://people.cs.kuleuven.be/~jantobias.muehlberg/stm17/.

2   Running Example, Infrastructure & Objectives

Figure 1 (source code in Fig. 2) shows a running example for the kind of system we consider: a sensor network on a parking lot with two parking spots. The infrastructure can be reused for multiple applications which can be provided by different stakeholders. Applications include parking guidance, parking lot utilization analysis, or detection of cars that violate parking rules. We show two of these applications: one (A_{Vio}) that detects and displays parking violations, and another (A_{Avl}) that displays the number of available parking spots.

The Shared Infrastructure. The infrastructure is a collection of *nodes* (N_i), where each node consists of a processor, memory, and a number of *I/O devices* (D_i). Multiple mutually distrusting stakeholders share the infrastructure to execute distributed *applications* (A_i). For simplicity, we assume processors are simple microprocessors such as the MSP430 used in our prototype.

An I/O device interfaces the processor with the physical world and facilitates (1) sensing some physical quantity (e.g., the state of a switch), (2) influencing some physical quantity (e.g., an LED), and (3) notifying the processor of some state change (e.g., a key being pressed) by issuing an interrupt.

In our running example, there are 5 nodes. Two of these $(N_{P1}$ and $N_{P2})$ are each attached to two input devices (a clock D_{Ti} and a car presence detector D_{Pi}),

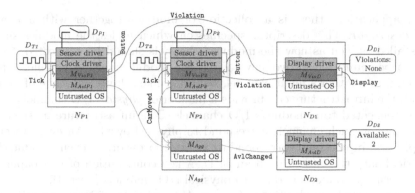

Fig. 1. Our running example with two applications, A_{Avl} (purple) and A_{Vio} (dark orange). Hardware (N_* and D_*) is trusted; the OS as well as the network are untrusted. E.g., the A_{Vio} deployer creates the three red PMs (cf. Fig. 2a) with a trusted compiler, attests the shared parking sensor-, clock- and display drivers and sets-up connections between the PMs. Remote attestation assures authentic execution of A_{Avl} and A_{Vio}. (Color figure online)

```
module VioP1
on Button(pressed):
  if pressed: taken = 1
  else:
    taken = 0
    count = 0
    Violation(0)
on Tick():
  if taken: count = count + 1
  if count > MAX: Violation(1)
module VioP2
# Similar to VioP1
module VioD
on Violation1(violated)
  v1 = violated
  if v1: Display(1)
  if v2: Display(2)
on Violation2(violated):
  # Similar to Violation1
```

```
module AvlP1
on Button(pressed):
  CarMoved(pressed)
module AvlP2
# Similar to AvlP1

module Agg
on CarMoved1(entered):
  p1 = entered
  num_avl = NUM_PARKINGS
  if (p1): num_avl = num_avl - 1
  if (p2): num_avl = num_avl - 1
  AvlChanged(num_avl)
on CarMoved2(entered):
  # Similar to CarMoved1

module AvlD
on AvlChanged(num_avl)
  Display(num_avl)
```

(a) A_{Vio} (b) A_{Avl}

Fig. 2. Source of the applications from Fig. 1. PMs are declared using the `module` keyword and span until the next `module` or the end of the file. `on` starts an event handler which can connect to an output of another PM, or to a physical I/O channel. Outputs are implicitly declared when invoked through a function call-like syntax.

and are installed on parking spots. Two other nodes (N_{D1} and N_{D2}) are connected to display devices (D_{Di}) and show the output of the applications. One node (N_{Agg}) is not connected to any I/O device but performs general purpose computation, e.g., aggregating data from multiple sensor nodes.

Modules and Applications. We use an event-driven application model and *modules* (M_i) contain input- and output channels. Upon reception of an event on an input channel, the corresponding event handler is executed atomically and new events on the module's output channels may be produced.

An application, then, is a collection of modules together with a *deployment descriptor*. This descriptor specifies on which nodes the modules should be installed as well as how the modules' channels should be connected. Channels can be connected in two ways. First, one module's output channel can be connected to another's input channel, behaving like a buffered queue of events. Second, the infrastructure can provide a number of *physical* I/O channels which can be connected to a module's I/O channels. The infrastructure must ensure that events on such channels correspond to physical events: An event received on a physical input could correspond to a button press or, an event produced on a physical output could turn on an LED. A key contribution of this paper is a way to securely connect modules to physical I/O channels (Sect. 4).

In our example applications (Fig. 1), A_{Vio} consists of three modules: two (M_{VioP1} and M_{VioP2}) are deployed on parking spots and detect single violations and one (M_{VioD}) aggregates and displays all violations. The two parking spot modules have two inputs that are connected to input devices provided by the infrastructure: one that produces events for cars entering and exiting the parking spot (D_{Pi}) and another that sends periodical timer events (D_{Ti}). As the source code (Fig. 2a) shows, these modules wait for a car enter event, then for a maximum number of timer events and then produce an output event to indicate a violation. These output events are connected to the inputs of M_{VioD} which in turn produces output events for all violations and sends them to the output display D_{D1}.

Attacker Model. We consider powerful attackers that can manipulate all the software on the nodes. Attackers can deploy their own applications on the infrastructure, but they can also tamper with the OS. Attackers can also control the communication network that nodes use to communicate with each other. Attackers can sniff the network, can modify traffic, or can mount man-in-the-middle attacks. With respect to the cryptographic capabilities of the attacker, we follow the Dolev-Yao model [5].

Attacks against the hardware are out of scope. We assume the attacker not to have physical access to the nodes, neither can they physically tamper with I/O devices. We also do not consider side-channel attacks against our implementation. While physical protection and side-channel resistance are important, they are orthogonal and complementary to the protection offered by our approach.

Security Objective. The deployer uses his own (trusted) computing infrastructure to compile the application A, to deploy the modules to the nodes in the shared infrastructure, and to configure connections between modules, and between modules and physical I/O channels. At run-time, an actual trace of physical I/O events will happen, and the deployer can observe an actual sequence of physical output events. We say that this sequence of outputs is *authentic* for an application A if it is allowed by A's modules and deployment descriptor in response to the actual trace of input events: the source code of A explains the physical outputs on the basis of actual physical inputs that have happened.

For instance for A_{Vio}, suppose we have physical events where a car arrives on parking 1, MAX clock ticks pass and then the display shows a 1. The trace of outputs is an authentic trace for A_{Vio}, because its source code allows for this display event given the physical input events. A trace for the same sequence of physical events, but now ending with the display showing a 2, is *not* authentic.

Our objective is to design a deployment algorithm such that the deployer can efficiently check authenticity of traces. If the deployer observes a trace of physical output events, and the authenticity check of the deployer succeeds, then our approach guarantees that this trace of output events is authentic.

This security notion rules out a wide range of attacks, including attacks where event transmissions on the network are spoofed or reordered, and attacks where malicious software tampers with the execution of modules. Other relevant attacks are *not* covered by this security objective. As discussed earlier, there are no availability guarantees – e.g., the attacker can suppress network communication. There are also no confidentiality guarantees: the attacker is not prevented from observing events. However, although this is not the focus of our design, our implementation *does* come with substantial protection of the confidentiality of the application's state as well as the information in events (Sect. 5).

3 Authentic Execution of Distributed Applications

We outline our requirements for the infrastructure w.r.t. security features, and show how these features are used effectively to accomplish our security goals.

Underlying Architecture: PMAs. Given the shared nature of the infrastructure assumed in our system model, we require the ability to isolate source modules from other code running on a node. Since an important non-functional goal is to minimize the TCB, relying on a classical omnipotent kernel to provide isolation is ruled out. Therefore, we assume the underlying architecture is a PMA [16].

While details vary between PMAs, isolation of software modules is understood as follows: A module must be able to specify memory locations containing data that are accessible by the module's code only (*data isolation*). The code of a module must be immutable and a module must specify a number of *entry points* through which its code can be executed (*code isolation*). For simplicity we further assume that both a module's code and data are located in contiguous memory areas called, respectively, its *code section* and its *data section*.

We also expect the availability of a compiler that targets PMs on the underlying architecture. The input to this compiler is as follows: (1) a list of entry point functions; (2) a list of non-entry functions; (3) a list of variables that should be allocated in the isolated data section; and (4) a list of constants that should be allocated in the isolated code section. The output of the compiler should be a PM suitable for isolation on the underlying architecture.

Besides isolation, we expect the PMA to provide a way to *attest* the correct isolation of a PM. Attestation provides proof that a PM with a certain identity has been isolated on the node, where the *identity* of a PM should give the deployer assurance that this PM will behave as the corresponding source code module.

After enabling isolation, the PMA is capable of establishing a confidential, integrity protected and authenticated communication channel between a PM and its deployer. Although the details of how this works may differ from one PMA to another, for simplicity we assume the PMA establishes a shared secret between a PM and its deployer and provides an authenticated encryption primitive. We refer to this shared secret as the *module key*. The authentication property of the communication channel refers to a PM's identity and hence to attestation. Thus, the PMA ensures that if a deployer receives a message created with a module key, it can only have been created by the corresponding, correctly isolated, PM.

Mapping Source Modules to PMs. To map a source module to a PM, we use the following procedure. First, each of the source module's inputs and outputs is assigned a unique *connection identifier*. The format of this identifier is unimportant as long as it uniquely specifies a particular input or output.

A table (`KeyTable`) is added to the PM's variables that maps connection identifiers to symmetric keys such that every connection has one key associated with it. These keys will be initialized to all zeros by the architecture, which is interpreted as an unconnected input or output. For establishing a connection, an entry point is generated (`SetKey`). This entry point takes a connection identifier and a key – encrypted using the module key – as input and updates the corresponding mapping in `KeyTable` if it is not already set (Fig. 3).

```
def SetKey(payload):
    try:
        conn_id, key = Decrypt(payload)
        if KeyTable[conn_id] == 0:
            KeyTable[conn_id] = key
    except: pass
```

Fig. 3. Pseudocode of the `SetKey` entry point using a Python-like syntax. Note that `Decrypt` uses the module key to decrypt the payload and throws an exception if the operation failed (i.e., the payload's MAC is incorrect is incorrect).

Since every connection needs to be protected from reordering and replay attacks, the compiler adds another table (`NonceTable`) to the PM's variables. This table maps connection identifiers to the current *nonce* for each connection.

All the module's event handlers are marked as non-entry functions. A callback table (`CbTable`) is added to the PM's constants that maps connection identifiers of inputs to the corresponding event handlers. This table is used by the entry point `HandleInput`, which is called when an event is delivered to the PM. `HandleInput` takes two arguments: a plain-text connection identifier and an encrypted payload. If `KeyTable` has a key for the given identifier it is used to decrypt the payload (using the *expected* nonce as associated data), which is then passed to the callback function stored in `CbTable`. If any of these operations fails, the event is ignored (Fig. 4). From a programmer's perspective, an input callback is only called for events that were generated by entities with access to valid connection keys.

```
def HandleInput(conn_id, payload):
  try:
    key = KeyTable[conn_id]
    if key != 0:
      cb = CbTable[conn_id]
      nonce = NonceTable[conn_id]
      cb(Decrypt(nonce, payload, key))
      NonceTable[conn_id] += 1
  except: pass
```

Fig. 4. Pseudocode of the `HandleInput` entry point. Erroneous accesses to the tables as well as errors during `Decrypt` cause exceptions. Thus, these events, as well as those for which no input key has been set, are ignored. `Decrypt` it takes a key and the expected associated data as arguments.

```
def HandleOutput(conn_id, data):
  key = KeyTable[conn_id]
  if key != 0:
    nonce = NonceTable[conn_id]
    NonceTable[conn_id] += 1
    payload = Encrypt(nonce, data, key)
    HandleLocalEvent(conn_id, payload)
```

Fig. 5. Pseudocode of the generated output wrapper. Since the compiler generates calls to this function and it cannot be called from outside the module, the connection identifier is always valid and no error checking is necessary.

Each call to an output is replaced by a call to `HandleOutput`. This function takes a connection identifier and a payload, encrypts the payload together with the current connection nonce (which is incremented afterwards) using the corresponding connection key and publishes it to the event manager (via `HandleLocalEvent`), passing it the connection identifier. If the output is currently unconnected, the output event will be dropped (Fig. 5).

To conclude, the following PM definition will be given as input to the PMA compiler: (1) `SetKey` and `HandleInput` as entry points; (2) input event handlers and `HandleOutput` as non-entry functions; (3) `KeyTable`, `NonceTable`, and module-global variables; and (4) `CbTable` and module constants as constants. Figure 6 shows the compiled memory layout of one of the example modules.

Untrusted Software on the Nodes. To support the deployment of modules and the exchange of events between modules, untrusted (and unprotected) software components need to be installed on the nodes, as outlined here.

Module Loader. The module loader is an untrusted software component running on every node. It listens for two types of remote requests: `LoadModule` and `CallEntry`. `LoadModule` takes a compiled PM as input, loads it into the PMA and returns the module's unique identifier together with all information necessary for attestation and module key establishment. What exactly this information is and how the attestation and key establishment is performed is specific to the used PMA. `CallEntry` takes a PM's identifier, the identifier of an entry point and potentially some arguments and calls the entry point with the given arguments.

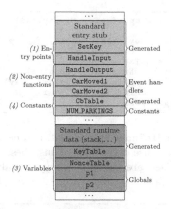

Fig. 6. Memory layout of the compiled version of M_{Agg} of A_{Avl} (Fig. 2b). The code-and data sections are shaded in light orange and purple, respectively. The numbers on the left labels correspond to the compiler inputs while the right labels indicate whether parts are implicitly generated by the compiler or correspond to source code. (Color figure online)

Event Manager. The event manager is another untrusted software component running on every node that is used to route events from outputs to inputs. It recognizes three types of requests: `AddConnection`, `HandleLocalEvent` and `HandleRemoteEvent`. A deployer can invoke `AddConnection` remotely to connect the output of a module to the input of another. How exactly inputs and outputs are identified is implementation specific but it will in some form involve specifying (1) a node address (e.g., an IP address); (2) a PM identifier; and (3) a connection identifier. As will become clear later, `AddConnection` only needs to be called on the event manager of the node where the output source module is deployed.

`HandleLocalEvent` is used by modules to publish an event; i.e., inside the output wrappers. The arguments are the module- and connection identifiers and the event payload. Based on the identifiers the event manager looks up the destination event manager and invokes its `HandleRemoteEvent` API, providing the identifiers of the input to which the request should be routed. For a `HandleRemoteEvent` request, the event manager will check if the destination module exists and, if so, invoke its `HandleInput` entry point, passing the connection identifier and payload as arguments.

Physical Input and Output Channels. We assume that the infrastructure offers physical input and output channels using *protected driver modules* that translate application events into physical events and vice versa. For input channels, these modules generate events that correspond to physical events and provide a way for application modules to authenticate the generated events. For output channels, a driver module (M_D) must have exclusive access to its device (D) and allow an application module (M_A) to take exclusive access over the driver. That is, the driver will only accept events – and hence translate them to physical events – from the application module currently connected to it. The infrastructure must also provide a way for the deployer of M_A to attest that it has exclusive access to M_D and that M_D also has exclusive access to D. The deployer must be able to attest M_D to ensure that it indeed only accepts events from the module currently having exclusive access and that it does not release this exclusive access without being asked to do so by the module itself.

Deployment. Deployment is the act of installing all application modules on their nodes and setting up the connections between outputs and inputs. All computations described in this section are run on the deployer's infrastructure and are therefore trusted. Communication is performed over an untrusted network.

In phase 1, the deployer starts by compiling each source module into a loadable image. Then, the deployment descriptor is used to find the node on which the module should be deployed and sends its module loader a `LoadModule` request. The deployer then performs the PMA-specific method of attestation and setting up the module key. At the end of this step, the deployer has a secure communication channel with each of its deployed source modules.

To complete phase 1, the deployer sets up the connections between modules (not yet the connections to physical I/O channels). The deployer will generate a unique connection key and send it to both endpoints of the connection. Sending the key to a PM is done by first encrypting it together with the connection identifier using the module key. This payload is then passed to the `SetKey` entry point using the module loader's `CallEntry` API.

Next (phase 2) the deployer sets up the connections to the physical I/O channels. The deployer first sets up the connection to physical outputs (phase 2a). This is the point in time from which we know that outputs will be authentic. Finally, all connections to physical inputs are set up (phase 2b).

Security Argument. Our goal is to ensure that all physical output events can be explained by the application's source code and the observed physical input events More precisely: *Consider a time frame starting at the end of phase 2a of deployment (Sect. 3), and ending at a point where the deployer starts an attestation of a specific protected driver module for an output device D_O. If this attestation succeeds, and if the deployer has observed a specific sequence of physical output events on D_O in the considered time frame, then there have been contiguous sequences of physical input events on the input devices connected to the application such that the observed outputs follow from these inputs according to the application source code semantics.*

As an example, consider A_{Vio} (Fig. 2a). If, after the application has been deployed, a "1" appears on the display, and if attestation confirms that the driver of the display is still in the expected state, then there must have been physical input events of a car arriving on parking spot 1 and `MAX` clock ticks.

Since output events can only be produced by the application's PMs; the assumption of a correct compiler then leads to the desired property. Because (1) a physical output event can only be produced by the corresponding device (D_O); (2) output drivers have exclusive access to their device; and (3) a PM (M_O) has exclusive access to the driver; only M_O can initiate physical outputs on D_O. The successful attestation of the output driver module after the outputs have been observed ensures that exclusive access was maintained over the entire considered time frame. The construction of PMs ensures that a module can only be invoked through its two entry points. Of these, only `HandleInput` can result in output events (Figs. 3 and 4). Since `HandleInput` authenticates its input, output events are always the result of correct input events. Since our deployment scheme only allows for two types of correct input events, physical input events and outputs from other modules, our security property follows.

4   Implementation

We have created a fully functional prototype of our design based on the hardware-only PMA Sancus [14], which we briefly introduce here. We provide both the necessary compiler extensions to compile source modules to Sancus PMs and the runtime components to deploy applications on Contiki [6] based networks. A novelty of our work are *driver PMs* that facilitate secure I/O.

Sancus. Sancus [14] is an MSP430-based PMAs, designed for low-cost and low-power embedded applications. As described in Sect. 3, Sancus divides PMs in two sections called the *public code section* and the *private data section*, and enforces strict access rules. A PM's code section can only be entered through a *single* entry point: its first instruction. The compiler assigns each user-defined entry point an integer identifier and adds an entry stub that evaluates such an identifier, dispatching to the correct entry point.

Sancus uses a three-level key hierarchy for remote attestation and secure communication. Every node contains a *node key*, which is only known by the owner of the node, the *infrastructure provider*. Every vendor who is to install PMs on a particular node is assigned a unique identifier. The second level of keys, *vendor keys*, is derived from the node key and these vendor identifiers. Finally, *module keys* are derived from a vendor key using a PMs *module identity*. This module identity – the concatenation of the contents of the module's code section and the load addresses of both its sections – is used for all authentication and attestation purposes. The module key is calculated by the Sancus hardware when a module is loaded and can also be calculated by the module's vendor. Since the hardware ensures that module keys can only be accessed by the corresponding PM, it is guaranteed that the *use* of a certain module key (e.g., by creating a MAC) functions as attestation of the module's identity.

This scheme works well for remote attestation but can be made more efficient for *local attestation*, i.e., the verification of a module's identity by another module running on the same node (called *secure linking* in Sancus terminology). Sancus provides an instruction that verifies the identity of a module wrt. a given MAC. A MAC, instead of a simple hash, is used to be able to store it in unprotected memory and is generated with the key of the module calling the attestation instruction. Unlike remote attestation, local attestation allows modules from different vendors to attest each other. Sancus assigns an integer *module identifier* to every PM, which is unique within a boot cycle. This can be used to speed-up local attestation by calling the attestation instruction only once.

Sancus defines secure communication as authenticated and integrity protected data exchange and provides modules with an instruction that uses the calling module's key to produce a MAC of some data. Modules can use this instruction to communicate securely with their vendor. Sancus' crypto engine uses HMAC with SPONGENT [4] as the underlying hash function to calculate MACs.

As our design requires the ability to create a *confidential* communication channel between a module and its vendor (Sect. 3), this engine did not suffice. We replaced the HMAC implementation with SPONGEWRAP [3] – an authenticated encryption with associated data mode. Our implementation can be configured to provide between 64 and 376 bits of security. The interface to the crypto engine is provided by two instructions: Encrypt takes a plaintext buffer, associated data (which will be authenticated but not encrypted), and a key and produces the ciphertext and an *authentication tag* (i.e., a MAC); Decrypt, given the ciphertext, associated data, tag and key, produces the original plaintext or raises an error if the tag is invalid. For both instructions, the key is an optional argument with the calling module's key as a default value. As with the original version of Sancus, this is the *only* way for a module to use its key.

Secure I/O on Sancus. This section describes how protected drivers can be implemented using Sancus. Remember that for output channels, we want an application module to have exclusive access to a driver (Sect. 3). This, in turn, implies that the driver should have exclusive access to the physical I/O device. Although for input channels the requirements are less strict – we only need to authenticate a device – for simplicity, we also use exclusive device access here.

Exclusive Access to Device Registers. Sancus, being based on the MSP430 architecture, uses (MMIO) to communicate with devices. Thus, providing exclusive access to device registers is supported out of the box by mapping the driver's private section over the device's MMIO region. There is one difficulty, however, caused by the private section of Sancus modules being contiguous and the MSP430 having a fixed MMIO region (i.e., the addresses used for MMIO cannot be remapped). Thus, a Sancus module can use its private section either for MMIO or for data but not for both. Therefore, a module using MMIO cannot use *any* memory, including a stack, severely limiting the functionality this module can implement.

We decided to solve this in software: Driver modules can be split in two modules, one performing only MMIO (mod-mmio) and one using the API provided by the former module to implement the driver logic (mod-driver). The task of mod-mmio is straightforward: for each available MMIO location it implements entry points for reading and writing this location, and ignores calls by modules other than mod-driver. This task is simple enough to be implemented using only registers for data storage, negating the need for an extra data section.

This technique lets us implement exclusive access to device registers on Sancus without changing the hardware representation of modules. Yet, it incurs a non-negligible performance impact because `mod-mmio` has to attest `mod-driver` on *every* call to one of its entry points. Doing the attestation once and only checking the module identifier on subsequent calls is not applicable because it requires memory for storing the identifier. We address this by hard-coding the *expected* identifier of `mod-driver` in the code section of `mod-mmio`. During initialization, `mod-driver` checks if it is assigned the expected identifier and otherwise aborts. `mod-driver` also attests `mod-mmio`, verifying module integrity and and exclusive access to the device's MMIO registers. On failure, `mod-driver` aborts as well.

Sancus did not support caller authentication [14], which we require for `mod-mmio` to ensure invocation by `mod-driver` only. We added this feature by storing the identifier of the *previously* executing module in a new register, and added instructions to read and verify this PM identity.

Secure Interrupts. On the MSP430, interrupt handlers are registered by writing their address to the interrupt vector, a specific memory location. Thus, handling interrupts inside PMs is done by registering a module's entry point as an interrupt handler. However, if the PM also supports "normal" entry points, a way to detect whether the entry point is called in response to an interrupt is required.

More generally, we need a way to identify *which* interrupt caused an interrupt handler to be executed. Otherwise an attacker might be able to inject events into an application by spoofing calls to an interrupt handler. To this end, we extended the technique used for caller authentication. When an interrupt occurs, the processor stores a special value specific to that interrupt in the new register to keep track of the previously executing module. This way, an interrupt handler can identify by which interrupt it was called in the same way modules can identify which module called one of their entry points. The processor ensures that these special values used to identify interrupts are never assigned to any PM.

Interfacing with Applications. One possibility to interface driver PMs with application PMs uses Sancus' secure linking feature (Sect. 4) for efficiency. The downside of our approach is that the application module has to be deployed on the same node as the driver. For simplicity, we discuss drivers for single physical events but the described techniques can easily be extended to drivers supporting multiple such events. Input drivers provide an entry point to register a callback function to be invoked when a physical event happens (`RegisterInputCb`). During the deployment phase, application modules call this entry point – using Sancus' secure linking feature – to register one of their entry points as a callback. The driver's identifier, which is the result of a successful secure linking step, is stored in the modules private data section. When a module's callback entry point is called, this identifier is compared with the result of the `CallerId` instruction to verify it was called by the expected driver.

Output drivers provide an entry point that allows modules to gain exclusive access (`AcquireOutput`). When called, this entry point checks if some module already has exclusive access and, if not, uses `CallerId` to store the identifier of the requesting module. It also offers an entry point for posting events which will check, again using `CallerId`, if the module posting the event has exclusive access.

During deployment, an application module first attests the output driver, storing its module identifier, and then calls `AcquireOutput`, aborting on failure. For attestation, the application modules provides an entry point for the deployer that attests that the module has exclusive access. This is implemented by comparing the driver PM's current module identifier with that of the module located at the location where the driver module was loaded at deployment time.

The reason this attestation procedure is secure is as follows. When an application module (M_A) attests a driver module (M_D) during deployment, M_A checks the correctness of M_D's code. This includes, among others, that the code only allows a single module to have access to the driver, and that it does not release this access without the module having exclusive access asking for it. If M_A records the module identifier of M_D after having attested it, M_A can later check if M_D still exists by simply validating the identifier of the PM loaded at the location where M_D was loaded during deployment. This works because Sancus ensures module identifiers are unique within a boot cycle. If M_A calls `AcquireOutput` on M_D and it succeeds, and later verifies that M_D still exists, M_A can be sure it still has exclusive access to M_D. This procedure also ensures that M_D has exclusive access to its underlying device.

Compiler and Untrusted Runtime. Our compiler implementation is a literal translation of the design outlined in Sect. 3. All modifications to the Sancus compiler are *extensions*, and all original Sancus features are still available to programmers (e.g., calling external functions or other PMs). On top of the existing annotations provided by the Sancus compiler for specifying entry points (`SM_ENTRY`), internal functions (`SM_FUNC`) and private data (`SM_DATA`), we added two new annotations: `SM_INPUT` and `SM_OUTPUT` for specifying inputs and outputs. Figure 7 shows an example module written in C using our annotations.

```
SM_OUTPUT(Violation);
SM_DATA int taken, count;
SM_INPUT(Button, data, len) {
  if (data[0]) {
    taken = 1;
  } else {
    taken = count = 0;
    char event = 0;
    Violation(&event, sizeof(event)); } }
SM_INPUT(Tick, data, len) {
  if (taken && ++count > MAX) {
    char event = 1;
    Violation(&event, sizeof(event)); } }
```

Fig. 7. A translation of module M_{VioP1} (Figs. 1 and 2a) to C using the annotations understood by our compiler.

`SM_OUTPUT` expects a name as argument (more specifically, a valid C identifier). For every output, the compiler generates a function with the following signature: `void name(char* data, size_t len)`. This function can be called to produce an output event. For input handlers, `SM_INPUT` generates a functions with the same signature as above. In this function, the programmer has access to a buffer containing the (unwrapped) payload of the event that caused its execution. For both inputs and outputs, the names provided in annotations are used in the deployment descriptor. The untrusted runtime consists the module loader and the event manager (Sect. 3), both running as regular Contiki [6] processes.

5   Evaluation and Discussion

To assess the runtime overhead and the size of the software TCB we have implemented and deployed A_{Avl} (Figs. 1 and 2b). Each node is configured to provide 64 bits of security. We install Contiki, our module loader and event manager, PM drivers for I/O devices (a button driver for the car sensors and a serial LCD driver for the display), and the application modules.

Table 1 shows the sizes of the different software components deployed on nodes. As can be seen, the majority of the code – about

Table 1. Size ("Src": source code, "Bin": binary size) of the software for running the evaluation scenario. The shaded components are part of the run-time software TCB.

Component	Src (LOC)	Bin (B)
Contiki	38386	14880
Event manager	598	1730
Module loader	906	1959
Buttons Driver	338	1016
LCD Driver	137	640
Parking Sensor	43	1383
Aggregator	84	1970
Display	31	1333
Deployment Descriptor	57	n/a

40 kLOC – is untrusted. A total of 633 LOC comprising of drivers and the actual application code is compiled to PMs and needs to be trusted, together with 57 LOC of the deployment descriptor. That is, only 1.7% of the deployed code base is part of the software TCB. When looking at the binary sizes of the these software components, the difference between infrastructure components (18.1 KiB) versus TCB (6.2 KiB, 25.5%) appears less prominent, which is mostly due to conditionally compiled code in Contiki and compiler generated entry points and stub code in PMs. Nevertheless, the reduction of the TCB when using our approach is substantial, leading to a considerably reduced attack surface on each node, and – importantly – the application owner does not need to trust *any* infrastructural software if he reviews the driver modules that his application uses.

We also performed a detailed performance analysis of this example application, the detailed results are given online in the supplements. For fast devices such as the button sensors, the overhead of our secure I/O approach can be quite large: the protected driver executes about 13 times slower than the unprotected one. However, not much effort was put in optimizing our implementation and we expect that significant performance gains are possible (e.g., the wrapper for encrypting output events uses `malloc` to create a buffer contributing about $30\mu s$ to the overhead). For slower devices such as the serial LCD, it is clear that the relative overhead drops significantly: the protected driver executes about

7% slower. Another type of overhead is due to the increased size of events. The sequence diagram shows that an event containing 2 bytes of useful data, will be 6 times as large. In general, the representation of events has a constant overhead of 10 bytes: 2 for the nonce and 8 for the MAC. Whether these overheads are acceptable will depend on the application. Yet, we feel that they are reasonable in the light of the security guarantees and TCB reduction provided by our approach.

Integrity versus Confidentiality. We have focused our security objective on integrity and authenticity, and an interesting question is to what extent we can also provide confidentiality guarantees. It is clear that, thanks to the isolation properties of protected modules and to the confidentiality properties of authenticated encryption, our prototype already provides substantial protection of the confidentiality of both the state of the application as well as the information contained in events. However, providing a formal statement of the confidentiality guarantees offered by our approach is non-trivial: some information leaks to the attacker, such as for instance when (and how often) modules send events to each other. This in turn can leak information about the internal state of modules or about the content of events. The ultimate goal would be to make compilation and deployment fully abstract [1] (indicating roughly that the compiled system leaks no more information than can be understood from the source code), but our current approach is clearly not fully abstract yet. Hence, we decided to focus on strong integrity first, and leave confidentiality guarantees for future work.

Hardware Attacks and Side-Channels. Although hardware attacks and side-channels are explicitly ruled out by our attacker model (Sect. 2), it is necessary to discuss the impact an attacker would have given access to such techniques.

An attacker that successfully circumvents the hardware protections on a node would be able to manipulate and impersonate all modules running on *that node*. That is, the attacker would be able to inject events into an application but only for those connections that originate from the compromised node. The impact on the application obviously depends on the kind of modules that run on the node. If it is an output module, the application is completely compromised since the attacker can now produce any output they want. If, on the other hand, it is one among many sensor nodes, the impact may be minor.

Given the kind of small microprocessors that we target, many side-channels such as cache timing attacks or page fault channels are not applicable. We leave an analysis of our implementation for side-channels for future work.

6   Related Work

A survey of hardware-based trusted computing architectures for isolation and attestation has been published in [8], and describes a number of platforms our approach could use. These range from Intel SGX over ARM's TrustZone to embedded architectures such as SMART and TyTAN. Notably, Sancus [14] is the only available embedded PMA, and the only open-source PMA overall. The secure compilation techniques for PMAs were proposed by Agten et al. [2].

Earlier techniques to establish a notion of trusted I/O paths are *BitE* [10], *Flicker* [9] and *Bumpy* [11]. Our approach improves over these by significantly reducing the size of the software TCB, from a full OS to less than 1 kLOC. By using Sancus as a PMA, we enable the integration of attestable software and I/O encryption directly into the input device. Techniques such as Flicker or SGX can be used to protect host software when communicating with Sancus nodes.

The VC3 system [15] is related to our work in the sense that they also provide strong security guarantees to the deployer of an application using SGX as a PMA, but they focus on correctness, confidentiality and completeness of Map-Reduce computations in a cloud-setting and hence do not need to deal with I/O.

The safe and secure deployment and use of devices in the domains of Wireless Sensor Networks (WSNs) and the IoT remains an open challenge. A number of schemes for distributed trust management for WSNs are surveyed in [7], which allow individual nodes to obtain trust values for neighboring nodes by observing these nodes' behavior. In [13], Sancus is used to securely inspect and assess the trustworthiness of unprotected software on WSN and IoT nodes directly. This kind of trust management is suitable to detect the systematic failure or misbehavior of nodes, but there are no inherent guarantees wrt. the authenticity of distributed computations being provided. We address this shortcoming by protecting all components of a distributed application throughout their life-cycle.

7   Conclusions

We have extended Sancus, a light-weight embedded protected module architecture with support for secure I/O, which enables the execution of reactive (event-driven) distributed applications on a shared infrastructure with strong authenticity guarantees and in the presence of capable attackers, while relying on a very small TCB. We foresee compelling use cases in IoT and control systems.

Acknowledgements. This research is partially funded by the Research Fund KU Leuven.

References

1. Abadi, M.: Protection in programming-language translations. In: Vitek, J., Jensen, C.D. (eds.) Secure Internet Programming. LNCS, vol. 1603, pp. 19–34. Springer, Heidelberg (1999). doi:10.1007/3-540-48749-2_2
2. Agten, P., Strackx, R., Jacobs, B., and Piessens, F.: Secure compilation to modern processors. In: CSF, pp. 171–185. IEEE (2012)
3. Bertoni, G., Daemen, J., Peeters, M., Van Assche, G.: Duplexing the sponge: single-pass authenticated encryption and other applications. In: Miri, A., Vaudenay, S. (eds.) SAC 2011. LNCS, vol. 7118, pp. 320–337. Springer, Heidelberg (2012). doi:10.1007/978-3-642-28496-0_19
4. Bogdanov, A., Knezevic, M., Leander, G., Toz, D., Varici, K., Verbauwhede, I.: The design space of lightweight cryptographic hashing. IEEE Trans. Comput. **99**(PrePrints), 1 (2012)

5. Dolev, D., Yao, A.C.: On the security of public key protocols. In: SFCS, pp. 350–357. IEEE (1981)
6. Dunkels, A., Gronvall, B., Voigt, T.: Contiki - a lightweight and flexible operating system for tiny networked sensors. In: Local Computer Networks, pp. 455–462. IEEE (2004)
7. Fernandez-Gago, M., Roman, R., Lopez, J.: A survey on the applicability of trust management systems for wireless sensor networks. In: SECPerU, pp. 25–30 (2007)
8. Maene, P., Götzfried, J., de Clercq, R., Müller, T., Freiling, F., Verbauwhede, I.: Hardware-based trusted computing architectures for isolation and attestation. IEEE Trans. Comput. (99), 1–14 (2017). http://ieeexplore.ieee.org/abstract/document/7807249/
9. McCune, J.M., Parno, B.J., Perrig, A., Reiter, M.K., Isozaki, H.F.: An execution infrastructure for TCB minimization. In: Eurosys, pp. 315–328. ACM (2008)
10. McCune, J.M., Perrig, A., Reiter, M.K.: Bump in the ether: a framework for securing sensitive user input. In: ATEC, USENIX (2006)
11. McCune, J.M., Perrig, A., Reiter, M.K.: Safe passage for passwords and other sensitive data. In: NDSS (2009)
12. Mühlberg, J.T., Cleemput, S., Mustafa, M.A., Van Bulck, J., Preneel, B., Piessens, F.: An implementation of a high assurance smart meter using protected module architectures. In: Foresti, S., Lopez, J. (eds.) WISTP 2016. LNCS, vol. 9895, pp. 53–69. Springer, Cham (2016). doi:10.1007/978-3-319-45931-8_4
13. Mühlberg, J.T., Noorman, J., Piessens, F.: Lightweight and flexible trust assessment modules for the internet of things. In: Pernul, G., Ryan, P.Y.A., Weippl, E. (eds.) ESORICS 2015. LNCS, vol. 9326, pp. 503–520. Springer, Cham (2015). doi:10.1007/978-3-319-24174-6_26
14. Noorman, J., Agten, P., Daniels, W., Strackx, R., Van Herrewege, A., Huygens,C., Preneel, B., Verbauwhede, I., Piessens, F.: Sancus: low-cost trustworthyextensible networked devices with a zero-software trusted computing base. In: USENIX Security Symposium, pp. 479–494. USENIX (2013)
15. Schuster, F., Costa, M., Fournet, C., Gkantsidis, C., Peinado, M., Mainar-Ruiz, G., and Russinovich, M. VC3: trustworthy data analytics in the cloud using SGX. In: Symposium on S&P, pp. 38–54. IEEE (2015)
16. Strackx, R., Noorman, J., Verbauwhede, I., Preneel, B., Piessens, F.: Protected software module architectures. In: Reimer, H., Pohlmann, N., Schneider, W. (eds.) ISSE 2013 Securing Electronic Business Processes, pp. 241–251. Springer, Wiesbaden (2013). doi:10.1007/978-3-658-03371-2_21

Exploring Botnet Evolution via Multidimensional Models and Visualisation

William Dash[1] and Matthew J. Craven[2(✉)]

[1] University of Bristol, Bristol BS8 1TH, UK
williamdash@dashsw.co.uk
[2] Centre for Mathematical Sciences, Plymouth University,
Plymouth PL4 8AA, UK
matthew.craven@plymouth.ac.uk

Abstract. A botnet is a program designed to perform a specific task using multiple computers connected in a network. In this paper we will focus on botnets being used to distribute malicious programs. In the real world, botnets have been shown to exhibit more aggressive and sophisticated behaviour than traditional malware. Botnets are used to infect computer networks and hence their success depends on the properties of the networks. We observe the behaviour of mathematical models used to describe botnets when botnet parameters are varied to understand if such variation is beneficial to their spread. We also introduce novel models for depicting botnet behaviour using master equations. These models, unlike previous ones, address nodes of distinct categories in a network as a sequence of probability distributions rather than a value at each time interval. We also contribute visualisations for these models. This paper is a substantial expansion of unpublished work the first author performed while on a Nuffield student research placement, with the second author the project supervisor.

Keywords: Botnet · Differential equation · Master equation · Visualisation · Complex systems security · Security in P2P (peer to peer) systems

1 Introduction

Despite the primary use of a botnet being a means of distributing malicious software, they were initially created to distribute computationally intensive tasks among a variety of devices, as in parallel processing. However, due to their ability to control large amounts of computer resources they have since become desirable in the distribution of malicious software. This makes botnets good for deploying software requiring large amounts of resources to be effective; an example of this is Distributed Denial of Service (DDoS).

As a result of the diverse capabilities of botnets and subtle, but aggressive, virus distribution they pose a large threat to modern cybersecurity. An example of such a case is the TDL-4 botnet [9]. As a rootkit, this modifies the master boot

© Springer International Publishing AG 2017
G. Livraga and C. Mitchell (Eds.): STM 2017, LNCS 10547, pp. 72–88, 2017.
DOI: 10.1007/978-3-319-68063-7_5

record of each infected node so that it is always loaded at startup. Such behaviour makes the botnet more difficult to eradicate than previous TDL generations. Another example is the Carna botnet [2]. Although Carna was used to collect data and not intended for malicious activities it became widespread. Comprised of around 420,000 nodes, it collected worldwide data regarding the geographical distribution of the usage of (it was claimed, all) IPv4 addresses.

Thus, as expressed in [1], modelling botnet behaviour and spread is crucial to preserve security. One method of modelling such spread as a threat is by using epidemiological models [1]. However, such models are often only comprised of the susceptible, infected, and recovered states (*SIR models*), due to the nature of diseases they are used to model. In contrast, botnets have a distinct lifecycle, which is described in [1] as follows: the payload (also know as the *worm*) is constructed by the botmaster and distributed across a network which proceeds to infect the maximum number of nodes possible. Each infected node receives commands from the command and control server of the payload and thus may begin or stop performing malicious tasks assigned by the botmaster at any time. After the malicious activities of a node are discovered by its true user, these activities may be terminated and the node has "recovered". However, depending on the botnet, nodes may be re-infected after recovery. Botnet size is often measured by the number of constituent nodes, from thousands to millions [7,8].

In terms of effectiveness and efficiency, several authors have proposed botnet modelling techniques. The work of [10] uses the CodeRed1v2 worm as a case study to model stochastic botnet behaviour. The work of [4] considers time zones in global botnet behaviour, and [12] considers interaction and co-operation between two botnets (and thus, many). Finally [11] considers statistical spread models of network subgraphs showing, by a search for subgraph isomorphisms in networks undergoing simulated network attacks, whether such subgraphs are likely caused by an initial botnet outbreak. Our work shall not consider these factors, as we wish our approach to be straightforward, focusing on interactions of nodes in distinct states within networks. The objective of this work is to firstly observe the behaviour of existing botnet models and then combine them with alternative epidemiological models. From this we derive more accurate and interesting probabilistic models describing botnet behaviour. Throughout, we detail model simulations and visualisations of botnet model results.

1.1   Modelling Contributions of this Paper

3D and 6D Probabilistic Models: Section 3 introduces a 3D probabilistic model based on the system of ODEs of [1]. Section 4 extends this, adding additional node states. This probabilistic approach is practical as it only considers integer numbers of items in each model state (often difficult with a - continuous - ODE approach). The approach also provides more information than models which produce fixed values for the number of nodes in each state on each iteration. This approach may also identify realistic worst and best case scenarios for any particular population/setting rather than just an expected value.

Extension to 7D Model and Applications to GSM Networks: In this paper Sect. 5 extends the work of Sect. 4 to a 7D botnet model in order to allow multiple worms to be distributed simultaneously by a botnet. It then goes on to show how our work, despite some limiting assumptions inherent in any model, may be applied to botnets propagating through GSM (Global System for Mobile Communications) networks based on the work from [6]. This approach of allowing a botnet to be able to distribute multiple worms in a population is advantageous as it has the models derived in Sects. 3 and 4 as a special case. Therefore this model simulates a more diverse range of scenarios than those models.

2   Using Sets of First Order ODEs

To begin, we review the ODE model proposed in [1], including suggested extensions/modifications, as a modified epidemiological model applied to botnets.

2.1   Model Setup

The botnet model proposed by [1] was based upon sets of ODEs developed for epidemiology, and comprises of the following classifications for each node:

S: Nodes vulnerable to infection by the worm being transferred by the botnet;

S_d: Nodes susceptible to the worm, but which are disconnected from the network;

I: Nodes infected by the worm and are able to infect other nodes, but show no signs of infection;

I_d: Infected nodes which are disconnected from the network;

V: Infected nodes which are executing the malicious task provided by the worm;

V_d: Infected nodes which previously executed malicious tasks but are disconnected from the network;

R: Previously infected nodes that have now permanently recovered.

The model assumes eleven connections between the possible nodes states. These are: a susceptible node becoming infected, disconnecting from the network and possibly reconnecting; similarly, a dormant infected node becomes active, disconnects or reconnects; an active infected node becomes dormant, temporarily or permanently recovers, or disconnects; a disconnected active infected node becomes dormant. As expressed in [1], this extended model is suited to botnets that transmit worms which mutate upon transmission or that contain multiple worms. This is highlighted by the transition from state V to S. This model proposed in [1] has the following parameters:

N, μ: Total population size, switching rate between hidden and active

b: Worm transmission rate

g, ρ: Permanent, temporary recovery rate

p: Apportioning coefficient of infected (dormant) nodes

σ: Switching rate between online and offline states

q: Apportioning coefficient of nodes connected to the network

The work of [1] provided a flow diagram, describing the transitions between each node in the configuration described above. We omit this in the present work; however, we may describe this model as a system of ODEs:

$$\frac{dS}{dt} = \frac{-b(I(t) + V(t))}{N}S(t) + \rho V(t) + \frac{\sigma}{1-q}S_d(t) - \frac{\sigma}{q}S(t); \quad \frac{dR}{dt} = gV(t)$$

$$\frac{dI}{dt} = \frac{b(I(t) + V(t))}{N}S(t) + \frac{\mu}{p}V(t) - \frac{\mu}{1-p}I(t) + \frac{\sigma}{1-q}I_d(t) - \frac{\sigma}{q}I(t) \qquad (1)$$

$$\frac{dS_d}{dt} = \frac{\sigma}{q}S(t) - \frac{\sigma}{1-q}S_d(t); \quad \frac{dI_d}{dt} = \frac{\sigma}{q}I(t) - \frac{\sigma}{1-q}I_d(t) + \frac{\sigma}{1-q}V_d(t)$$

$$\frac{dV}{dt} = \frac{\mu}{1-p}I(t) - \left(\frac{\mu}{p} + g + \rho + \frac{\sigma}{q}\right)V(t); \quad \frac{dV_d}{dt} = \frac{\sigma}{q}V(t) - \frac{\sigma}{1-q}V_d(t)$$

Although the input parameters are given above, we must consider the initial numbers of nodes in all classes. The work of [1] showed that $I(0) > 0$ (i.e., there are nodes able to infect the network). Further, from parameter experimentation, it is crucial that $S(0) \geq 0.9N$ in order for the botnet to be able to grow to a sufficiently large size. Also, [1] showed the need for $V(0) = R(0) = 0$, to allow us to view the entire life cycle of the botnet from its initial network penetration. This model assumes that all nodes in the population are online and connected to the network being infected at the start of the simulation, allowing the botnet to initially enter the population and ensuring it does not necessarily die out immediately. Hence the starting values $S_d(0) = 0$, $I_d(0) = 0$, $V_d(0) = 0$ have also been used in our model simulations. The simulation was coded in Python, with the GNUPlot package used to visualise the results in the next subsection.

2.2   Visualisation

In Figs. 1 and 2 the green line represents the proportion of class S nodes, orange class S_d, dark blue class I, yellow class I_d, light blue class V, brown class V_d and red class R. A simulation output is shown in Fig. 1. In this, the model used example parameters: transmission rate $b = 0.5$, recovery rate $g = 0.25$,

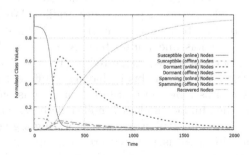

Fig. 1. Simulation results of the current model for 2000 iterations where $N = 100$. (Color figure online)

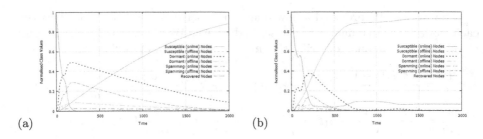

(a)   (b)

Fig. 2. The result of 2000 model iterations with b being fBm using value noise. On the left Eq. (2) is used, and on the right Eqs. (2)–(3) are used. (Color figure online)

hidden-active switching rate $\mu = 0.1$, apportioning coefficient $p = 0.1$, temporary recovery rate $\rho = 0.01$, proportion of online nodes $q = 0.9$, and online-offline switching rate $\sigma = 0.09$.

Figure 1 shows a distinct peak where around 64% of the population are dormant infected nodes (class I). These nodes then tend to recover at a shallower rate than their infection. This is a combined result of the low values of parameters μ, ρ and g compared to b and the assumption that nodes can only recover once they have moved into class V. In addition, a single region of growth, followed by decay, for class I nodes is shown. This non-repetitive behaviour is caused by the small values of parameters ρ and σ compared to g, which causes most nodes to move from class V to class R, rather than iterating through any previous states.

To observe scenarios that the current model depicts we begin by varying some of the more influential parameters of this simulation. However, as stated in [1], it is clear that model behaviour is independent of population size, and so the most interesting variables concern the transition speeds (b, g, ρ, p and q) between each class. The functions used in our simulations will be examples only. At this stage, we focus on the parameters concerning the initial infection and recovery of nodes in the model. Thus we assume the botnet has a constant level of aggression (p is constant) and the variables b, g, ρ, q are functions of time, t.

First, we vary the parameter b using fractal Brownian motion (fBm) initialised with value noise with time as seed. This definition is more suitable than a simple constant as the propagation of botnets across a network depends on a number of clearly variable factors (e.g., network traffic). We initialise the fBm with value noise as opposed to (the more common) Perlin noise as we require a 1D noise function ($b(t)$ has one parameter). Also, to produce results more applicable to real-life botnets we, as suggested in [1], consider user response to the presence of a botnet. We model this by having a different proportion, q_v, of online class V nodes and assume the infection of a node is only detected when the node is active. As the number of class V nodes increases so do the number of users being informed, spreading the word and informing a given (for simplicity, fixed) number of other infected users how to recover nodes.

These people then recover nodes and exhibit the same behaviour as their predecessors. This shows, as in standard population growth models, exponential growth in the number of people recovering nodes. Assuming each user corresponds to a single node and that the first user attempt to recover nodes is by removal from the network, the proportion of infected (active) nodes that are not online is exponential in V_n (the normalised number of class V nodes) and the proportion of online node users, q_v, decays exponentially. We use the function

$$q_v(t) = \exp\left(-100V(t)/N\right) \tag{2}$$

to simulate this relationship. Figure 2a illustrates a simulation using (2). We extend this approach by assuming that progressively fewer users are able to temporarily and permanently repair (recover) nodes respectively. For this we use exponential functions to describe both relationships, meaning they exhibit similar behaviour to q_v. However, in order to represent the difference in difficulty of temporarily and permanently recovering a node we give each function distinct coefficients. We formalise this by the (example) equations

$$\rho(t) = \exp\left(V(t)/N - 1\right) \text{ and } g(t) = 0.5\exp\left(V(t)/N - 1\right), \tag{3}$$

and implement Eqs. (2)–(3) in Fig. 2b. Both results indicate a decrease in the peak number of infected nodes. Observe that Fig. 2a also contains fewer class S nodes (in green) when in stable equilibrium than Fig. 2b. This means the ability to recover an infected node, even temporarily, is more advantageous in reducing overall infection of the network than just disconnecting the node.

Of course, this model may be considered constrained by its fixed population size as it assumes no node is destroyed and that the botnet does not expand to other networks or populations. The model is also restricted by its lack of consideration of individual nodes; treating the total population as a single entity and consequently allowing for non-integer numbers of nodes in all classes.

3   A 3D Botnet Model

We now apply a simplified version of the Sect. 2 model to multidimensional probabilistic modelling.

3.1   Multidimensional Modelling

So far we have used ODEs from a single type of biological model. However, producing a more realistic and accurate botnet behaviour model requires alternative approaches. One such approach, [5], constructs a multidimensional probability distribution of all possible combinations of node states a population may contain at any time. However, the model of [5], in the form of a master equation, was designed to consider epidemics conforming to a standard SIR progression, meaning each node is in one of those three states. Hence this model is not directly applicable to botnets due to its limited number of states. However, by extending the number of model states, and so the number of dimensions in the probability distribution, we produce a distinct type of botnet model to that of Sect. 2.

3.2   Model Explanation

This model is expressed and then simulated using a master equation. Under master equation notation, the number of equations to be evaluated is a function of population size, N. That is, a master equation acts as a generalised equation for each combination of S, I and V values that may exist within a given population. In order to produce a suitable master equation, we must consider a reduced set of possible transitions that occur between node states defined in the model of Sect. 2. We also allow for a variable-sized population. To do so, we use the following assumptions analogous to [5]: each time a new node is added to the population it is susceptible to the botnet, and each node may die or be removed from the population regardless of type. Using these additional transitions, shown in the flow diagram (Fig. 3), the following events may occur within the model. A node may be added to the population, a susceptible node becomes infected (dormant), an infected (dormant) node becomes active, an infected (active) node becomes dormant, an infected (active) node recovers from the infection; or finally, a node in either the S, I or V category dies.

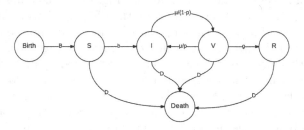

Fig. 3. Flow diagram showing the inter-class transfer rates for the current model.

Expressing transitions as equations requires two new parameters from [5]. The first is the rate, B, at which new population nodes are added, and the second is the rate, D, at which nodes die or are removed. Each such transition changes the probability that each S, I, V combination occurs in the population, and so the master equation includes terms describing each event. In reality if any such transition occurs to a node combination then a new node combination is produced, represented in our model by reduction of the likelihood of the original combination occurring and increase of the likelihood of the resulting combination occurring. Thus each S, I, V combination (Table 1) has pairs of terms, one representing the source decreasing the probability and the other its source of increase. Each term has a coefficient of the likelihood of its parent S, I, V combination occurring. Thus, when the likelihoods of new S, I, V combinations are calculated, the probability of each parent combination is considered (each iteration of the model depends upon the last). Each parent combination that results in a new combination, along with the causal event, are listed below.

Table 1. Relative S, I and V combination of each event corresponding to a source of increase in probability for each unique combination of node types in a population.

A node is added to the population	$S - 1, I, V$
A susceptible node becomes infected (dormant)	$S + 1, I - 1, V$
An infected (dormant) node becomes active	$S, I + 1, V - 1$
An infected (active) node becomes dormant	$S, I - 1, V + 1$
An infected (active) node recovers from the infection	$S, I, V + 1$
A susceptible node is removed from the population	$S + 1, I, V$
An infected (dormant) node is removed from the population	$S, I + 1, V$
An infected (active) node is removed from the population	$S, I, V + 1$

The node combinations in Table 1 represent the original combination of nodes that each transition occurs to in order to produce the node combination: S, I, V. For example, if a node was added to the population, then the number of nodes would increase by 1. In addition, every time a new node is added it is added to the susceptible category. Thus the number of nodes in class S will increase by 1 and the other classes would remain unaffected. In order to produce the final combination of S, I, V we subtract 1 from the S term. This is so that we compensate for the addition of 1 to S caused by this transition, hence producing the original combination $S - 1$, I, V. Using the flow rates from Sect. 2 and the new parameters from Sect. 3 we produce a master equation to describe the transitions (the inputs and outputs for each S, I, V combination) shown below.

$$\frac{dP_{S,I,V}}{dt} = -\left(\frac{bS(I+V)}{N} + \frac{\mu}{1-p}I + \frac{\mu}{p}V + gV + BN + DS + DI + DV\right)P_{S,I,V}$$
$$+ \frac{b(S+1)(I-1+V)}{N}P_{S+1,I-1,V} + \frac{\mu}{1-p}(I+1)P_{S,I+1,V-1} \qquad (4)$$
$$+ \frac{\mu}{p}(V+1)P_{S,I-1,V+1} + g(V+1)P_{S,I,V+1} + B(N-1)P_{S-1,I,V}$$
$$+ D(S+1)P_{S+1,I,V} + D(I+1)P_{S,I+1,V} + D(V+1)P_{S,I,V+1}$$

When simulating the current model we set $P_{45,5,0}$ to one and the probability of all other S, I, and V combinations to zero. This was so that the number of infected nodes in the population is sufficiently large that the botnet is able to grow to a reasonable size and that the constraints explained in Sect. 2 are satisfied. In addition, as the current model allows for dynamically sized populations, the additional constraints: $S + I + V \leq N$ and S, I, $V \geq 0$ will be applied to all corresponding simulations. This is so that the population size in the simulation is bounded above and below, making it easier to simulate. Therefore the parameter N will now denote the maximum population size in all further simulations. A simulation output of the current model is shown in Figs. 4a–c, with transmission rate $b = 0.5$, recovery rate $g = 0.1$, hidden-active switching rate $\mu = 0.1$, apportioning coefficient $p = 0.5$, population increase rate $B = 0.0005$ and population decrease rate $D = 0.0005$.

3.3   Visualisation

The current model produces a 3D probability distribution, and would require a 3D output device in order to display all data produced in its raw form. We thus reduce the 3D distribution by effectively removing V combinations from the data. This is done by summing the probabilities assigned to positions with the same S and I combination but different V combinations. We repeat this process with the remaining combinations of node classes to produce three separate 2D probability distributions (effectively projections). Results are shown for susceptible and dormant infected nodes (Fig. 4a), susceptible and active infected nodes (Fig. 4b), and dormant infected and active infected nodes (Fig. 4c).

Although the distributions of Figs. 4a–c contain a significant number of entries with negligible probability it does not contain any zero elements. In addition, each of the node types in this distribution has a distinct concentration. Specifically, in Figs. 4a and b the susceptible nodes have a standard deviation of approximately 5.21. In Figs. 4a and c the infected (dormant) nodes have a standard deviation of around 4.61. Also, the infected (active) nodes in Figs. 4b and c have a standard deviation of around 2.71. The higher variation of nodes in class S, in comparison to classes I and V, is likely to be a result of the initial conditions and population increase rate used in the simulation. This model shows a very different approach to botnet modelling than the previous model, as

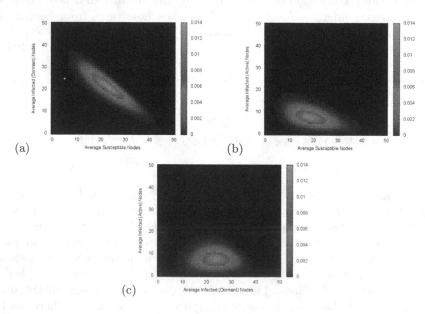

Fig. 4. The resulting distributions of the current model on iteration 2670 where $N = 50$ for each S and I combination (top left), each S and V combination (top right), and each I and V combination (bottom). The heat map corresponds to the probability of a given combination occurring in the population.

it is probabilistic. Consequently, modelling real life botnets with this model may require more discipline. In addition, the current model is somewhat restricted by its simplicity and may be extended to include more node states.

4   A 6D Model

We now extend the model from Sect. 3 to allow nodes to temporarily connect and disconnect from the network/population being targeted by the botnet.

4.1   Model Explanation

The new model implements the more diverse behaviour exhibited by the model from Sect. 2 by making use of additional classifications of nodes. However, in order to do so we must change the number of dimensions of the probability distribution that we produce (since each node type is represented across an axis perpendicular to all others). As a result we produce a 6D master equation as there are six different node states being modelled. Making identical assumptions about the behaviour of offline states to the model of Sect. 2, we describe how the states in the current model transition to and from one another (Fig. 5). Just as when deriving the model of Sect. 3 we need to consider all possible events or transitions that may occur within the model and their corresponding relative S, S_d, I, I_d, V and V_d combinations (Table 2).

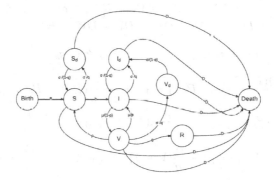

Fig. 5. Flow diagram describing transitions between node states for the current model.

Using the flow rates for each of the events (defined in Sects. 2–3) we formalise the model as a 6D master Eq. 5, describing the inputs and outputs for each state combination. In this equation we use the notation $P_{S+1,S_d-1,*}$, for example, to mean that the states S and S_d have changed and all other states stay the same, and $P_* = P_{S,S_d,I,I_d,V,V_d}$.

Table 2. Relative S, S_d, I, I_d, V and V_d combinations for each event corresponding to a source of increase in probability of each unique combination of nodes in a population.

Node added to population	$S-1$, S_d, I, I_d, V, V_d
Susceptible node switches to being in an offline state	$S+1$, S_d-1, I, I_d, V, V_d
Offline susceptible node switches to online	$S-1$, S_d+1, I, I_d, V, V_d
Susceptible node becomes infected (dormant)	$S+1$, S_d, $I-1$, I_d, V, V_d
Offline infected (dormant) node switches to being online	S, S_d, $I-1$, I_d+1, V, V_d
Online infected (dormant) node switches to being offline	S, S_d, $I+1$, I_d-1, V, V_d
Infected (dormant) node becomes active	S, S_d, $I+1$, I_d, $V-1$, V_d
Infected (active) node becomes dormant	S, S_d, $I-1$, I_d, $V+1$, V_d
Infected (active) node temp. recovers from botnet payload	$S-1$, S_d, I, I_d, $V+1$, V_d
Infected (active) node switches to being offline	S, S_d, I, I_d, $V+1$, V_d-1
Offline inf. (active) node becomes offline inf. (dormant)	S, S_d, I, I_d-1, V, V_d+1
Infected (active) node permanently recovers from infection	S, S_d, I, I_d, V+1, V_d
Susceptible node is removed from the population	$S+1$, S_d, I, I_d, V, V_d
Offline susceptible node removed from population	S, S_d+1, I, I_d, V, V_d
Infected (dormant) node removed from population	S, S_d, $I+1$, I_d, V, V_d
Offline infected (dormant) node removed from population	S, S_d, I, I_d+1, V, V_d
Infected (active) node removed from population	S, S_d, I, I_d, $V+1$, V_d
Offline infected (active) node removed from population	S, S_d, I, I_d, V, V_d+1

$$\frac{dP_*}{dt} = -\left(\begin{array}{c} \frac{\sigma}{1-q}S_d + \frac{\sigma}{q}S + \frac{bS(I+V)}{N} + \frac{\sigma}{1-q}I_d + \frac{\sigma}{q}I \\ +\frac{\mu}{1-p}I + \frac{\mu}{p}V + \rho V + \frac{\sigma}{q}V + \frac{\sigma}{1-q}V_d + gV \\ +DS + DS_d + DI + DI_d + DV + DV_d + BN \end{array}\right) P_*$$

$$+\frac{\sigma}{1-q}(S_d+1)P_{S-1,S_d+1,*} + \frac{\sigma}{q}(S+1)P_{S+1,S_d-1,*} \qquad (5)$$

$$+\frac{b(S+1)(I-1+V)}{N}P_{S+1,I-1,*} + \frac{\sigma}{1-q}(I_d+1)P_{I-1,I_d+1,*}$$

$$+\frac{\sigma}{q}(I+1)P_{I+1,I_d-1,*} + \frac{\mu}{1-p}(I+1)P_{I+1,V-1,*} + \frac{\mu}{p}(V+1)P_{I-1,V+1,*}$$

$$+\rho(V+1)P_{S-1,V+1,*} + \frac{\sigma}{q}(V+1)P_{V+1,V_d-1,*} + \frac{\sigma(V_d+1)}{1-q}P_{I_d-1,V_d+1,*}$$

$$+g(V+1)P_{V+1,*} + D(S+1)P_{S+1,*} + D(S_d+1)P_{S_d+1,*}$$

$$+D(I+1)P_{I+1,*} + D(I_d+1)P_{I_d+1,*} + D(V+1)P_{V+1,*}$$

$$+D(V_d+1)P_{V_d+1,*} + B(N-1)P_{S-1,*}$$

Using previous constraints gives $P_{9,0,1,0,0,0}=1$ and a zero probability of all other combinations initally. As in Sect. 3 we apply $S+S_d+I+I_d+V+V_d \leq N$ and S, S_d, I, I_d, V, $V_d \geq 0$ to bound the numbers of nodes in each class. A simulation output is shown in Fig. 6a, with rates $b = 0.5$, $g = 0.1$, $\mu = 0.1$, $B = 0.0005$, $D = 0.0005$, $\rho = 0.01$ and $\sigma = 0.09$ (c.f. Sect. 2.1). The apportioning coefficient was $p = 0.5$ and proportion of online nodes was $q = 0.9$.

4.2   Visualisation

To visualise model simulations we found it best to view them as a combination of two-dimensional distributions, as in Sect. 3. However, this gives $\binom{6}{2} = 15$ distinct 2D distributions. So we decided to only view the distributions containing an online and offline state pair, producing only three images, but at the same time allowing us to view each node state. Figures 6a–c show these visualisations.

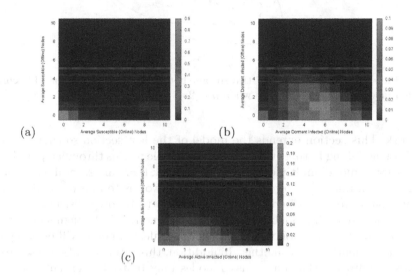

(a)   (b)

(c)

Fig. 6. The probability distribution on iteration 2670 of the current model ($N = 10$) of each S and S_d combination (top left), each I and I_d combination (top right), and each V and V_d combination (bottom).

Here the number of class I nodes has a larger standard deviation (1.71) than the number of class V nodes (1.47). But, unlike the results of Sect. 3, the number of class S and S_d nodes have much smaller standard deviations than any other classes (1.13 and 0.22 respectively). The extended number of node states makes this model more general than that of Sect. 3. The current model also uses a discrete approach so that only integer numbers of nodes can exist in certain states (as per Sect. 3). The combination of these two characteristics is absent in the other models derived in this paper, meaning the current model may more realistically model botnet behaviour. However, the data produced may be more difficult to visualise and interpret than previous model data.

5   Extensions

Although the work of Sects. 3 and 4 introduced new models, they only focussed on the behaviour of a botnet transferring a single worm propagating through

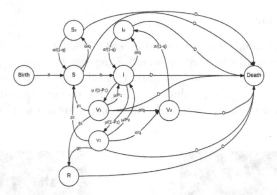

Fig. 7. Flow diagram describing transitions between node states for the current extended model in the special case when $n = 2$.

a network. This section extends the model of the last section so that it will be capable of modelling botnets that transmit multiple worms through a population.

In order to model multiple worms in a network there are several assumptions that have been made on how the botnet assigns worms to infected nodes. So far we have considered each node in the population to be only distinguishable by their state within each model; hence, each I state node is indistinguishable to the Botmaster. In this extension we assume that all infected nodes will be assigned a worm independently of one another. In addition, this extension also preserves the previous assumption that only class I nodes may be told to execute malicious activities by the C & C server. So, in this model each infected (active) state will be unable to directly transition to one another. As a result of the above assumptions, this model will not contain state V as used in previous models. Instead we use V_1, V_2, ..., V_n to denote all the possible infected node states considered in this extended model. As a result the parameters p, ρ and g are no longer used and instead each V_i state has its own associated p_i, ρ_i and g_i values. Using the new states and parameters, we may construct Fig. 7 (and so a 7D master equation, omitted) for the special case $n = 2$ of this extended model.

This model demonstrates one of the many ways in which the models from Sects. 3–4 may be generalised to produce more diverse botnet models. However, the models introduced in this paper are only suitable for modelling perfect populations in which network parameters remain constant. In the next subsection we detail an implementation of the above extended model to depict a botnet propagating across a GSM network.

5.1   Simulation Setup

We now use this model to simulate a botnet that operates on mobile phones. In particular this botnet will use multiple worms, will be transferred over WiFi and has the objective of disruption of the GSM network to which the infected phones are connected. The botnet uses the strategy described in [6], which is to send excessive numbers of requests to the home location register (HLR) in the network. The HLR within a GSM network is a database of the details of everyone authorised to use the network. All requests within the network need to interact with the HLR in order to be processed, making it a clear attack target.

Here, the V_1 state represents a worm that excessively issues insert_call_forwarding requests to the HLR. This was chosen as, according to [6], this is the most effective request for attacking an HLR. However [6] also shows this request has a low occurrence in a typical GSM network, making any infected devices easily identifiable. To complement this, the V_2 state represents a worm that excessively issues update_location requests to the HLR. The results of [6] indicate this request is less strenuous on the HLR. However, [6] also indicates that in a typical GSM network the number of insert_call_forwarding requests issued is approximately one seventh of the number of update_location requests. So, we reasonably assume that seven times more malicious devices issuing insert_call_forwarding requests are identified and recovered (temporarily or permanently), as they are more conspicuous, than devices issuing update_location requests ($\rho_1 = 7\rho_2$ and $g_1 = 7g_2$). We also assume it is easier to temporarily recover an infected device than to recover it permanently (giving constraints $\rho_1 > g_1$ and $\rho_2 > g_2$). As a result, the values $\rho_1 = 0.7$, $\rho_2 = 0.1$, $g_1 = 0.35$ and $g_2 = 0.05$ were used.

The objective of this botnet is to exceed maximum total HLR throughput on the targeted network. Here this is equivalent to maximising the number of nodes in classes V_1 and V_2. However, the commands being issued and hence the strain put on the HLR by nodes in classes V_1 and V_2 are different. Interpreting Fig. 5 in [6], nodes in class V_1 are approximately 1.5 times more strenuous on the HLR than nodes in class V_2. Therefore the objective of the botnet is to maximise $1.5V_1 + V_2$ on each iteration of the simulation. Hence a suitable objective function of this botnet is $V_{obj} = 1.5V_1 + V_2$. This function will be used to produced a probability distribution from the results of the current model in the visualisation subsection. By Fig. 5 of [6], it is also reasonable to assume that in this case $p_1 = 1.5p_2$. In this example we have $p_1 = 0.3$ and $p_2 = 0.2$. All the remaining parameters are identical to those of Sect. 4. For the simulation, using the same constraints as previously gives the starting condition $P_{9,0,1,0,0,0,0} = 1$ and the constraint $S + S_d + I + I_d + V_1 + V_2 + V_d \leq N$ with non-negative summands.

5.2   Visualisation

As in Sect. 4, we display several of the 2D projections of the resulting 7D distribution. We produce plots of S with S_d and I with I_d. We also present a plot of V_{obj} with V_d, to allow comparison to the results of the Sect. 4 model, and a plot of V_1 with V_2 to allow comparison of both worms being transferred. Figures 8a–d show outputs for transmission rate $b = 0.5$, recovery rates $g_1 = 0.35$ and $g_2 = 0.05$, hidden-active switch rate $\mu = 0.1$, population increase/decrease rate $B = 0.0005$ ($D = 0.0005$), apportioning coefficients $p_1 = 0.3$ and $p_2 = 0.2$, temporary recovery rates $\rho_1 = 0.7$ and $\rho_2 = 0.1$, proportion of online nodes $q = 0.9$ and offline-online switch rate $\sigma = 0.09$.

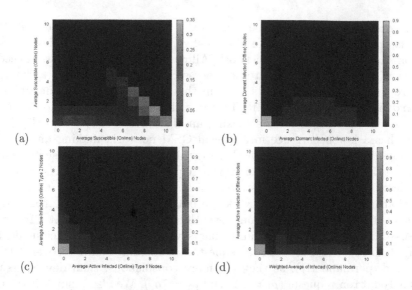

Fig. 8. The probability distributions on iteration 2670 of the extended model ($N = 10$) of each S and S_d combination (top left), each I and I_d combination (top right), each V_1 and V_2 combination (bottom left) and each V_obj and V_d combination (bottom right).

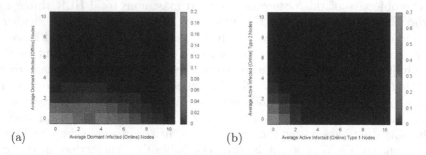

Fig. 9. The probability distribution on iteration 540 of the current model ($N = 10$) of each I and I_d combination (left), and each V_1 and V_2 combination (right).

These results show significantly larger variation in the number of class S and S_d nodes, with standard deviations 2.25 and 0.93 respectively, in comparison to the Sect. 4 results. This may result from the larger values of ρ_1 and ρ_2 used, as it causes more infected nodes to become susceptible again. Although Figs. 8a–d allow us to compare this model to that of Sect. 4, they show little information about the new states introduced. To address this we refer to Figs. 9a–b, which are distributions from the same simulation on iteration 540. These results indicate that the simulation parameters cause the infection to progress through the population faster than simulations of Sects. 3 and 4. This is clear from the fact that on iteration 2670 the distribution for all classes except S and S_d approaches zero. This indicates the population has reached a stable equilibrium by iteration 2670, in which infected nodes are no longer present. In addition, Fig. 9b shows a higher expected number of class V_2 nodes (0.32) in comparison to those in class V_1 (0.20). This would suggest that the large values of ρ_1 and g_1 in comparison to ρ_2 and g_2 respectively are more influential in this simulation than the larger value of p_1 compared to p_2.

This implementation gives one illustration of how to make the models derived in this paper more applicable to real world scenarios. However, in order to asses how accurate the current model is, it is recognised that it needs to be compared to real world data.

6   Conclusion and Further Work

This work introduced the use and visualisation of 3D, 6D and 7D probabilistic master equations to depict a botnet lifecycle and to evaluate the likelihood of a given result occurring, given certain parameters. Section 3 highlights how the ability to recover infected nodes (temporarily or permanently) is far more advantageous than simply disconnecting them when attempting to reduce the damage caused by a botnet. The extensions of Sect. 5 also emphasise that the models introduced in this paper are constrained by their ideal nature. The work also shows how models may be tailored to more specific networks or scenarios.

To extend this work we will consider how the behaviour of the population changes when individual nodes or sections of a population have different properties to each other. This ability would account for the scenario in which offline botnets fail to receive updated instructions from the Botmaster and hence have different properties to the rest of the population when they come back online. We could also consider links between offline states other than to and from their corresponding online states. The work may also be extended by a comparison to publicly-available data obtained from real life botnet infections (e.g., [3]). Using a genetic algorithm (GA), for example, the model parameters given in this work could be adjusted to fit a specific real world data set such as this. A possible cost function for such a GA could be derived as follows.

Denote X as a state in the model, A as the set of all model states, $E[X]$ as the expected number of nodes in class X, and X_1 as the actual number of nodes in class X from the data set being used. Clearly for all $X \in A$ we wish to make $E[X] - X_1$ as close to zero as possible. This is equivalent to minimising $\sum_{X \in A} [(E[X] - X_1)^2]$ (the squaring operation solves potential negativity issues).

However, the number of nodes in class X varies with time, t, and so for all $t \in \mathbb{R}^+$ we wish to minimise $\sum_{X \in A} [(E[X(t)] - X_1(t))^2]$. This is equivalent to wishing to minimise the integral $\int_0^\infty \sum_{X \in A} [(E[X(t)] - X_1(t))^2] \, \mathrm{d}t$.

Using this GA approach with suitable mutation and crossover operators may yield a suitable parameter fitting method. This may allow for an assessment of how the dynamic properties of the system vary in actuality and would assist in making this theoretical work even more representative of real life botnets.

Acknowledgements. The authors acknowledge the kindness of the Nuffield Foundation for making this work possible, and the generous research support of Plymouth University.

References

1. Ajelli, M., Lo Cigno, R., Montresor, A.: Compartmental differential equation models of botnets and epidemic malware (extended version), University of Trento report T.R. DISI-10-011, 2–3, 9 (2010)
2. Anon: Internet Census 2012: Port Scanning/0 Using Insecure Embedded Devices (2013). (Carna Botnet) http://census2012.sourceforge.net/paper.html
3. CAIDA Datasets. http://www.caida.org/research/security/#Datasets
4. Dagon, D., Zou, C., Lee, W.K.: Modeling botnet propagation using time zones. In: Proceedings of the 13th NDSS, vol. 6, pp. 2–13 (2006)
5. Keeling, M.: Population Dynamics MA4E7, Warwick University, 50 (2004). http://homepages.warwick.ac.uk/~masfz/Pop_Dyn/Handouts.pdf
6. Lin, M., Ongtang, M., Rao, V., Jaeger, T., McDaniel, P., La Porta, T., Traynor, P.: On cellular botnets: measuring the impact of malicious devices on a cellular network core. In: Proceedings of the 16th ACM Conference on Computer and communications Security, pp. 223–234 (2009)
7. Nordlohne, C.: Measuring Botnet Prevalence: Malice Value, preprint (2015). http://acdc-project.eu/wp-content/uploads/2015/05/malice-value2.pdf
8. Rajab, M., Zarfoss, J., Monrose, F., Terzis, A.: My botnet is bigger than yours (Maybe, Better than Yours): why size estimates remain challenging. In: Proceedings of the 1st USENIX Workshop in Hot Topics in Understanding Botnets, April 2007
9. Rodionov, E., Matrosov, A.: The Evolution of TDL: Conquering x64, eSeT (2011). https://www.welivesecurity.com/media_files/white-papers/The_Evolution_of_TDL.pdf
10. Rohloff, K., Başar, T.: Stochastic behavior of random constant scanning worms. In: Proceedings of the 14th International Conference in Computer Communications and Networks, pp. 339–334 (2005)
11. Rrushi, J., Mokhtari, E., Ghorbani, A.: Early stage botnet detection and containment via mathematical modeling and prediction of botnet propagation dynamics. University of New Brunswick Technical report TR10-206 (2010)
12. Song, L.P., Jin, Z., Sun, G.Q.: Modeling and analyzing of botnet interactions. Physica A **390**, 347–358 (2011)

Facing Uncertainty in Cyber Insurance Policies

Per Håkon Meland[1,2](✉), Inger Anne Tøndel[1,2], Marie Moe[2],
and Fredrik Seehusen[2]

[1] Norwegian University of Science and Technology, Trondheim, Norway
{per.hakon.meland,inger.anne.tondel}@ntnu.no
[2] SINTEF Digital, Trondheim, Norway
{per.h.meland,inger.a.tondel,marie.moe,fredrik.seehusen}@sintef.no

Abstract. Cyber insurance has gained less ground in Europe than in
the U.S., but with emerging laws and regulations, the prospect of considerable fines for security breaches is pushing many organisations into this
market. A qualitative interview study in Norway reveals the main uncertainty factors for organisations that have little experience with the cyber
insurance consideration process, and how they perceive the products,
process and expected support in case of a cyber incident. These uncertainty factors can be reduced by being aware of typical coverage gaps,
exclusions and loss types that are commonly found in cyber insurance
products.

Keywords: Cyber insurance · Risk management · Gap analysis · Exclusions · Coverage · Negotiation

1 Introduction

Cyber insurance is an expanding market, fuelled by the growing number of cyber
threats as our society becomes increasingly dependent on interconnected digital
technology. In fact, Lloyd's City Risk Index [16] and the World Economic Forum
[28] both consider cyber attacks to be one of the top risks facing the world today.
Cyber insurance can be defined as the "transfer of financial risk associated with
network and computer incidents to a third party" [5], and is meant to take care
of incidents that have low frequency and high impact.

In the U.S., there is and has been a considerable up-take of cyber insurance.
A recent survey by Hiscox [14] reports that 55% of U.S. respondents state they
have cyber insurance. Looking at Europe, the situation is a bit different. According to a survey by Marsh & McLennan Co, only 13% of European companies
have purchased this [19]. Why nine out of ten cyber insurance policies in the
world are in the U.S., can probably be explained by more than ten years of
state breach notification laws [7]. The situation is likely to become more similar
in Europe, when emerging data protection regulations take effect in the near
future [9]. For this reason, many organisations are now preparing to enter this
market, but this is a new and challenging task for them, since there are not
well-established practices for considering cyber insurance.

© Springer International Publishing AG 2017
G. Livraga and C. Mitchell (Eds.): STM 2017, LNCS 10547, pp. 89–100, 2017.
DOI: 10.1007/978-3-319-68063-7_6

The main contribution of this paper is a study of the demand side view of cyber insurance, driven by the following research questions:

1. What are the main uncertainty factors in the consideration phase as perceived by the demand side?
2. How can these uncertainties be reduced?

Section 2 gives an overview over the related work for this topic. The former research question is studied in Sect. 3 through qualitative interviews with Norwegian organisations, who only have very little experience with this new type of product. For the latter research question, we analyse and discuss these uncertainties in Sect. 4 with experiences found in a more global perspective to see whether or not they are well-founded, and what can be done to reduce them. Section 5 provides a conclusion to the work.

2 Related Work

There have already been several publications covering various challenges for the demand side of cyber insurance. Bandyopadhyay [2] have developed nine hypotheses on adoption of cyber insurance by organisations. He claims that organisations likely to adopt and utilise cyber insurance are recognized by high intensity of state of the art technology, business critical information systems, central management of cyber risks, efficient intra-organisational communication and collaboration, and imposed regulations. Those who are less accommodating typically have high security experience, high risk appetite, and a volatile business environment.

A survey by the Ponemon institute [21] provides some more empirical insight in which factors are most important when deciding whether or not to buy cyber insurance. For instance, 70 % of their respondents reported increasing interested in cyber-insurance policies after experiencing an incident. Among those that do not plan to buy insurance, the following main reason were given: "Premiums are too expensive" (52 %) and "Too many exclusions, restrictions and uninsurable risks" (44 %). Bandyopadhyay [3] has also argued that overpricing due to information asymmetry has been the primary reason for the limited growth of the cyber insurance market seen from the demand side. Additional barriers have been explained in separate studies by ENISA [12], U.S. Department of Homeland Security [23] and MARSH [17], such that firms already think they are covered by their existing general business interruption policies. Mr. Brew from Liberty International Underwriters [22] lists the following reasons why more customers do not buy cyber insurance:

- Cost and revenue concerns: Some see cyber security as a luxury purchase.
- Uncertainty: Will they actually pay out if there is an event? Untested market.
- High risk appetites: Technology entrepreneurs are risk takers, and do not see insurance as a necessary investment.
- Maturity: Companies are unaware of the availability of cyber insurance (and also about cyber security risk exposure).

A recent joint global study [20] by Swiss RE and IBM Institute for Business Value concluded with a very simple reason why companies were not buying cyber insurance; *they simply had not explored it.* This study included 1005 organisations from 15 industries in over 50 countries.

As can be seen from the literature, there can be many reasons why cyber insurance is still regarded as somewhat "immature, with room for improvement" [15]. The polices themselves tend to have varying form, content and vocabulary, which makes it difficult to grasp coverage and terms, as well as compare policy offerings from different insurers [18]. Though many organisations presumably seem to have taken an informed decision when deciding upon cyber insurance, a significant portion is also sitting on the fence because they do not feel competent to make any decision due to *uncertainty.* In the next section, we explore some of these uncertainty aspects in more detail.

3   Interview Study

3.1   Method

During the autumn of 2016, we conducted a series of ten in-depth interviews with representatives from Norwegian organisations. Since only a very few Norwegian organisations currently have cyber insurance, the limited market made it difficult to design a larger empirical study. Still, we were able to obtain representation from different industries, such as finance, media, retail, critical infrastructure and IT. Most of these organisations are large by Norwegian standards, but a few were also medium size in the range of one hundred employees. Six out of the ten organisations had experience with a cyber insurance consideration process. Out of these, one organisation had acquired, two were still considering and three had decided not to invest in this option. The remaining four expressed their needs and thoughts if they were to start such a process.

We consider this setting to be representative for the Norwegian market and similar areas. Norway is considered to be technologically advanced and an example of a society that depends heavily on information systems, and thus, a society exposed to cyber threats. For instance, Norwegians use digital services to a large extent, well above EU average, and companies have a high on-line presence [10]. There is also a steady course towards a cashless economy where almost all transactions are done electronically [26]. Figure 1 illustrates a sample of digital maturity factors compared to the rest of Europe.

Each of the interviews lasted about one hour, and had a semi-structured form where one researcher asked the questions, and another made notes and additional remarks. All the results were also digitally recorded, transcribed and coded in a set of a priori main categories with emerging sub-categories. The complete results of the interviews are out of scope for this paper, but we have extracted the main uncertainty aspects with respect to *products*, consideration *process* and expected *support* in the case of an incident.

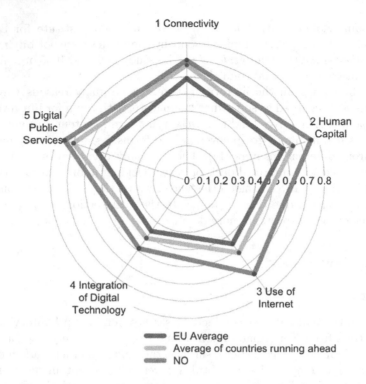

Fig. 1. The digital agenda scoreboard for Norway (2016) [10].

3.2   Results

Products. In general, the cyber-insurance products and market are perceived as immature by those organisations that have considered to buy cyber-insurance. Characteristics put out by the informants include "there are different definitions to the term cyber risk", "the market is premature", "products are not prepared thoroughly", "there's lot of fancy words that we don't know the real meaning of". One informant had asked if their regular insurance company could provide this product for them, but they did not have anything readily available. In this case, the insurance company made one on-the-fly especially for this organisation.

The most important thing that make cyber insurance interesting seem to be coverage and limit. Price is less important. The informants seem to all agree that insurance is for catastrophes, that is incidents with high consequence and low likelihood. With today's cyber insurance products, coverage is perceived as low and not enough for to cover catastrophe costs. In addition, a cyber insurance will only cover parts of the real incident cost. Many of the companies we have talked to are mostly worried about reputation loss and loss of market position, and thus future income. Their impression was that these types of costs were not covered by an insurance. Many express that the cyber insurance products are difficult to understand, and that many aspects are unclear, illustrated by quotes such as "for the time being, there is a lot of promise-ware" and "it is a product where it is not easy to get a concrete feeling of what is covered and not". Also, some informants were critical to the competence of the insurance companies in this field, mentioning: "When we asked technical questions about security, they could not really answer" and "... they don't know what they are selling".

There was a clear trend that the informants seemed unsure about the real benefits of the existing products. In addition, the products are perceived as expensive compared to other insurance products. One informant characterised the premium as "random", meaning it seems arbitrary what price you get based on the risk and the security measures of the company. This can be summed up by the following statement from one informant: "It is not everything that appears attractive and realistic for us to use. And the extent of coverage you will get in case of a break-in or an incident is a bit diffuse. They [insurance agents] say media support and so on, but what do they mean by that? It is very difficult to know the extent of that. In my opinion, the whole concept of cyber insurance is a bit vague and hard to grasp. The only thing that is concrete is the annual premium you have to pay".

Process. When the organisations started the process of considering cyber insurance, the natural first step for them had been to assess their own cyber risk. Though most of the informants explain that their organisation already has some form of risk assessment practice that includes cyber, this does not seem to be enough to serve as a foundation for making decisions on whether or not to buy cyber coverage. Many of the organisations we talked to were still in the process of performing a more thorough risk assessment of their cyber risk, and a decision to buy cyber insurance was still pending from that assessment. However, as of now, they were still uncertain about their needs. The process of evaluating products was perceived complex and challenging for several reasons. First, as this is a new product, there is a general risk that no one picks up on it and takes responsibility for evaluating its relevance for the organisation ("it could easily fall between two stools").

Second, risk managers or similar roles that handle other types of insurance products do not know that much about cyber. Thus, they need more support from brokers than what is the case with most other types of insurance products. They also need to interact with IT people internally, something they are not used to, and this exposes them to a field very different from their own main competence. A few notable quotes from the interviews:

- "... it is a new area, and vague because you do not know enough about computers and do not have the fantasy to understand what is happening"
- "...sounded a bit like science fiction the first time I heard about it"
- "...you suddenly enter a technological world that is much more complicated than sitting and reading nice contracts"

Third, as explained before, products are perceived to be immature and terms are often unclear. It was stated: "Terms should be clearer than they are right now. It seems that the insurance guys have just put up a list of things that would be nice to have. It does not say anything about at what level, and if there are any requirements on proof. Do we have to document all our security measures?" and "what does it mean to have a firewall or antivirus? What are the requirements to the firewall or antivirus? Does it e.g. have to be patched? What about gathering evidence after an incident? The policy does not say anything about this". Additionally, those that claim to know the cyber insurance market well, stated that this is developing rapidly, both when it comes to products and terms, and as a result, it is challenging to keep up to date.

Those companies with a lot of internal competence on insurance would actually prefer cyber as part of existing coverage, and not as a stand-alone product. One informant stated: "Then you can work with insurance companies that already know you, and it is cheaper". Another argued the following: "It is a small extension you do in an existing program, while buying a stand-alone product, which is offered on a broad scale, is a totally different scenario. There is extra work to for us to support them with their analysis, I'd rather work with those that already know our risk exposure".

As part of the negotiation with insurance companies, self-evaluation forms and questionnaires are frequency used. The organisations that have experience with these consider them to be relevant, but with the following remarks:

- "The form seems very high level, maybe because the policies are only meant to cover low pay-outs."
- "These forms are not suitable for complex, heterogeneous organisations, such as ours, with many locations for our different offices. There must be a dialogue."

One of the informant emphasised that their key success factor was obtaining a better understanding of the total risks that the organisation faced, and existing insurance coverage. This was stated as: "The most important thing we did in the beginning was this gap-analysis: what do we have, what do we lack when it comes to insurance". This was an activity in which they invested a lot of time together with their broker.

Support. Though practical support from insurance companies in the case of an incident was not something most informants talked much about, there was an agreement on the following two things:

- It would be interesting to them if they would get access to highly specialised competence on the specific technology they are using.
- If such help should be useful, there must be a close relationship between the insurer and insuree over time, and an openness, "so they will know us and know how things are. They should not have to do a lot of research to understand us before they can start implementing countermeasures and limit damages".

Access to specialised competence and ability to have a close relationship were not something that the informants necessarily perceive to be part of current products, but something that would make the products more interesting. As of now, they are not sure if this is the kind of support that is offered. Additionally, there are uncertainties related to pay-out. This was related to lack of experience and unclear products (as explained above). One informant explained that they consider cyber insurance products to stem from the U.S. These [insurance] companies are perceived to have other ranges of pay-outs than what's common in Norway. This can impact the trust towards the product and process effort in case there is an incident.

4 Reducing Uncertainty

A cyber insurance is not a silver bullet, and can never be a complete replacement for risk modification as a part of a risk management plan. Any organisation considering cyber insurance should focus on what kind of coverage they need to address their residual risk, and harmonise this with other insurances [13,25]. But in order to do this, a lot of the uncertainty aspects from the previous section must be overcome. There is a lot of uncertainty related to the products themselves. Besides the novelty of the product, this is also caused by the fact that such policies are not standard products, but a result of a negotiation between the insuree and insurer. The negotiation phase is used to tailor standard products to more specific coverage and establish a price for individual insurees [15]. This includes defining exclusions, carve-backs, premium, payouts or support actions in the case of cyber events, cover limits (or caps), etc. To quote Siemens and Beck [25]; "buying an off-the-shelf policy can result in disaster". A negotiation would also be used when renewing policies, but for cyber insurance in particular, many organisations are doing this for the first time. The products themselves are therefore very much reliant on the process, and the support is a result of what has been agreed upon.

In the following sub-sections, we show what to be aware of when negotiating coverage of gaps, exclusions and loss.

4.1 Closing the Gaps

A gap analysis for information security is usually performed to discover potential gaps between what level of security you have in place and requirements from regulations and standards, or in simple terms, *comparing where you are against where you want to be*. We noted from our interviews with Norwegian organisations, that when they were mentioning gap analysis, this was mainly about *determining whether or not the organisation was under-insured for cyber events*.

Most organisations already have a portfolio of insurance products in place, and general liability, property and crime insurances can in many cases cover a number of cyber events. However, they are not designed to fully cover all the potential costs and losses related to cyber risk [15]. In fact, there are significant cyber-related risks that remain largely uninsurable or the coverage is modest compared with the overall exposure [27]. With little experience on claim from traditional insurances and cyber policies, there is a lot of uncertainty about

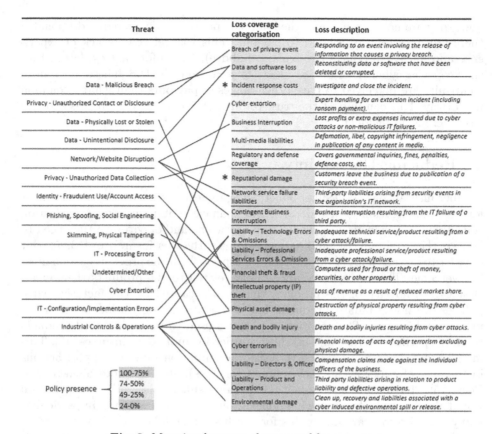

Fig. 2. Mapping between threats and loss coverage

loss coverage gaps. Therefore, it is important to have an idea of what risks are typically insurable and non-insurable, sort out the ones that can cover the needs, and prepare clarifying questions for the negotiation table.

In Fig. 2, we have combined two datasets to illustrate how cyber threats can be mapped to insurance coverage. The column to the left contains a threat categorisation from Advisen[1] ordered by registered loss amount. For instance, "Data - Malicious Breach" accounts for 622 cases with a total loss amount of $5,311,075K, while "Industrial Controls and Operations" accounts for merely two cases with a total of $85K. The rightmost two columns show typical loss coverage categories as defined in a study by Cambridge Centre for Risk Studies [6]. These 19 categories extend an original cyber loss categorisation scheme developed by a steering group of 15 insurance companies, several industry organisations and government agencies [17]. There was quite a variation on coverage in the

---

[1] The dataset we have received from Advisen is dated November 2016 and contains 33023 world-wide cyber loss events. Romanosky has described the origins of this data in [24].

26 UK insurance products that was examined (two-thirds of what was estimated to be on the market). The colour scheme in Fig. 2 indicates how commonly the losses were part of the policies. Due to the lack of an official vocabulary for cyber threats and losses, there is a significant degree of interpretation in this mapping, especially for the lower coverage segment. Also, note that a single threat category can lead to more than one type of loss. Especially "Incident response costs" and "Reputational damage" would have so many threat links that we did not include them in the figure.

In an ideal world, the most expensive threats would normally be present in cyber insurance policies, but as the figure shows, this is currently not the situation. It may also be that a policy contains coverage that is not relevant or necessary for the organisation that considers the insurance. It is therefore recommended to create an individual risk profile that can be used to compare expected threat exposure with what the policy offers to cover.

4.2 Checking for Exclusions

It is typically in the lower coverage segment in Fig. 2 that you will run into a world of exclusions that organisations must review, both for their existing policies and those under consideration. For instance, "cyber terrorism" is an ambiguous term, and probably more related to the people or group behind the threat, along with the associated motivation (e.g. political, religious, ideological or similar purposes), rather than the action itself. Many organisations would assume that any DDOS attack would be covered by Business Interruption, but according to [8], such claims could be rejected on the basis of a terrorism exclusion if there is a hacktivist group behind.

Besides war and terrorism exclusions, that are typically found in any type of insurance policy, there are exclusions that are particular for cyber insurance. The following check-list is based on reports from the Association of British Insurers [1] and Thomas Bentz from Holland & Knight [4]:

- **Court jurisdiction** - The territories of U.S. and Canada tend to be excluded from cyber insurance policies purchased in Europe.
- **Claims by related entities** - Claims related to loss of data belonging to employees (personal data), contractors and partial owned subsidiaries are not normally included.
- **Bodily injury and property damage** - As can be seen from the loss coverage categories in Fig. 2, tangible assets tend to be excluded. General liability policies may already cover the direct expenditures, but probably not subsequent lawsuits.
- **Crime vs cyber insurance** - Consequences that are meant to be covered by a crime insurance policy, such as attacks leading to theft of money, will not be reimbursed by a cyber insurance ("Financial theft & fraud" loss coverage category).
- **Mechanical/electronic failure** - Claims due to computers that stop working. Should be limited to malicious acts causing the computers to fail for the policy to respond.

- **Laptop exclusions** - Coverage for portable electronic devices tends to be excluded, especially if they do not encrypt their contained data.
- **Patent, software, copyright infringement** - We have already seen that IP theft belong to the lower coverage segment. Carve-backs (exclusion overrides) can be negotiated to cover claims caused by non-management employees and third parties.
- **Employment practices** - Incident arising from poor or insecure employment processes are often excluded or can shrink the policy's limits.
- **Employee benefit plan breaches** - Often referred to ERISA exclusions in the U.S., breach of data found in e.g. pension plans and health benefit plans, can be a special condition that is not covered.
- **Prior acts** - Since there may be a long time between time of breach and time of discovery, exclusions can limit the covered incidents originating from before policy inception and long tailed consequences.
- **The insured vs insured** - Such exclusion state that a claim made by one insured against another insured is not covered, however, there can be carve-backs for various reasons such as violation of privacy.

4.3   Clarifying Loss

It is also useful to clarify what costs are covered for different types of cyber events. The data material from Advisen divides this into the following four categories, which we have detailed using definitions from Allianz [11]:

- **Response costs** - E.g. forensic investigations, identifying and preserving lost data, advice on legal and regulatory duties, notification costs according to legal and regulatory requirements, determining the extent of indemnification obligations in contracts with third party service providers, credit monitoring services and other remedial actions required after a loss of data, public relations expenses to handle negative publicity.
- **Economic loss** - E.g. loss of business income caused by a targeted attack, indemnity for stolen funds, indemnity for cyber extortion.
- **Litigated cases** - Defense costs and damages for which the insured is liable.
- **Fines and penalties** - Monetary fines and penalties levied by regulators arising from a loss of data.

Considering these categories, the Advisen data show that *response costs* has the highest average cost, while *economic loss* has the lowest, averaging about one third of response costs. Any organisation should during the negotiation get a clear definition about what kind of costs are covered for different types of incidents, and check these caps.

5   Conclusion

Cyber insurance has gained less ground in Europe than in the U.S., but with emerging laws and regulations, the prospect of considerable fines for security breaches is pushing many organisations into this market. What remains to see is: Can these organisations properly navigate through the still immature and obscured maze of cyber insurance products, or will they be easy prey for insurance companies offering policies that will not be worth much in the case of cyber events?

We have shown that the demand side struggles with several uncertainty factors when it comes to cyber insurance, and this has hindered the confidence in the product and market adoption process. Our qualitative interview study was based in Norway, but we believe that the same observations are found wherever regulations have not been a strong driving force yet. With an expected increase in this market, there is a need for better guidance in the consideration processes, as well as clearly defined and understandable terms and conditions for the product. This especially includes the identification of security gaps within the organisation, and coverage gaps, exclusions and loss types for the cyber insurance policy.

It was also found during the interview studies, that even for organisations that did not end up buying an insurance, there were still positive effects from the consideration process, since it brought attention and awareness of cyber security to the management level and across the organisation.

Acknowledgments. This research has been performed as part of the inSecurance project funded by SINTEF Digital. We would like to thank the representatives from all the organisations that participated in the interviews for sharing their experiences with us, and discussions with representatives from brokers and insurance companies. A final gratitude to Professor Guttorm Sindre at NTNU for feedback and comments.

References

1. Association of British Insurers: Making sense of cyber insurance: a guide for SMEs. Technical report, ABO (2016)
2. Bandyopadhyay, T.: Organizational adoption of cyber insurance instruments in it security risk management: a modeling approach, Proceedings, P. 5 (2012)
3. Bandyopadhyay, T., Mookerjee, V.S., Rao, R.C.: Why IT managers don't go for cyber-insurance products. Commun. ACM **52**(11), 68–73 (2009)
4. Bentz, T.: Negotiating key cyber exclusions. Insurance Day (2015). https://www.insuranceday.com/news_analysis/legal_focus/negotiating-key-cyber-exclusions.htm
5. Böhme, R., Schwartz, G.: Modeling cyber-insurance: towards a unifying framework. In: Workshop on the Economics in Information Security (WEIS) (2012)
6. Cambridge Centre for Risk Studies: Managing cyber insurance accumulation risk. University of Cambridge, Technical report (2016)
7. Cohn, C., Barlyn, S.: European, Asian companies short on cyber insurance before ransomware attack (2017). http://www.reuters.com/article/us-cyber-attack-insurance-idUSKCN18B00H
8. CRIF: Cyber insurance and the terrorism exclusion (2014). http://www.cyberriskinsuranceforum.com/content/cyber-insurance-and-terrorism-exclusion
9. DG Justice and Consumers: Reform of EU data protection rules (2016). http://ec.europa.eu/justice/data-protection/reform/index_en.htm

10. Digital Single Market: Digital scoreboard (2016). https://ec.europa.eu/digit al-single-market/digital-scoreboard
11. Dobie, G., Collins, S.: A guide to cyber risk - managing the impact of increasing interconnectivity. Technical report, Allianz (2015). http://www.agcs.allianz.com/ assets/PDFs/risk%20bulletins/CyberRiskGuide.pdf
12. ENISA, Robinson, N.: Incentives and barriers of the cyber insurance market in Europe. Report 28th June 2012. http://www.enisa.europa.eu/activities/Resilience-and-CIIP/national-cyber-security-strategies-ncsss/incentives-and-barriers-of-the-cyber-insurance-market-in-europe/at_download/fullReport
13. Gordon, L.A., Loeb, M.P., Sohail, T.: A framework for using insurance for cyber-risk management. Commun. ACM **46**(3), 81–85 (2003)
14. Hiscox: The hiscox cyber readiness report (2017). https://www.hiscox.co.uk/ cyber-readiness-report/docs/cyber-readiness-report-2017.pdf
15. Hurtaud, S., Flamand, T., de la Vaissiere, L., Hounka, A.: Cyber insurance as one element of the cyber risk management strategy February 2015. https://ww w2.deloitte.com/lu/en/pages/risk/articles/cyber-insurance-element-cyber-risk-ma nagement-strategy.html
16. Lloyd's, Cambridge Centre for Risk Studies: Lloyds City Risk Index 2015–2025 (2015). http://hwww.lloyds.com/cityriskindex/
17. Maude, F.: The role of insurance in managing and mitigating the riske (2015). https://www.marsh.com/uk/insights/research/uk-cyber-security-role-of-insuranc e-in-managing-mitigating-risk.html
18. Meland, P.H., Tøndel, I.A., Solhaug, B.: Mitigating risk with cyberinsurance. IEEE Secur. Priv. **13**(6), 38–43 (2015)
19. Nikolaeva, M., Rivet, M.: French central bank chief urges insurers to step up cyber risk coverage (2017). http://www.reuters.com/article/us-france-insura nce-idUSKBN1591Q9
20. Pain, L.D., Anchen, J., Bundt, M., Durand, E., Schmitt, M.: Cyber: In search of resilience in an interconnected world (2016). http://www.swissre.com/library/ archive/Demand_for_cyber_insurance_on_the_rise_joint_Swiss_Re_IBM_study_shows. html
21. Ponemon: Managing cyber security as a business risk: Cyber insurance in the digi-tal age. Report, Ponemon Institute, August 2013. http://www.ponemon.org/blog/ managing-cyber-security-as-a-business-risk-cyber-insurance-in-the-digital-age
22. Protection, National, Directorate, Programs: Cyber risk culture roundtable read-out report, Technical report. U.S. Department of Homeland Security (2013)
23. Protection, National, Directorate, Programs: Cybersecurity insurance workshop readout report, Technical report. U.S. Department of Homeland Security (2012)
24. Romanosky, S.: Examining the costs and causes of cyber incidents. J. Cybersecur. **2**(2), 121–135 (2016)
25. Siemens, R., Beck, D.: How to buy cyber insurance. Risk Manag. **59**(8), 40 (2012)
26. Svanemyr, S.: Kontantene forsvinner i butikkene (Norwegian) (2016). https:// tinyurl.com/j7qaqe9
27. Swiss Re Institute: Cyber: getting to grips with a complex risk. Technical report, Swiss Re (2017). http://www.swissre.com/library/sigma_01_2017_en.html
28. World Economic Forum: The global risks report 2016, 11st edn. (2016). http:// www3.weforum.org/docs/GRR/WEF_GRR16.pdf

Authorization

How Much is Risk Increased by Sharing Credential in Group?

Hiroaki Kikuchi[✉], Niihara Koichi, and Michihiro Yamada

Graduate School of Advanced Mathematical Sciences, Meiji University,
4-21-1 Nakano, Tokyo 164-8525, Japan
{kikn,niihara}@meiji.ac.jp

Abstract. Insider threats are one of the biggest issues in information management. In practice, the hardest challenge is protecting information assets from malicious insiders. There have been many studies to clarify the factors influencing insiders to perform malicious activities. However, a user study based on a questionnaire cannot be expected to reveal the honest opinions of potential malicious insiders who may give false answers to such studies. In addition, it is hard to observe the comprehensive searches of malicious activities in insider incidents, because available data about incidents are limited. To overcome the difficulties in studying malicious activities in insider threats, we propose a new approach employing epidemiological methodologies with (1) risk amplification, and (2) a logistic model for malicious incidents. We employed a total of 200 subjects from crowd-sourcing services and observed every step that they employed to perform a given task in an environment motivating them to malicious activities (risk amplification). We applied a logistic regression to identify the odds ratio of in favor of malicious activity among those exposed to a factor divided by the odds when not exposed to it. Our experiment shows that a credential shared in group increases the risk of malicious insiders by 3.28 with statistical significance ($p < 0.1$).

1 Introduction

Insider threats are one of the biggest issues in information management. In practice, the hardest challenge is to protect information assets from malicious insiders. There have been many studies to clarify the factors influencing users to perform malicious activities. Leon et al. showed through an online survey how privacy practices affect users' willingness to allow the collection of behavioral data and identified classes of information that most people would not share [4]. Fagan and Kahn introduced a rational decision model and identified key gaps in perception between people who follow common security advice and those who do not [1]. They collected 290 survey responses to the known security recommendations, i.e., updating software, a password manager, two-factor authentication, and changing passwords frequently. Hausawi conducted a survey study to ask security experts about the behavior of end-users [7]. According to these studies, the most negative behavior is sharing credentials in groups. Individuals may

© Springer International Publishing AG 2017
G. Livraga and C. Mitchell (Eds.): STM 2017, LNCS 10547, pp. 103–117, 2017.
DOI: 10.1007/978-3-319-68063-7_7

behave maliciously when they are grouped under group credential and so can *hide* their individual identity within a group umbrella.

However, a user study [2,3] based on questionnaire should not be exposed to reveal the honest opinions of potential malicious insiders who may give false answers to such studies. In addition, it is hard to observe the comprehensive searches of malicious activities in insider incidents, since available data about incidents are limited.

To overcome the difficulties in studying malicious activities in insider threats, we propose a new approach using epidemiological methodologies with (1) risk amplification, and (2) a logistic model for malicious insiders. Our goal is to identify the significant factors in motivating employees to conduct malicious activities. Employees' willings to follow security policies may be affected by environmental conditions. For example, they are likely to ignore security rules with too many requirements, under tight schedule, and with low payment. Among environmental factors, we focus on those that help an employee feel free to use arbitrary activities without monitoring. If employees find that no equipment monitors their activities, they are more likely to cheat on their duties without detection.

In this study, we conducted an experiment in which subjects were asked to complete a given task under varying monitoring conditions. We employed a total of 200 subjects from crowd-sourcing services and observed steps that they performed a given task in an environment motivating them to malicious activities. We applied a logistic regression to identify the odds ratio of the malicious activity among those exposed to a factor divided by the odds when not exposed to that factor. Our experiment shows that sharing credentials in group increases the risk of malicious insiders by 3.28 with statistical significance ($p < 0.1$).

2   Background and Related Work

There were many studies on insider threats.

Capplli *et al.* classified insider threats into three groups: insider IT sabotage, insider theft of intellectual property, and insider fraud [19]. The present work deals with insider fraud.

Cohen and Felson [15] presented the 'routine activity theory,' which argues that most crimes have three necessary conditions: a likely offender, a suitable target, and the absence of a capable guardian. Cressey [16] proposed the fraud triangle model to explain the factors present in every fraud situation: perceived pressure, perceived opportunity, and rationalization. Greitzer *et al.* [13,17] provided some indicators of insider threats based on published case studies and discussions with experienced human resources professionals. According to these studies, various hypothesized causes of insider threats exist. However, because there are so many potential causes of malicious insider threats, which ones have the greatest effect on insider behavior remains unclear [5,6].

Capplli et al. proposed a MERIT model related to insider threats based on investigations of criminal records [20]. Nurse et al. proposed a framework

for characterizing insider attacks [21]. Their models are convenient for administrators in solving the problems and analyzing the risks associated with insider
threats. We demonstrated experimentally that placing participants in environments with low levels of surveillance is more likely to lead to insider threats [14].
There were many studies for detecting typical behaviors of malicious insiders
[8–12]. Hausawi conducted an interview study to survey security experts about
the behavior of end-users [7]. According to these studies, the most negative
behavior is sharing credentials in group. However, how much group sharing credentials increases the risk of insider threats remains unclear.

In this paper, we investigate the relationship between sharing credentials in
group and the risk of malicious insider threats.

3   Methodology

3.1   Study Design

Our goal is to identify the significant factors in motivating employees to conduct
malicious activities. An employee's willings to follow security policies may be
affected by environmental conditions. For example, they are likely to ignore
security rules that have too many requirements when schedules are too tight,
and salaries are too low. Among environmental factors, we focus on those that
help an employee feel free to perform arbitrary activities without monitoring. If
employees find that no equipment monitors their activities, they are more likely
to cheat without detection.

In this study, we conducted an experiment in which subjects were asked to
complete a given task under varying conditions of monitoring. We observed how
they behaved in a given environment and quantified the risk of malicious insiders
by counts of malicious activities in each of environment. The set of subjects was
divided into the following (mixed) groups;

- Group **sharing credentials**. Subjects are given a single common credential,
  e.g., "administrator" or "guest", to have access to resources. Even if a subject
  makes a mistake, the activity is logged with the common identity and the
  subject cannot be identified, except that one of the group did it. Hence,
  sharing credentials could spoil the traceability of transactions. Knowing that
  their activities cannot be distinguished, a potential insider might frequency
  perform malicious activities more frequently.
- Group assigned to **individual credentials**. Ordinarily, subjects are given
  individual credentials (identity and password) and use them to sign in to
  a website before completing a task. Hence, they are supposed to follow an
  instruction of task and no malicious activity would be taken in the group.
- Group with **ID indicated**. The website explicitly indicates the subject's
  identity at the top of the page so that subjects can notice that they sign-
  in with individual credentials. The indication of identity reminds them to
  consider that all behaviors will be logged with their identity.

– Group **no ID indicated**. This is the opposite of the ID indicated group. Because no identity is indicated, subjects may not be sure whether their activities are monitored.

We investigate differences in the number of malicious behaviors in these groups. Our research question is *whether individuals do behavior more malicious behaviors when group identity is shared than individual can be identified.* To determine the question, we test the null hypothesis

H_0: The proportion of subjects who behave maliciously among the group where subject share a common credential is identical to the proportion of malicious subjects assigned in individual credentials.

against the following alternative hypothesis:

H_1: The subjects sharing common group credentials are more likely to perform malicious activities.
H_2: The subjects without their identities indicated are more likely to perform malicious activities.

3.2 Subjects

To investigate the differences between groups, we collected a total of 198 subjects using Lancers Inc.[1], the Japanese crowd-sourcing service, in October 2016. We required Lancers' certified workers who had enrolled in the service with their official certificates of Japanese residence. All subjects who completed the given task were paid 250 JPY (equivalent 2.2 USD), which is typical for a task that takes approximately 20 min to complete.

We assigned subjects round robin to one of four groups, $A, B, C,$ and D, corresponding to hypotheses H_1 and H_2 as defined in Table 1. For example, all subjects in group A shared the same identity "Guest" which was not identified while they completed a task. If both hypotheses are true, group A is most likely and group D is least likely to participate in malicious activities. For groups B and D, we assigned individual identities of the form "user$nnnnn$" where n is a random decimal digit. The number of subjects in group D is the smallest because some of them withdrew from the task.

After reviewing and signing to a consent form, subjects answered demographic questions. Table 3 shows the demographics of our subjects[2]. We found that the subjects' attributes were randomly distributed over the four groups without any significant skew.

---

[1] http://www.lancers.jp.
[2] We plan to make all data publicly available from our website http://windy.mind. meiji.ac.jp/kiknlab2014/paper.html in a way that does not compromise anyone's privacy.

3.3   Micro-task of Testing Website

To simulate the experience of working in an IT company, we instructed the subjects to evaluate the performance of a target website providing a search service and gave them a specified query list of 70 (Japanese) words to test. We explained to them that the aim was to test the usability of a developed website and we wished to know the performance when many queries were sent in a short period. Subjects were required to test at least 50 queries out of the given 70 words, but were allowed to complete their task even though they had not yet tested the minimum number of queries.

After testing the query search of the website, the subjects were asked some questions such as the correctness of the query, the performance of the response, and their experience using the website. The search service was implemented using Google API and the query lists were collected randomly from websites. For experimental purposes, we added a few unusual words to the list.

3.4   Difficulties in Observation

Although we could see all of the steps that our subjects took in the given task, it was not easy to observe malicious activities for several reasons. The followings are difficulties that we faced in observing malicious activities in our experiment.

- *No motivation.* The subjects were hired on an experimental and short-term contract. Hence, they were not motivated to take risks to perform malicious activities that could be detected easily and result in canceling their payment. If they found any difficulty in their task, they could simply cancel their agreement. These are differences between the experiment and a real business environment. Without suffering persistent long-term stress in the working environment, people may not want to behave maliciously.
- *Monitor without identity.* We wanted to observe how subjects behave when they find that no one monitors them. This is a contradictory requirement. Without assigning unique identities, there is no way to distinguish some subjects. Alternatively, we may use Http cookies or hidden links embedded in the website to track target subjects. However, if we use this tracking technique, an advanced subject could suspect the use of tracking and behave as if they were monitored.
- *Small effect of individual credentials.* We expected that subjects assigned individual credentials would be less likely to work maliciously. However, they did not take the credentials serious, even when unique identities were given because they knew the identities were issued for an experimental purpose and only for one-time use. In an experiment, there is little difference between shared and individual credentials.

3.5   Risk Amplification

To overcome the difficulties caused by limited motivation of malicious behavior in the experimental environment, we used a distorted environment, called *risk*

Table 1. Hypotheses and groups

Group	H_1 (account)	H_2 (ID indication)	N
A	Shared	No	52
B	Individual		52
C	Shared	Yes	46
D	Individual		48

Table 2. Schedule of delays with respect to iteration s

Iteration s	Delay [s]	Copy-and-paste
1–4	0	
5–12	1	
13–18	2	
19–22	3	
23–30	4	
31–32	20	
33–36	2	
37–40	9	
41–42	20	Disabled
43–44	5	Disabled
45–46	9	Disabled
47<	5	Disabled

Table 3. Demographics of our subjects

Demographic	A	B	C	D	Total
Gender					
Male	28	30	23	28	109
Female	24	22	23	20	89
Age					
<19	0	0	1	0	1
20–29	8	2	7	6	23
30–39	18	19	17	22	76
40–49	16	24	14	14	68
50–59	6	5	6	5	22
60<	4	2	1	1	8
Occupation					
Office worker	16	17	6	9	48
Government	1	0	0	0	1
Self-employed	13	13	15	16	57
Part-time worker	7	5	2	5	19
Homemaker	6	10	13	8	37
Student	0	0	1	1	2
Unemployed	5	6	4	6	21
Other	4	1	5	3	13
N	52	52	46	48	198

amplification, in which subjects are required to work in an environment with some obstacles. If a subject behaves maliciously under the risk amplification condition with a certain probability, he or she could act malicious in an ordinary condition with smaller but proportional probability. The observed probability is useful to estimate the true magnitude of risk in arbitrary conditions. Risk amplification allows us to make small probabilities look larger so that we can examine risks of relevant conditions.

Scheduled Delay. To frustrate subjects with the website response, we manipulated the performance of the website as scheduled in Table 2. The duration of delay varies with iteration of query, s. For example, the response is delayed by 20 s at the 31st and 32nd iterations. Meanwhile, subjects might consider that some intensive computations were happening at the web server and thus be motivated to complete their task before testing the minimum number of queries, which is treated as a malicious activity.

Disabled Copy-and-Paste. Similar to the scheduled delays in Table 2, we used Javascript to disable the copy-and-paste function of the browser for iterations greater than 40 ($s > 40$). We chose a few unusual long words for the query list so that subjects would want to copy and paste to test them without carefully typing the long word. Hence, they might become irritated by the suddenly disabled copy-and-paste and be motivated to replace the annoying unusual word with random words, which is regarded as a malicious activity.

No Indication of Iteration. The iteration counts s were not available to subjects to make them believe that the iterations were not significant in completing task. We accepted any completion report before or after the minimum number of queries (50) and allowed subjects to answer questions about usability of the website, even if they had not tested the full 50 queries, which is counted as a malicious activity.

3.6   Tracking Subjects

To track subjects sharing credentials in group and monitor all activities made without unique individual identities, we assigned unique query lists to subjects. By matching the log of tested queries with the query lists assigned to the subjects, we could identify exactly who sent the queries and examine whether they performed any malicious activities while testing the target website.

For those who had individual credentials, tracking was trivial. We required them to sign in to the target website using their Lancers ID for which the payment was made. The use of the official ID helped convince them that their activities were monitored by their employer, and that any fault in their duties could cancel the payment. Thus, individual credentials encouraged subjects to refrain from behaving maliciously.

In these ways, we enlarged the difference of effect in malicious activities between shared and individual credentials and quantify how much risk is increased with sharing group credential against assigning individual ones.

3.7   Malicious Activities

1. *Completing a task with fewer iterations.* In this activity, the task was completed earlier than expected by testing fewer than the minimum 50 iterations.
2. *Replacing given words (queries) with random ones.* When a query does not exactly match any of the words assigned to the subject, we regard it as malicious behavior by the subject who typed in a random word. This malicious activity occurs when the subject wishes to proceed without typing a long unusual word. Similar activities such as querying with null strings or typing error are also classified into this category.
3. *Privileged Access.* Subjects were instructed that privileged access was prohibited in the experiment where we prepared a fake "administrator" link. Therefore, if a subject tried to click a privileged link to modify the records of the task, we regarded it as malicious.

4   Study Results

4.1   Elapsed Time

Figure 2 shows the cumulative processing time T_i [s] with respect to iterations s of querying (indicated as search count). We show typical behaviors of four representative users in different colors. In general, the elapsed time increases monotonically with iteration, but it sometime increases sharply. For example, the blue line rises at $s = 41$, which was caused by the scheduled delay mentioned in Sect. 3.5.

The typical behaviors of the subjects are classified into the following four patterns:

1. Terminating task before testing the required number of iterations ($s < 50$). User 1 indicated in red is malicious.
2. Terminating the task when a constrains is encountered (scheduled delay or disabled copy-and-paste). User 3 in green stops querying at around $s \geq 41$ when a response is delayed by 20 s. This is labeled as malicious.
3. Completing a task as soon as the minimum iteration is satisfied. User 2 indicated in blue is legitimate.
4. Completing task by testing all 70 words in a given list. User 4 indicated in blue, plotted always as the highest of the four, is legitimate (Fig. 1).

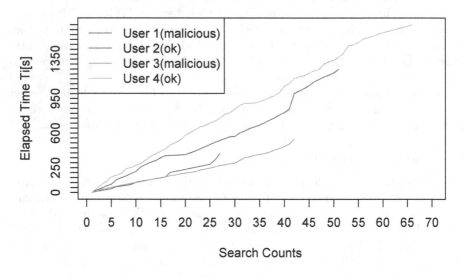

Fig. 1. Elapsed times for a sample of users against iteration (Color figure online)

4.2   Malicious Activities

Table 4 shows the number of malicious subjects, defined as those who performed at least one of the malicious activities, defined in Sect. 3.7. We find slightly decreasing tendency of malicious activities in the order of groups $A > B > C > D$, as assumed in hypothesis, H_1: subjects sharing a common group credential (A, C) are more likely to behave maliciously than those who sign-in with individual credentials (B, D).

Table 4. Malicious activities

Activity	A	B	C	D	Total
(1) Fewer iteration	11	8	9	7	35
(2) Random queries	5	3	1	2	11
(3) Privileged access	1	1	0	0	2
N	17	12	10	9	

Table 5. Malicious subjects with fewer iteration

Demographic	A	B	C	D	Total
Gender					
Male	7	5	6	6	24
Female	4	3	3	1	11
Age					
<19	0	0	1	0	1
20–29	1	0	1	2	4
30–39	6	1	3	3	13
40–49	0	3	2	1	6
50–59	1	2	1	0	4
60<	3	2	1	1	7
Occupation					
Office worker	3	3	2	2	10
Government	1	0	0	0	1
Self-employed	4	0	3	3	10
Part-time worker	1	0	0	0	1
Homemaker	1	2	1	0	4
Student	0	0	1	1	2
Unemployed	1	2	0	1	4
Other	0	1	2	0	3
N	11	8	9	7	35

The most frequent malicious activity is (1) completing task with fewer iterations, which is followed by (2) replacing required with random words, and (3) privileged access. We show the demographics of malicious subjects in Table 5. The number of malicious subjects is generally proportional to the population of each demographic groups (we show hypothesis testing later). However, note that older subjects are more frequently detected as malicious than younger ones. For instance, the seven (87.5%) out of eight subjects over 60 years of age were malicious users. By investigating the log of their behaviors, we observed that they usually spent a longer time on and often duplicated the same query.

Since they might be unfamiliar with this type of task and might have lost their way before completing it, we should exclude the older subjects as outliers and focus on the younger ones.

4.3 Cumulative Relative Frequency

A cumulative relative frequency, $Cu(s)$, defined as the fraction of subjects who completed the task at iteration s as a proportion of the group, gives more detailed malicious behaviors. Figure 2 shows the changes in cumulative relative frequencies of the four groups A, B, C and D. We show a vertical dotted line at $s = 50$ which is the threshold iteration for regarding subjects as malicious.

The higher the frequency is, the more subjects completed the task, and more malicious activity occurred in the group. For example, group A has $Cu(s < 50) = 0.21 = 21/52$, which means that 21 subjects out of 52 members of A did not satisfy the minimum requirement of 50 queries (malicious subjects). The tendency of increased malicious activities with shared credentials is enhanced when we examine the subset of workers aged 30 through 39, as shown in Fig. 3. The fractions of malicious subjects, $Cu(s < 50)$, of groups A, B, C and D are $0.33, 0.05, 0.18$, and 0.14, respectively. We note that there were more malicious subjects in group A than any other group. Therefore, the environmental condition of the group, i.e., sharing group credentials without ID indication, must have an effect in increasing the risk of insider threats.

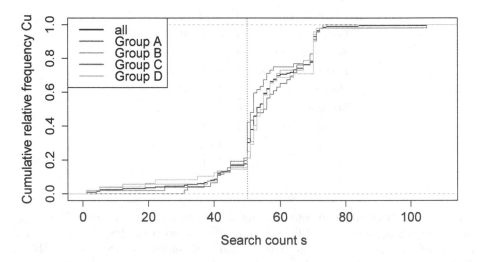

Fig. 2. Cumulative relative frequencies of groups (all members)

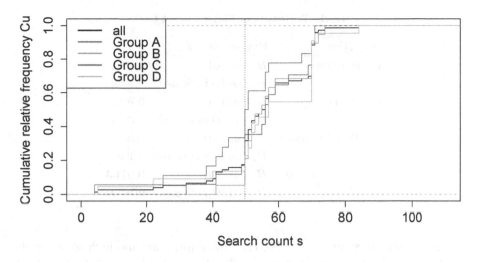

Fig. 3. Cumulative relative frequencies of groups (for subjects aged 30–39)

4.4 Hypothesis Testing (Fisher's Exact Testing)

To test the null hypothesis H_0 that two proportions of malicious subjects with/without sharing group credentials (groups A plus C) are identical, we used the Fisher's exact test. To carry out the test, we have the 2×2 contingency tables for each malicious activity as shown in Table 6, where there are total of eight contingency tables computed to test hypothesis H_1 (sharing identity) and H_2 (indication of identity). Based on the observation in Sect. 4.3, we added another table for the subset of malicious subjects restricted to 30–39 years of age.

For a hyper-geometric distribution with 1 degree of freedom, we have the probabilities followed by the counts in the contingency tables in Table 7.

Table 6. Contingency tables of counts of malicious subjects

Activities	Malicious	H_1 (shared ID)		H_2 (no ID indicated)	
		Shared	Individual	Not Indicated	ID indicated
		$A + C$	$B + D$	$B + D$	$C + D$
Fewer iteration	Yes	20	15	19	16
	No	78	85	85	78
Random query	Yes	6	5	8	3
	No	92	95	96	91
Privileged access	Yes	1	1	2	0
	No	97	99	102	94
Fewer iteration (30's)	yes	9	4	7	6
	No	26	37	30	33

Table 7. Results of Fisher's exact test

Activities	Hypothesis	p
Fewer iteration	H_1 (shared)	0.3551
	H_2 (no ID indicated)	0.8539
Random query	H_1 (shared)	0.7662
	H_2 (no ID indicated)	0.2201
Privileged access	H_1 (shared)	1.0000
	H_2 (no ID indicated)	0.4987
Less iteration (30s)	H_1 (shared)	**0.0763**
	H_2 (no ID indicated)	0.7659

With the significance level $p < 0.05$, the probabilities are too high to reject the null hypothesis for this case. However, with $0.05 < p < 0.1$, we can reject the null hypothesis that there is no association between the malicious activities in the subset in their 30s and the condition of sharing group credential, hence we conclude that there is evidence of an association between sharing group credentials and malicious activities.

Our experiment did not reveal quite strong confidence to the hypothesis that sharing group credential increases malicious behaviors. We think the reason of this caused by small subsets of subjects such as over-60-years group in Table 5. We don't think that they intended to do maliciously but unfortunately they were recognized as malicious according to our criteria of malicious behaviors. Moreover, they are not eligible for our study that aims to identify significant factor in insider threats in industry. Hence, we should design an experimental condition more carefully for selection proper subset of workers.

4.5   Logistic Regression

To quantify the risk introduced by sharing credentials, we performed a multivariable logistic regression analysis on the subset of subjects aged their 30s. Our logistic regression model has a dependent variable for the outcome of malicious activity of (1) fewer iteration and multiple independent variables; x_1, a sharing group credential, x_2, a gender, occupations such as x_3, "part-time worker", x_4, "office worker", and so on, as shown in Table 8. Let p be probability that individuals in their 30s will perform malicious activity of completing the task with fewer iteration. The logit of our model is

$$\log \frac{p}{1-p} = -16.75 + 1.189x_1 + 1.165x_2 + \cdots + 12.90x_7,$$

where the coefficient of x_1 (sharing group credential) is statistically significant with 90 % ($Pr < 0.1$) confidence level. Therefore, the estimated odds ratio of

Table 8. Results of logistic regression (* shows the significant level of $Pr < 0.1$)

	Variables	Coefficient	Std. Error	z value	$Pr(> |z|)$
	(Intercept)	-16.75	1455.39	-0.012	0.991
1	sharing ID	**1.189**	0.675	1.760	0.0784*
2	Male	1.165	0.902	1.292	0.196
3	Part-time worker	14.40	1455.40	0.010	0.992
4	Office worker	13.94	1455.40	0.010	0.992
5	Self-employed	13.80	1455.40	0.009	0.992
6	Homemaker	14.17	1455.40	0.010	0.992
7	Unemployed	12.90	1455.40	0.009	0.993

having malicious activity (fewer iteration) for subjects sharing credentials versus those who have individual credentials is

$$\widehat{OR} = \frac{Pr(mal.|sharing)}{1 - Pr(mal.|sharing)} \Big/ \frac{Pr(mal.|individual)}{1 - Pr(mal.|individual)}$$
$$= e^{1.189} = 3.28,$$

which implies that the risk of malicious activity when credentials are shared is about three times higher than when they are not.

5   Conclusions

We have proposed a new approach to identify significant factors in insider threats. In our proposed method, a set of subjects work on a simple task, and we observes how many malicious activities are performed in varying conditions. We propose a distorted environment, called *risk amplification*, in which subjects are required to work in the presence of some obstacles. Subjects who behave maliciously under the risk amplification condition with a certain probability can be expected to behave maliciously in ordinary conditions with smaller but proportional probability. The observed probability is useful to estimate the true magnitude of risk in arbitrary conditions.

We quantified the risk introduced by sharing group credentials, by performing a multi-variable logistic regression analysis. Our experimental results showed that the estimated odds ratio of having malicious activity among subjects who share credentials is 3.28 compared with those who do not. We conclude that the risk of malicious activity occurring when sharing credentials is about three times higher than that when not.

Our future works include a future investigate primal factors to make subject motivate malicious activities, and a generalization of our experimental results to real one. Since our experiment has some limitations, e.g., the duration of observation, the number of subjects, the kinds of tasks, and the environment, we plan to conduct a long-term experiment where subjects have more chances to behave maliciously.

References

1. Fagan, M., Khan, M.M.H.: Why do they do what they do?: a study of what motivates users to (not) follow computer security advice. In: Proceedings of 12th Symposium on Usable Privacy and Security (SOUPS 2016), pp. 59–75 (2016)
2. Rao, A., Schaub, F., Sadeh, N., Acquisti, A., Kang, R.: Expecting the unexpected: understanding mismatched privacy expectations online. In: Proceedings of 12th Symposium on Usable Privacy and Security (SOUPS 2016), pp. 77–96 (2016)
3. Ion, I.,Reeder, R., Consolvo, S.: "... no one can hack my mind": comparing expert and non-expert security practices. In: Eleventh Symposium on Usable Privacy and Security (SOUPS 2015), pp. 327–346 (2015)
4. Leon, P.G., Ur, B., Wang, Y., Sleeper, M., Balebako, R., Shay, R., Bauer, L., Christodorescu, M., Cranor, L.F.: What matters to users? Factors that affect users' willingness to share information with online advertisers. In: Proceedings of the SOUPS 2013. ACM (2013)
5. Aurigemma, S., Panko, R.: A composite framework for behavioral compliance with information security policies. In: Proceedings of the 2012 45th Hawaii International Conference on System Sciences, pp. 3248–3257. IEEE Computer Society (2012)
6. Renaud, K., Goucher, W.: The curious incidence of security breaches by knowledgeable employees and the pivotal role a of security culture. In: Tryfonas, T., Askoxylakis, I. (eds.) HAS 2014. LNCS, vol. 8533, pp. 361–372. Springer, Cham (2014). doi:10.1007/978-3-319-07620-1_32
7. Hausawi, Y.M.: Current trend of end-users' behaviors towards security mechanisms. In: 4th International Conference on Human Aspects of Information Security, Privacy, and Trust, pp. 140–151 (2016)
8. Spitzner, L.: Honeypots: catching the insider threat. In: Proceedings of 19th Annual Computer Security Applications Conference, pp. 170–179 (2003)
9. Azaria, A., et al.: Behavioral analysis of insider threat: a survey and bootstrapped prediction in imbalanced data. IEEE Trans. Comput. Soc. Syst. 1, 135–155 (2014)
10. Legg, P.A., et. al.: Caught in the act of an insider attack: detection and assessment of insider threat. In: IEEE International Symposium on Technologies for Homeland Security (2015)
11. Legg, P.A.: Visualizing the insider threat: challenges and tools for identifying malicious user activity. In: 2015 IEEE Symposium on Visualization for Cyber Security (VizSec), pp. 1–7 (2015)
12. Greitzer, F.L., et al.: Identifying at-risk employees: modeling psychosocial precursors of potential insider threats. In: 2012 45th Hawaii International Conference on System Science (HICSS), pp. 2392–2401 (2012)
13. Greitzer, F.L., Frincke, D.A.: Combining traditional cyber security audit data with psychosocial data: towards predictive modeling for insider threat mitigation. In: Probst, C., Hunker, J., Gollmann, D., Bishop, M. (eds.) Insider Threats in Cyber Security. Advances in Information Security, vol. 49, pp. 85–113. Springer, Boston (2010). doi:10.1007/978-1-4419-7133-3_5
14. Niihara, K., Kikuchi, H.: Primary factors of malicious insider in E-learning model. In: HCI International 2016 - Posters' Extended Abstracts: 18th International Conference. Proceedings, Part I, pp. 482–487 (2016)
15. Cohen, L.E., Felson, M.: Social change and crime rate trends: a routine activity approach. Am. Sociol. Rev. 44(4), 588–608 (1979)
16. Cressey, D.R.: Other People's Money: A Study in the Social Psychology of Embezzlement. Free Press, Glencoe (1953)

17. Greitzer, F.L., et al.: Identifying at-risk employees: modeling psychosocial precursors of potential insider threats. In: 2012 45th Hawaii International Conference on System Sciences, pp. 2392–2401 (2012)
18. Fagade, T., Tryfonas, T.: Security by compliance? A study of insider threat implications for Nigerian banks. In: Tryfonas, T. (ed.) HAS 2016. LNCS, vol. 9750, pp. 128–139. Springer, Cham (2016). doi:10.1007/978-3-319-39381-0_12
19. Cappelli, D., Moore, A., Trzeciak, R.: The CERT Guide to Insider Threats: How to Prevent, Detect, and Respond to Information Technology Crimes. (Theft, Sabotage, Fraud). Addison-Wesley Professional, Boston (2012)
20. Cappelli, D., et al.: Management and Education of the Risk of Insider Threat (MERIT): System Dynamics Modeling of Computer System. Carnegie Mellon University, Software Engineering Institute (2008)
21. Nurse, J.R.C. et al.: Understanding insider threat: a framework for characterising attacks. In: 2014 IEEE of the Security and Privacy Workshops (SPW), San Jose, CA, pp. 214–228 (2014)

Smart Parental Advisory: A Usage Control and Deep Learning-Based Framework for Dynamic Parental Control on Smart TV

Giacomo Giorgi, Antonio La Marra, Fabio Martinelli, Paolo Mori, and Andrea Saracino$^{(\boxtimes)}$

Istituto di Informatica e Telematica, Consiglio Nazionale delle Ricerche, Pisa, Italy
{giacomo.giorgi,antonio.lamarra,fabio.martinelli,paolo.mori, andrea.saracino}@iit.cnr.it

Abstract. Parental Control functionalities currently included in Smart TVs, DBS decoders and Pay TV services are cumbersome to use, not flexible and, in the end, are seldom used. This paper presents a framework for dynamic enforcement of parental control policies on Smart TV contents. The framework exploits an extended version of the Usage Control model able to dynamically grant, suspend and resume the right to access a content, based on the content classification and on the age of people currently in front of the Smart TV. An accurate age estimation is performed by mean of a cascade of two deep learning networks. We present an implementation of the proposed framework in a smart home environment, showing both simulated and real experiments for accuracy in classification and performance analysis.

1 Introduction

In the last years, Smart TVs have had a dramatic increase in their diffusion, due to the availability of a very large number of different models from the main home appliances vendors at really affordable prices. A Smart TV is a television which embeds an operative system (OS), is able to install manufacturer and third party applications (apps), and is generally connected to the Internet. Thus, Smart TVs are able to provide a set of additional functionalities compared to standard televisions, including Video on Demand, Internet TV, Multimedia services, Video Streaming, Social Networks, etc.

Given the plethora of multimedia contents which are available through Smart TVs and due to their ease of access, issues arise when children and minors in general have the possibility to access these contents. In particular, a relevant number of available video media contents are classified as Adult Only or require the presence of an adult for a minor to safely watch the content.

This work has been partially funded by EU Funded projects: H2020 C3ISP, GA #700294, H2020 NeCS, GA #675320, and EIT Digital HII Trusted Data Management with Service Ecosystem.

© Springer International Publishing AG 2017
G. Livraga and C. Mitchell (Eds.): STM 2017, LNCS 10547, pp. 118–133, 2017.
DOI: 10.1007/978-3-319-68063-7_8

The relevance of the problem is confirmed by the fact that, Smart TVs themselves and some apps or content provider already include some machineries to enforce parental control. However, these solutions are mainly based on manual settings of channels, programs or time slots which should be accessible or not to the children, where the forbidden contents are generally protected through a PIN or a password. This makes the parental control service cumbersome to use, since adults are not willing to insert a password/PIN any time they wish to watch a program or content not meant for children. Moreover, these approaches have limited flexibility, not considering, for example, those programs which are accessible to minors only if watched in presence of an adult. For this use case, is also not considered the case in which the adult can temporarily leave the minor to watch the program/content, without actively pausing it. We argue that these parental control policies can be automatically and effectively enforced by exploiting *access* and *usage control* models.

In this paper we present a Smart Parental Advisory: a Usage Control-based framework to enforce advanced and dynamic parental control policies on Smart TV contents. The proposed framework exploits Smart TV's built-in camera (or a pluggable webcam) to continuously monitor the users watching (or in front of) the TV, and a cascade of two deep learning network to estimate in real time the age of those users. We present the design and training of the two deep learning networks, used respectively to recognize the number of current users and to estimate their age. Afterward, we will present the full framework as implemented in a smart home environments which integrates a usage control system able to dynamically enforce the parental control policies directly on the smart TV, by granting, suspending and resuming the right to watch a specific content, based on metadata directly extracted from the content itself. Furthermore, a complete evaluation of the system performance is performed by statistical, simulated and real experiments. Finally, a performance analysis to show the viability of the approach is presented.

The rest of the paper is organized as follows: in Sect. 2 we report notions on the concepts usage control and on the guidelines for parental advisory exploited in this work. Section 3 describes in detail the framework logical architecture, the workflow and details of the implementation in a smart home environment. In Sect. 4 are reported and discussed the results related to face classification and age estimation accuracy of deep learning networks, afterward results on a simulated scenario and a real one are reported. Section 5 compares Smart Parental Advisory with related works. Finally Sect. 6 briefly concludes presenting some future directions.

2   Background

This section reports background notions on the instruments exploited in this work, in particular we will report a brief description of the usage control model and of the classification standards for multimedia contents.

2.1   The Usage Control Model

The Usage Control (UCON) model [13,15] goes beyond traditional access control models by introducing *mutability* of attributes and new decision factors besides *authorizations*: *obligations* and *conditions*. Mutable attributes represent features of subjects, resources, and of the environment which are not static (as in the traditional access control models), but they change their values as a consequence of the normal operation of the system [14]. Some mutable attributes change their values because the policy includes attribute update statements that are executed before (*pre-update*), during (*on-update*), or after (*post-update*) the execution of the access. Other mutable attributes change their values because of actions performed by the subjects. For instance, the number of people in front of a TV is a mutable attribute of the environment which changes its value when further people go in front of the TV or people who are in front of the TV go away.

Since mutable attributes change their values during the usage of an object, the usage control model allows to define policies which are evaluated before (*pre-decision*) and continuously during the access to the object (*ongoing-decision*). Hence, in the Usage Control model it is crucial to be able to detect an update of a mutable attributes, in order to perform the continuous evaluation of the policy and to promptly react to attribute changes causing policy violations by taking proper actions, e.g., by suspending the related accesses which are in progress.

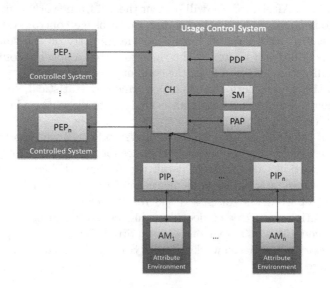

Fig. 1. Usage control system architecture

The framework proposed in this paper exploits the Usage Control Systems (UCS) based on the XACML reference architecture [12] presented in [2,9], which is shown in Fig. 1. In the XACML reference architecture, the Policy Enforcement Points (PEPs) embedded in the controlled system intercept the execution of security relevant operations, and they invoke the Context Handler (CH), which is the frontend of the Usage Control system. The *Policy Information Points (PIPs)* are the components invoked by the CH to collect the attributes required for the evaluation of the policy retrieved from the Policy Administration Point (PAP). Attributes are managed by Attribute Managers (AMs), sometimes called Attribute Providers or Attribute Stores, which provide the interfaces to retrieve and, in case of mutable Attributes, to update their current values. Each scenario where the Usage Control system is exploited requires its specific set of AMs and, consequently of PIPs configured to properly interact with them. With respect to the XACML reference architecture, in the Usage Control system PIPs are also in charge to detect when the value of attribute change, in order to trigger the policy re-evaluation for the involved ongoing accesses, which are managed by the Session Manager (SM).

The workflow regulating the continuous evaluation of a Usage Control policy is the following. When the subject *s* tries to execute a security relevant action *a*, the PEP suspends its execution and retrieves the information related to this access (subject and resource IDs, etc.). The PEP sends the *TryAccess* message with the data previously collected to the Usage Control system, which performs the *pre-decision* process and returns the result to the PEP (*permitaccess* or *denyaccess*) which enforces it. If the execution of *a* is permitted, the PEP sends the *StartAccess* message to the Usage Control system as soon as *a* is started, to start the *on-decision* phase. Again, the Usage Control system performs the first evaluation of the Usage control policy. From this moment on, as long as the action *a* is in progress, the Usage Control service evaluates the Usage Control policy every time an attribute changes its value. If the policy is violated, the Usage Control system sends the *SuspendAccess* message to the PEP, in order to suspend the execution of the access and take proper countermeasures. The values of the attributes could change several time, and each time the policy is evaluated exploiting the new values. When an access has been suspended but the policy is satisfied again as a consequence of a further change in the value of the attributes, the Usage Control system sends the *ResumeAccess* message to the PEP, in order to resume the execution of the access and perform the proper obligations. Eventually, the PEP will detect the termination of the access performed by the subject who initiated it, and will notify the Usage Control system sending the *endAccess* message. For a detailed description of the Usage Control system and of the interactions among its components, please refer to [2].

2.2 TV Parental Guidelines

Multimedia contents, such as movies and TV programs, are classified according to standards to advise the intended audience about features which might be considered dangerous or offensive to a set of spectators. In this work we refer to the American standard for parental guidelines[1], which are based on two parameters, namely the *Audience* and the *Content Label*.

---

[1] http://www.tvguidelines.org/resources/TV_Parental_guidelines_Brochure.pdf.

The audience parameter may assume one of the following values:

- **Y** for all children: this means that the program is not expected to frighten younger (2–6) children.
- **Y7** older children: this program is designed for children age 7 and above. Some of this programs may also have the FV content label (see below) in case of fantasy violence is more combative than other programs.
- **G** general audience: it is a program for all ages. Even if this program is not specifically designed for children, most parents may let younger children watch this program unattended.
- **PG** parental guidance: many parents may find this program unsuitable for younger children (the theme may call for parental guidance).
- **14** parents strongly cautioned: many parents may find this program unsuitable for children under 14 yr old. They are also urged against letting children unattended.
- **MA** mature audience: this program is specifically designed to be viewed by adults.

Content Label indicates if a show might contain violence, sexual explicit contents, mature language, etc. Each content can thus have assigned one or more of the following values:

- **D** suggestive dialogue
- **L** coarse or crude language
- **S** sexual situations
- **V** violence
- **FV** fantasy violence

The presence of one or more among D, S and L moves define a program or content whose intended audience is PG, 14 or MA.

3   Smart Parental Advisory

We designed and implemented a framework where a Smart TV is instrumented with a camera (embedded in the TV or external) which constantly takes pictures of the spectators. These pictures are elaborated to detect whether there are children alone (i.e., without adults) watching the TV. This component exploits two deep learning neural networks: one to recognize the number of people in the video, and the other to estimate their age. This information is represented as two mutable attributes of the environment, i.e., an attribute which represents the number of adults and the other which represents the number of children. The idea is that a video with PG classification starts to be played on the TV only if there is (at least) an adult in front of it. As soon as the adult goes away, the Usage Control system detects a change in the related attribute. This change triggers the re-evaluation of the previous policy, which results in a policy violation and then in the stop of the reproduction. When an adult comes back in front of the TV, the attribute which represents the number of adults changes its value again.

Consequently, the Usage Control system performs a further evaluation of the usage control policy which, this time, is satisfied. Hence, the Usage Control system issues the resume command, which is enforced by our framework by resuming the video playback.

The proposed system is highly customizable and configurable, and more complex policies taking into account further attributes (e.g., provided by other sensors installed in the Smart Home environment) could be easily defined and enforced. For instance, the policy could force the shut down of the TV when nobody is watching it in order to save energy.

In the following of this section the general architecture of the proposed smart home parental control framework is presented and the components are detailed.

3.1 Logical Architecture

The logical architecture of our framework is depicted in Fig. 2.

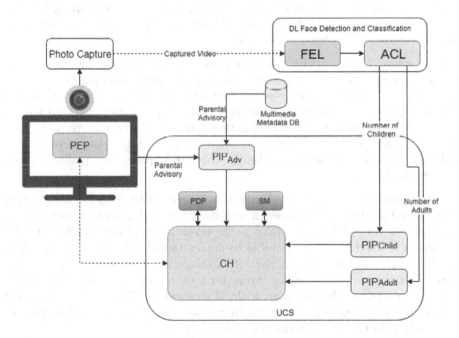

Fig. 2. Architecture of the smart parental advisory framework

As shown, the main actor initiating the workflow is the PEP, which directly communicates with the UCS when a content is being opened, i.e., the user is turning on the TV, changing channel, or opening a content through an application. Hence, the PEP initiates the request phase, by invoking the TryAccess and StartAccess functions. The Photo Capture component monitors periodically the area from which spectators should be watching the TV. The images which are captured periodically are sent to the Deep Learning Face Detection and Classification component, which is made by a cascade of two deep learning networks: the *Face Extraction Layer* (FEL), which extracts from the captured picture the faces of the spectators, and the *Age Classification Layer* (ACL), which estimates the age for each extracted face. The number and the age of spectators are thus used as attributes for the evaluation of the usage control policy, performed by the UCS. More specifically, the mutable attributes provided from the face detection and classification components are the Number of Children and the Number of Adults currently in front of the TV. The UCS also exploits the non-mutable attribute related to the classification for parental advisory of the current content, which can be extracted directly from the SmartTV, when available, extracted from the file of the content, or looked up automatically on external DB such as IMDB. Based on the UCS response, the PEP will permit or deny the playback of the content, being able to *revoke* the right to visualize the content as soon as the context does not match the policy anymore, and to *resume* the visualization when the context becomes compliant again. This will ensure, for example, that the reproduction of a content classified as PG, stops automatically as soon as there are no more adults in front of the TV, and is resumed automatically when an adult comes back in front of the TV.

Photo Capture: The SmartTV's built-in camera is used to take pictures at regular intervals in order to continuously monitor the users watching the TV. The choice of performing the capture at specific intervals is done to limit the power consumption and the processing time on a device which however should still be considered constrained on the side of performance. In the current version of our framework, the picture is taken as-is, i.e., no further processing is performed on the picture after it has been taken in order to improve the quality, remove possible blurring, etc.

Face Extraction Layer: The Face Extraction Layer (FEL) is an implementation of the Max-Margin Object Detector (MMOD)[2] with features extracted by a Convolutional Neural Network (CNN). The layer is offered by the CNN MMOD tool presented in dlib v19.2[3] suitable to detect faces in the images. The CNN provided by the tool detects if a part of an image is a face or not. The network begins with three downsampling layers used to reduce the size of the image by 8× and outputs a feature map with 32 dimensions. The results are passed through four convolutional layers which compute the features used to pass to the Max-Margin Object detection loss layer (Fig. 2).

Age Classification Layer: The Age Classification Layer (ACL) is a deep learning solution used as age estimator of a single face image. The network used is based on the Deep EXpectation architecture (DEX) [16], which uses the deep VGG-16 architecture composed by 13 convolutional layers with 3×3 filters to extract features from input image of size 256×256. The convolutional results are passed to three fully connected layers followed by a softmax layer composed

---

[2] https://arxiv.org/abs/1502.00046.
[3] http://dlib.net/.

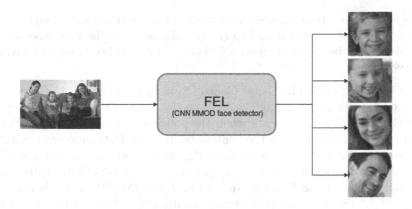

Fig. 3. FEL architecture.

by 101 softmax normalized neurons, one for each age class, used to predict the age similarity score. The DEX training starts from a CNN pre-trained on the large ImageNet dataset for image classification in order to exploit the acquired capability to discriminate 1000 object categories in images. Fine-tuning the pre-trained CNN on labeled face images extracted from the IMDB-WIKI dataset[4] is used to adapt the network to estimate 101 ages.

Our strategy consists in modifying the DEX architecture changing the number of output neurons from 101 to 2 in order to distinguish only two classes of age ([0–14] and [15–100]), and training the new architecture on a smaller, but with a better age distribution, dataset (Adience Db) starting from the weights of the model obtained from the network trained on the IMDB-WIKI dataset on 101 classes of age as shown in Fig. 4.

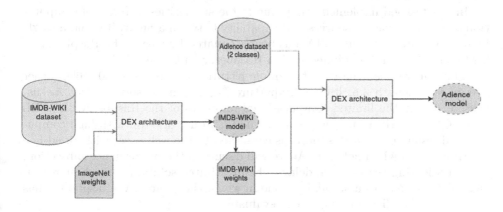

Fig. 4. IMDB-WIKI model fine tuned with Adience database.

---

[4] https://data.vision.ee.ethz.ch/cvl/rrothe/imdb-wiki/.

We performed a training session of the last two Fully connected layers of the network in order to fit the model to the new dataset and the new classification. The training has been executed on a GeForce GTX1080 board and it converged after five epochs.

Usage Control System: The Usage Control System is integrated in the parental control framework by including the PEP on the SmartTV, which monitors and blocks the streaming of contents when the policy is not matched. The PIP_{Adv} extracts the information from the content being played/streamed retrieving the parental recommendation directly from the content metadata, when available (natively offered in Android TVs[5]), or querying external databases with content information such as the Internet Movie Database (IMDB), which is accessible through SQL[6] queries. The other two PIPs directly interact with the ACL to receive the number of adults and children currently in front of the TV.

Testbed Implementation and Smart Home Simulation. The Smart TV can be considered by definition a component of a smart home environment. In fact, being connected to the home network, it can easily communicate with other devices connected to the same network. Hence, it is possible to exploit the different functionalities and computational power of the device for providing additional joint functionalities and improving the whole system performance. In [8] we have presented a distributed P2P architecture for implementing usage control in smart home environments, which could be exploited by our implementation of Smart Parental Advisory. In particular, since the Smart TV should be considered, from the point of view of performance, a relatively constrained device, running the FEL, ACL and UCS components directly on it might impose a considerable overhead and might result in poor performance. To this end, we consider the possibility of outsourcing these functionalities to other nodes of the smart home network.

In our testbed implementation, due to the similarities in terms of computational power, storage resources and capability between a Smart TV and a single board computer, the Smart TV has been simulated by means of a Raspberry Pi 3 Model B Vers. 1.2, equipped with a Raspberry Pi Camera 5MP.

The camera has been used to sample pictures of resolution 650×650 (other specs.: focal length 3.6, ISO 200, aperture $f/2.9$, shutter speed 1/16). As discussed, due to the limited computational resources of the Raspberry, the FEL and ACL networks run, together with the UCS on a desktop with high computational resources. The Raspberry is connected to the webserver with an ad-hoc WiFi or with a wired network. As we will discuss in the performance subsection, even considering the network delays, the distributed solution is much more efficient with respect to a standalone one in which the smart TV (Raspberry) has to perform classification and policy evaluation.

---

[5] https://developer.android.com/reference/android/media/tv/TvContentRating.html.

[6] https://github.com/ameerkat/imdb-to-sql.

Data Extraction and Policy Enforcement. The policy enforcement is performed by the PEP, which, as shown in Fig. 2, is embedded in the Smart TV. In our simulated scenario, the PEP is embedded into the Raspberry and it is able to intercept the execution of any video opened, extract the video information rating from the metadata and act on the execution process on the basis of the UCS decision. The interception phase is done by using *iNotify*, which is a file watcher mechanism in the Linux kernel, which monitors and notifies all the system call related to file system operations related to a specific directory. Since in our experiments the monitored content is a video, iNotify is set to monitor all operations which are related to files with video extension and we retrieve the PID of the related processes. Hence, the PEP which is used to stop and resume its execution exploits the library commands of the VLC media player[7] to block or resume the video execution according to the UCS decision. In our implementation the parental advisory information are extracted by querying the IMDB server, using the metadata extracted directly from the video file.

4   Results

This section reports the results of the experiments we conducted, divided in: classification accuracy for the FEL and ACL networks computed on a face dataset, simulation experiments where Smart Parental Advisory has been tested on a video simulating the stream of the smart TV camera, and real experiments with real spectators.

4.1   Classification Results

The FEL based on the CNN MMOD tool provided by dlib is trained on the dlib face detection dataset[8]. This dataset contains the faces extracted from the *face scrub dataset*[9] and the *VGG dataset*[10]. The testing phase, instead, is performed on the *FDDB dataset* [6] that contains 5.171 annotated faces in 2.845 images taken from the *Faces in the wild dataset* [5]. The DEX network used to implement the ACL has been trained by exploiting the *IMDB-WIKI dataset*[11]. This dataset has been chosen since it is the largest one with real ages and gender annotation, for a total of 460.723 face pictures from 20.284 celebrities extracted from IMDb and 62.328 pictures extracted from Wikipedia.

As shown in Fig. 5, the ages are not well balanced, with an almost complete lack of images in the age range [0–15] and [70–100]. Due to this issue, a fine tuning has been performed on the DEX network using the *Adience db* [4] dataset, which contains 26.580 face images from 2.284 subjects divided in 8 different age ranges, equally distributed. The datasets have been filtered, removing images

---

[7] http://www.videolan.org/vlc/index.it.html.
[8] http://dlib.net/files/data/dlib_face_detection_dataset-2016-09-30.tar.gz.
[9] http://vintage.winklerbros.net/facescrub.html.
[10] http://www.robots.ox.ac.uk/~vgg/data/vgg_face/.
[11] https://data.vision.ee.ethz.ch/cvl/rrothe/imdb-wiki/.

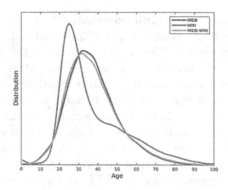

Fig. 5. Ages distribution in the IMDB-WIKI dataset

Table 1. Accuracy of DEX on Adience db

	[0–2]	[4–6]	[8–12]	[15–20]	[25–32]	[38–43]	[48–53]	[60–100]	Total
# faces	2.199	1.587	1.297	866	3.269	1.471	591	606	11.886
# corrects	2.046	1.321	709	807	3.250	1.468	591	606	10.798
# errors	153	266	588	59	19	3	0	0	1.088
Accuracy	93%	83%	54%	93%	99%	99%	100%	100%	**90.125%**

with multiple faces belonging to different age ranges or images wrongly labeled, obtaining thus a dataset consisting of 5.949 faces in the age range [0–12] and 5.937 faces in the age range [15–100].

The True Positive Rate (TPR) of the FEL on the FDDB dataset, as reported in [3], is 0.879134 with 90 false positive detection on 2.845 images. The accuracy of the ACL is computed on the Adience db dataset testing the DEX network trained on the IMDB-WIKI dataset and the DEX network fine tuned on the Adience db dataset. The results we obtained are reported, respectively, in Tables 1 and 2.

The overall accuracy obtained in our experiments is more than 90% in this 8 classes classification problem, where the labels reflects the one used in the dataset. The majority of errors falls in the [8–12] category. However, it is worth noting that adolescents in this age range might be difficult to categorize even for a human eye, due to different growth speed.

Table 2 shows that the fine tuning considerably increases the accuracy, strongly reducing the errors also for the most critical age ranges. Moreover, it is worth noting that the problem that has been considered in this set of experiments is more complex than the one related to the enforcement of the majority of parental control policies. As a matter of fact, in our experiments we will consider the ability to discern people with more than 14 years old from people with less than 14 years old.

Table 2. Accuracy of DEX fine tuned on Adience Db

	[0–2]	[4–6]	[8–12]	[15–20]	[25–32]	[38–43]	[48–53]	[60–100]	Total
# faces	219	158	129	86	326	147	59	60	1.184
# corrects	216	139	98	74	324	146	59	60	1.116
# errors	3	19	29	12	2	1	0	0	66
Accuracy	98%	87%	75%	86%	99%	99%	100%	100%	**93%**

4.2   Simulation Scenario

The simulative experiments have been used to evaluate the capability of the framework to estimate the age of spectators from a video stream, simulating what the Smart TV camera is continuously monitoring. To this aim, we have selected a video[12] portraying a family (mother and father) with a child in front of a webcam, who are considered spectators of the Smart TV. This video is divided in shares where the whole family is in front of the camera, shares with the child alone and parts with parents only. The whole video has been reproduced three times, supposing that the spectators will be watching at first a content with classification Y, afterward a content with classification PG, and finally one with classification MA. The usage control policy we enforced is the following:

1. If the content *Parental Advisory* is equal to PG, at least one *adult* must be continuously present in front of the TV to allow the streaming.
2. If the content *Parental Advisory* is equal to MA, no children must be in front of the TV to allow the streaming.

The duration of the video is 5 min and 3 s with a resolution of 1280×720 at 25 fps. Setting an interval extraction frames of 5 s, 60 frames have been extracted, of which 24 portraying only adults, 11 representing the child alone, and 25 showing the adults and the child together. Out of 115 faces globally present in the 60 frames, the FEL was able to correctly detect 111 faces, thus achieving an accuracy of 96%.

As we can see from Fig. 6 the faces undetected, surrounded by red boxes, represent peculiar cases such as face cut, people not looking in the direction of the TV, or people too far from the camera.

The ACL was able to correctly estimate the age of 99 out of 111 faces, thus achieving an accuracy of 89%. In particular, 10 times an adult face (out of 74) has been classified as a child and only 2 times the child has been recognized as an adult. To improve the accuracy we have modified the classified images by cropping the faces extracted by the FEL, with an additional 40% of margin around the detected face. This has dramatically increased the accuracy, with a number of correctly classified faces of 110 out of 111. Thus the impact on the

---

[12] https://www.youtube.com/watch?v=7cRJHdCrLMY.

Fig. 6. Faces misclassified by the FEL. (Color figure online)

user experience would have been minimal since the TV program would have only been blocked one time for few seconds, during the reproduction, according to policy 1 and 2.

4.3   Real Scenario

A real scenario has been reproduced in an house setting, physically connecting the raspberry with the camera to a smart TV without camera. One of the recorded pictures is depicted in Fig. 7, portraying a father with his daughter in front of the TV. The pictures have been collected at the same rate of the simulated use case. The frames which have been collected are the following: 3 frames with only one adult, 12 frames with only one child, and 13 frames with the adult and the child.

The FEL was able to detect 41 faces over 41, thus achieving an accuracy of 100%, whereas the ACL was able to correctly classify 38 over 41 ages with 92% of accuracy, with the adult misclassified 3 times and the child only once. As expected, in the real use case the overall accuracy is slightly lower, due to the lower image quality, still the effect on the user experience would have been

Fig. 7. Real experiment setting.

quite limited. The same policies used for the simulated experiments have been considered also for the real scenario, having thus the stream blocked 3 times.

4.4 Performance Analysis

This section describes the performances of our parental control system, analyzing the time overhead introduced by each component, needed to estimate the delay for enforcing UCS decisions.

FEL Performance. The time required to extract faces is reported for three different cases: the time to extract faces from a frame of the simulated testbed, the time to extract faces from a frame of the real use case, and the time to extract faces from a frame with a large number of people, minimum 5. The average measured time is, respectively, of $T_{sim} = 1.50$ s, $T_{real} = 1.86$ s and $T_{mul} = 2.09$ s.

ACL Performance. The time required to classify faces is calculated for the video tester on 111 faces. The network requires 2.37 s for the weights initialization (only the first time) and 3.46 s to classify 111 images. The mean time to classify one face is 0.031 s.

Network Time. The network time is the time required to send an image from the raspberry to the server. The mean time computed on 60 images sent is of 0.19101 s.

UCS Time. The UCS time considers the whole overhead introduced by the UCS for policy (re-)evaluation when an attribute is changed in such a way that the previous access decision for the ongoing content changes. The Stop Reproduction Time (SRT) is the time necessary to stop the reproduction of a video in case the policy is not respected any more (revoke), whilst the Resume Reproduction Time (RRT) is the time necessary to resume the reproduction of the video when the policy is once again matched. Their value are, respectively, $T_{SRT} = 3.46$ s and $T_{RRT} = 3.89$ s. Hence, the time in which the system would remain in a state that is not consistent is equal to T_{SRT} or T_{RRT} plus the only not negligible time, which is FEL overhead. Then, it is possible to conclude that a violation would not last for more than 5 s.

5 Related Work

A framework which exploits the embedded camera in a smart TV for user authentication is presented in [11]. By authenticating users the framework also performs parental control enforcement, however, differently from Smart Parental Advisory the age recognition is based on the manual assignment of the age to the recognized face. On the other hand, our framework performs age recognition automatically, without exploiting the identity. Hence, Smart Parental Advisory is able to recognize new adults and children without the need of retraining it for any new spectator, being thus more general. A similar machinery to the one of [11] has been patented for commercial use in [7]. Deep learning for face recognition has been used with high accuracy in [17]. However, this work only focuses on classification aspects, without considering parental control aspects. A recent work focused instead only on age estimation is the one presented in [1], where deep learning algorithms have been used to automatically infer the age of people from face pictures. In our work instead the process of age recognition is more challenging since the faces on which the age is estimated are extracted from live streams.

Usage control for data management has been used for controlling dynamically the right to use files on mobile devices and in the cloud respectively in [9,10]. These works are mainly focused on the description of the usage control framework infrastructure, presenting generic policies. The present work describes instead a real application of the usage control in a real environment, with effects not only on security, but safety as well.

6   Conclusion and Future Work

Enforcing parental control on smart TVs in a dynamic, effective and seamless way is a challenging task. To remove the necessity of relying on passwords and PIN codes, in this paper we have presented Smart Parental Advisory, a framework which exploits deep learning to extract and estimate the age of spectators in front of the TV. The framework relies then on usage control to evaluate and enforce policies at runtime, blocking the content reproduction or channel streaming automatically, as soon as the policy conditions are violated. The effectiveness of the framework and viability of the approach has been proven through both simulated and real experiments. The current implementation, especially in the side of photo capture and elaboration is a mere proof of concept and its improvement is planned as a future work. In particular we plan to improve the quality of the captured image using High Dynamic Range (HDR) technique, to further improve the accuracy. Other planned work concern the usage of a larger set of people for experimental evaluation, together with additional and more complex policies which might include attributes extracted from other devices in the house, such as additional cameras to monitor the presence of people in the room and not only those in front of the TV.

References

1. Dong, Y., Liu, Y., Lian, S.: Automatic age estimation based on deep learning algorithm. Neurocomputing **187**, 4–10 (2016). Recent Developments on Deep Big Vision
2. Carniani, E., D'Arenzo, D., Lazouski, A., Martinelli, F., Mori, P.: Usage control on cloud systems. Future Gener. Comput. Syst. **63**, 37–55 (2016)
3. Dlib: High quality face recognition with deep metric learning (2017). http://blog.dlib.net/2017/02/high-quality-face-recognition-with-deep.html
4. Eidinger, E., Enbar, R., Hassner, T.: Age and gender estimation of unfiltered faces. Trans. Inf. Forensics Secur. **9**(12), 2170–2179 (2014)

5. Huang, G.B., Ramesh, M., Berg, T., Learned-Miller, E.: Labeled faces in the wild: a database for studying face recognition in unconstrained environments. Technical report 07–49, University of Massachusetts, Amherst, October 2007
6. Jain, V., Learned-Miller, E.: FDDB: a benchmark for face detection in unconstrained settings. Technical report UM-CS-2010-009, University of Massachusetts, Amherst (2010)
7. Kwoh, D.S., Mankovitz, R.J.: Apparatus and method for total parental control of television use, January 17 1995. US Patent 5,382,983
8. La Marra, A., Martinelli, F., Mori, P., Saracino, A.: Implementing usage control in internet of things: a smart home use case. In: Proceedings of the 16th IEEE International Conference on Trust, Security and Privacy in Computing and Communications (IEEE TrustCom-17) (2017, to appear)
9. Lazouski, A., Mancini, G., Martinelli, F., Mori, P.: Usage control in cloud systems. In: The 7th International Conference for Internet Technology And Secured Transactions, (ICITST-2012), pp. 202–207 (2012)
10. Lazouski, A., Martinelli, F., Mori, P., Saracino, A.: Stateful data usage control for android mobile devices. Int. J. Inf. Secur. **16**, 1–25 (2016)
11. Lee, S.H., Sohn, M.K., Kim, J., Kim, B., Kim, H.: Smart TV interaction system using face and hand gesture recognition. In: 2013 IEEE International Conference on Consumer Electronics (ICCE), pp. 173–174, January 2013
12. OASIS: eXtensible Access Control Markup Language (XACML) version 3.0, January 2013
13. Park, J., Sandhu, R.: The $UCON_{ABC}$ usage control model. ACM Trans. Inf. Syst. Secur. **7**(1), 128–174 (2004)
14. Park, J., Zhang, X., Sandhu, R.: Attribute mutability in usage control. In: Research Directions in Data and Applications Security XVIII, IFIP TC11/WG 11.3 Eighteenth Annual Conference on Data and Applications Security, pp. 15–29 (2004)
15. Pretschner, A., Hilty, M., Basin, D.A.: Distributed usage control. Commun. ACM **49**(9), 39–44 (2006)
16. Rothe, R., Timofte, R., Van Gool, L.: DEX: deep expectation of apparent age from a single image. In: 2015 IEEE International Conference on Computer Vision Workshop (ICCVW), pp. 252–257 (2015)
17. Taigman, Y., Yang, M., Ranzato, M., Wolf, L.: DeepFace: closing the gap to human-level performance in face verification. In: Proceedings of the IEEE Conference on Computer Vision and Pattern Recognition, pp. 1701–1708 (2014)

A Consistent Definition of Authorization

Audun Jøsang[⊠]

University of Oslo, Oslo, Norway
josang@ifi.uio.no

Abstract. A shared understanding of terms and concepts is a condition for meaningful discussions in any domain of scientific investigation and industrial development. This principle also applies to the domain of information security. It is therefore problematic when central terms are assigned inconsistent meanings in the literature and mainstream textbooks on information security. In particular, this is case for the concept of 'authorization' for which the security community still has not arrived at a clear and common understanding. We argue that there can only be one interpretation of authorization which is consistent with fundamental security concepts. Consistent definitions of security terms are important in order to support good learning and practice of information security. The proposed definition of authorization is not only consistent with other fundamental security terms, it is also simple, logical and intuitive.

Keywords: Cybersecurity · Security education · Authorization · Access control · Authentication · IAM

1 Introduction

The concept of *authorization* is fundamental in the domain of information security. For example, the term is used in the definitions of 'confidentiality', 'availability' and 'access control' in the prominent international standard ISO/IEC 27000 *Information security management systems Overview and vocabulary* [8]:

- *Confidentiality* is the property that information is not made available or disclosed to unauthorized individuals, entities, or processes.
- *Availability* is the property of being accessible and usable upon demand by an authorized entity.
- *Access control* means to ensure that access to assets is authorized and restricted based on business and security requirements.

However, there is significant confusion regarding the interpretation of "*authorized*" or "*authorization*", and the term is not defined in the said standard, which is problematic. One can guess that the standards committee thought it was unnecessary to define the term 'authorization' because its meaning is commonly and well understood. However, its usage with relation to information security is not well understood in the literature, as shown in the following section.

© Springer International Publishing AG 2017
G. Livraga and C. Mitchell (Eds.): STM 2017, LNCS 10547, pp. 134–144, 2017.
DOI: 10.1007/978-3-319-68063-7_9

2 Illustrating the Confusion Around the Concept of Authorization

In the quest for the meaning of the term *"authorized entity"* in ISO/IEC 27000 it is useful to look up the common meaning of the verb *"to authorize"* by consulting a general dictionary such as Merriam-Webster's online dictionary[1]

– *To authorize is to endorse, empower, justify, or permit by, or as if by, some recognized or proper authority (such as custom, evidence, personal right, or regulating power).* (Merriam-Webster)

An essential conclusion from the above definition of *"to authorize"* is that *only authorities can authorize.* A follow-up question is then, what is an authority? With regard to the security services confidentiality, availability and access control, it seems obvious that the authority emerges from the management level in the organisation where policies are being specified. As an example, people working in the HR department in a company need access to staff profiles containing name, address, salary, etc., whereas staff working in other units do not need and therefore should not have access to each others profiles. This policy is actually an *access policy* which in turn is translated into access control rules in computer systems. To specify that access policy is the act of authorizing people in the HR department to access staff profiles stored on the company's network. Once the policy has been specified, the HR staff are authorized to access staff profiles. It also requires that the policy is translated into access control rules which then are used by the system to enforce the access policy. Access control can thus be described as the process of enforcing the access policy, which is done by the system. The system thus enforces the access policy specified by the (human) authority.

2.1 The Unsatisfactory Definition of Authorization in X.800

The security standard X.800 *Security Architecture for Open Systems Interconnection for CCITT Applications* [9] gives a definition of the concept of authorization. A security standard which defines the concept of authorization is interesting because it could potentially remove confusion about the meaning of authorization in the context of security, but unfortunately the standard fails to do so. X.800 defines authorization as follows.

– *Authorization is the granting of rights, which includes the granting of access based on access rights.* (X.800)

Note that X.800 in fact gives two alternative interpretations of authorization, namely (1) *"granting of rights"*, and (2) *"granting of access"*. The standard thus recognises that there is a difference between *"granting of rights"* and

---

[1] https://www.merriam-webster.com/dictionary/.

"granting of access" which is important. Sadly, the standard says that term 'authorization' covers both interpretations, which is unfortunate because it necessarily leads to confusion.

The *"granting of rights"* is the act of defining an access policy. The *"granting of access"* is the enforcement of the access policy which is equivalent to access control, i.e. access is granted when an access request is allowed according to the policy, but is of course rejected when an access request is not allowed according to the policy. We find it unacceptable that the standard assigns two very different interpretations to the term 'authorization' because it leads to difficulty in the learning and application of security, and to confusion in discussions and the literature of the security community.

In order to illustrate the significance of the difference between *"granting of rights"* and *"granting of access"* the next section illustrates how these two functions represent totally different steps in the general IAM (Identity and Access Management) architecture which includes both authentication and access control functions.

2.2   A Framework for Identity and Access Management

User authentication is a fundamental security component for secure service access, whether the service is provided online through the Internet or in a closed local network. Failed authentication, where an attacker is able to take on the identity of another entity and get unauthorized access to restricted and sensitive resources, is a serious security threat that can have significant negative consequences. Authentication assurance expresses the certainty of correct authentication in a network or domain, as specified by prominent authentication assurance frameworks [1, 6, 7].

Once the system or service provider has determined the user's identity the user can proceed with accessing resources or requesting services for which the user has been authorized. Typically, any single user is only authorized to access a limited set of services and resources. The system therefore needs to to apply access control which consists of deciding whether access requests to services or resources are permitted according to the authorization policy, and then to enforce that decision by either rejecting access in case the user is not authorized, or granting access in case the user is authorized.

The term IAM[2] (Identity and Access Management) denotes the security technologies that enable the intended authorized individuals to access the right resources at the right times for the right reasons. IAM can be described in terms of three separate phases where each phase contains a set of steps, as illustrated in Fig. 1.

The configuration phase covers the registration, provisioning and authorization steps. Registration consists of specifying a new account with a unique name, and populating the account with relevant data about the user. The provisioning step consists of providing the user with information, credential(s) and optionally

---

[2] http://www.gartner.com/it-glossary/identity-and-access-management-iam/.

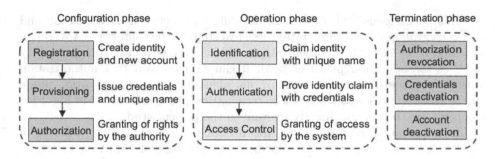

Fig. 1. Phases of identity and access management

a token for authenticating to access the account. In case biometric authentication is to be used, this step also includes collecting biometric templates to be used for authentication. Authorization which is the last step of the configuration phase consists of specifying the user's access permissions in the form of an AC (Access Control) Policy. Authorization must obviously be specified, or delegated, by an authority in the organization, and results in the definition of AC rules in the system that controls access to resources. The configuration phase is revisited whenever necessary for updating identity, credentials or authorization attributes.

After initial completion of the configuration phase, the user entity is able to use the credentials, and optionally a token, authenticate and log in to the account during the operation phase of IAM, and can engage in trusted interactions as an authenticated user. Although authentication can be seen as a single step in the operation phase, the correctness and assurance of authentication depends not only on the correctness of the authentication step, but also on the registration step, and on the provisioning step during the configuration phase. Should any of these steps fail, then authentication will fail in general, as described by the various authentication assurance frameworks [1,6,7].

Similarly, the correctness of access control requires that the correct identity has been authenticated, that an appropriate access policy has been defined in the authorization step, and that this policy is correctly enforced in the access control step. Hence, the correctness and assurance of access control depends on the correctness and assurance of IAM in general.

The termination phase is included for completeness, but it can also be considered as part of the configuration phase. It is useful to distinguish between the steps of access revocation and credentials revocation. If access is revoked, the user can still log in by using the authentication credentials. On the other hand, if the credentials are revoked, the user is no longer able to log in, and will obviously no get access. However, even if the credentials have been revoked it is still possible that the user is authorized for access. The reason for credential revocation can e.g. be that the credentials have been stolen by attackers. The user must then be provisioned with new credentials in order to authenticate and log in to the account.

This paper focuses on describing the difference between authorization and access control, and Fig. 1 illustrates these two steps in the context of IAM. It can for example be seen that authentication and access control are complementary steps of the operation phase of IAM. It can also be seen that authorization must take place during the configuration phase prior to the operation phase where access control takes place. The termination phase is included in Fig. 1 for completeness, but is not directly relevant to the present study.

An important conclusion to be drawn from Fig. 1 is thus that *"granting of rights"* and *"granting of access"* represent specific steps of IAM that belong to different phases in the IAM architecture. Keeping the steps clearly separate is essential for making IAM meaningful. Confusing these two steps can have serious consequences for the interpretation and application of information security services, as described in the following section.

2.3 The Consequence of Authorization Confusion

Using the same term 'authorization' to describe the *"granting of rights"* and the *"granting of access"* obviously can lead to serious confusion, as the scenario below illustrates.

Scenario A: Inconsistent interpretation of authorization

1. You crack somebody's password on a system, and use it to access private resources owned by that user.
2. The login screen gives the warning: *"Only authorized users may access this system, offenders will be prosecuted"*, but you know how to get out of trouble if you get busted.
3. You get caught, accused of performing unauthorized access, and taken to the police.
4. You argue: *"Text books and standards on information security state that the system authorizes users when they access the system. Hence, I was authorized because I got access to the system."*
5. Case dismissed, you go free.

While this absurd scenario could be an advantage for attackers, it certainly would be bad for the defenders of computer networks. It is therefore disappointing that international security standard like X.800 cultivate this confusion. Unfortunately, many other standards and text books on security do the same. Below are some examples.

2.4 Authorization Confusion According to the ABAC Standard

ABAC (Attribute-Based Access Control) is the most recent and most advanced model for access control, which generalises previously defined AC models such as MAC (Mandatory Access Control), DAC (Discretionary Access Control) and RBAC (Role-Based Access Control). In 2014 NIST[3] published the standard SP800-162 *Guide to Attribute Based Access Control (ABAC) Definition and Considerations* [5]. This framework for ABAC came very timely because standards and best practice for ABAC were missing, while at the same time many stakeholders in sectors such as e-health and construction wanted to implement ABAC to allow more open and distributed AC solutions.

Obviously, authorization is a central element of ABAC. The NIST standard SP800-162 provides these definitions related to authorization:

- *Access control or authorization is the decision to permit or deny a subject access to system objects (network, data, application, service, etc.) Note that ABAC can be used without identification information, and authentication method is not addressed in this document. The terms access control and authorization are used synonymously throughout this document.*
- *Privileges represent the authorized behavior of a subject; they are defined by an authority and embodied in policy or rules. For the purposes of this document, the terms privileges and authorizations are used interchangeably in that they are meant to convey ones authority and implicit approval to access one or more objects.*

The ABAC standard thus defines 'authorization', 'access control' and 'privileges' as synonymous. It appears that 'privileges' denotes 'authorizations', and that 'access control' is the same as access control according to IAM of Fig. 1, hence the ABAC standard confuses the concepts of 'authorization' and 'access control' in the same way as the standard X.800 does.

2.5 Authorization Confusion According to the CISSP All-in-One Exam Guide

CISSP (Certified Information Systems Security Professional) is an industry certification popular amongst security consultants and people in the IT security community. The CISSP curriculum is relatively technical and very broad, so candidates who want to sit the exam to obtain the certification typically study text books specifically written to help prepare for the exam. One of the most popular CISSP preparation books is the *CISSP All-in-One Exam Guide* which was published in its 7th edition in 2016 [4].

This text book pretends to present the concept of authorization as having one meaning, but the description of the term clearly reveals two different interpretations. For example, in the 2nd paragraph on p. 725 in CISSP All-in-One Exam Guide (7th Ed.) it says:

- *"If the system determines that the subject may access the resource, it authorizes the subject"*.

---

[3] National Institute of Standards and Technology.

The interpretation above is clearly that of *"granting of access"* according to IAM of Fig. 1. However, the 3rd paragraph on the same page the book says:

- *"A user may be authorized to access the files on the file server, but until she is properly identified and authenticated, those resources are out of reach."*

The interpretation above is clearly that of *"granting of rights"* according to IAM of Fig. 1. Hence, the CISSP All-in-One Exam Guide confuses the concepts of 'authorization' and 'access control' in the same way as the standard X.800 does.

3   The Origin of the Confusion

The interpretation of 'authorization' as *"granting of access"* can be traced back to the concept of AAA (Authentication, Authorization, and Accounting) as implemented in the network protocol RADIUS (Remote Authentication Dial-In User Service). This networking protocol supports centralised management of authentication, access control, and accounting for users who access network services. RADIUS was developed by Livingston Enterprises, Inc. in 1991 as an access server authentication and accounting protocol and later defined as the IETF standard RFC2865 in 2000 [11]. As RADIUS had some shortcomings, a new and more advanced protocol called Diameter was defined by IETF as RFC6733 in 2012 [2].

The Diameter standard states: *"The Diameter base protocol is intended to provide an Authentication, Authorization, and Accounting (AAA) framework for applications such as network access or IP mobility in both local and roaming situations."*

Both RADIUS and Diameter have been widely adopted and implemented, in particular by prominent network equipment manufacturers such as Cisco. As a result, Cisco and other companies have distributed technical and marketing documentation that widely promotes the AAA concept, where the middle 'A' stands for 'authorization' in the sense of *"granting of access"*. Many network security experts therefore understand 'authorization' with that meaning. Unfortunately, this interpretation is inconsistent with fundamental security concepts as explained above.

To remedy this situation it would of course be possible to re-interpret the middle 'A' as *"access control"*, which would make the AAA concept perfectly compatible with fundamental security definitions.

4   A Consistent Definition of Authorization

An IETF standard which predates those of RADIUS and Diameter is the RFC2196 from 1997 called *Site Security Handbook* [3]. RFC2196 states:

"Authorization refers to the process of granting privileges to processes and, ultimately, users. This differs from authentication in that authentication is the

process used to identify a user. Once identified (reliably), the privileges, rights, property, and permissible actions of the user are determined by authorization.

Explicitly listing the authorized activities of each user (and user process) with respect to all resources (objects) is impossible in a reasonable system. In a real system certain techniques are used to simplify the process of granting and checking authorization(s)." (RFC2196)

This description and interpretation of authorization makes sense, because it defines authorization as the *"granting of rights"* in line with the IAM architecture of Fig. 1. Unfortunately, it seems that this Site Security Handbook of 1997 [3] has been overlooked by subsequent IETF standards such as RADIUS and Diameter.

While not being an authoritative source of information because anybody can edit, Wikipedia can be useful as a guide to the most up-to-date definition and description of concepts. In particular, the concept of 'authorization' is described as follows:

"Access control in computer systems and networks rely on access policies. The access control process can be divided into the following phases: policy definition phase where access is authorized, and policy enforcement phase where access requests are approved or disapproved. Authorization is the function of the policy definition phase which precedes the policy enforcement phase where access requests are approved or disapproved based on the previously defined authorizations.". (Wikipedia: 'Authorization', accessed on 30.01.2017)

We propose the following definitions of 'authorization' and 'access control' which are in line with the article on Wikipedia.

- **Definition 1:** *Authorization is the specification of access policies.*
- **Definition 2:** *Access control is the enforcement of access policies.*

These definitions are consistent with the definitions of e.g. confidentiality, availability and access control in ISO/IEC 27000 [8], and eliminate the possibility of confusion described in Sect. 2 above. These definitions are also compatible with the now 20 years old *Site Security Handbook* [3].

Let us revisit the example from Sect. 2.3 about accessing a system with a cracked password, and interpret it in light of the definition of authorization from Definition 1.

Scenario B: Consistent interpretation of authorization

1. You crack somebody's password on a system, and use it to access private resources owned by that user.
2. The login screen gives the warning: *"Only authorized users may access this system, offenders will be prosecuted"*, but you hope that you will not get busted.
3. Unfortunately, you get caught, accused of performing unauthorized access, and taken to the police.

> 4. The police argues: *"The account you accessed was not yours, and you were not authorized to access it. In addition, the login screen informed you that only authorized users are allowed to access it. Hence, you acted in direct breach of the stated policy when you accessed the system without authorization."*
> 5. You have no excuse, you get convicted and go to jail.

The above scenario illustrates how the consistent interpretation of authorization according to Definition 1 prevents any misunderstanding, and makes it clear that a hacker using a cracked password is not authorized when using it to access a system. This scenario validates Definition 1's consistency with the fundamental security concepts of confidentiality, integrity and availability.

5   The Role of Authorization in Identity and Access Management

In order to illustrate how authorization and access control fit together in IAM (Identity and Access Management) Fig. 2 illustrates a scenario which covers both the configuration phase and the operation phase of IAM. The indexes on the arrows indicate the order in which each action is executed. The notions PAP (Policy Administration Point), PDP (Policy Decision Point) and PEP (Policy Enforcement Point) are defined in the OASIS standard XACML (eXtensible Access Control Markup Language) [10].

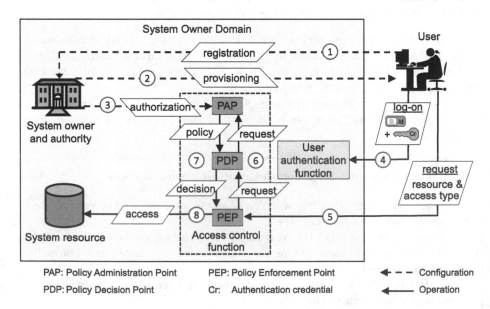

Fig. 2. Scenario of authorization and access control IAM

In the scenario, the user must first be registered with the domain owner (1), and receive the necessary credentials through provisioning (2). Now follows the authorization step where the access policy is specified for the user at the PAP (3). Next follows the operation phase where the user logs on (4) and requests access (5). Then the access policy is fetched from PAP (6), the policy is analysed and a decision is made at the PDP (7), and the decision is enforced by PEP, which grants access (8) assuming that the decision was positive. These steps are illustrated in Fig. 2.

In the above scenario there is a clear separation between the functions for specifying the access policy (authorization) and its enforcement (access control). e-Health scenarios with complex policies for access to patient journals are good examples where it is crucial to clearly understand the distinction between authorization and access control. For example, patients can play a role in defining the access policy for their own medical journals, e.g. by giving consent to how their medical data can be processed and accessed. This access/consent policy must then be translated into rules that the system can use to enforce the access/consent policy.

6   Conclusion

We have shown that there is considerable confusion around the interpretation of authorization related to identity and access management. Several definitions of authorization in prominent international standards are incompatible with the fundamental security concepts of confidentiality, integrity and availability. We have proposed to define authorization as *"the specification of access policies"* which is consistent with other fundamental security concepts and which is also perfectly intuitive. There is solid precedence from 1997 for having this clear and consistent definition of 'authorization'. The confusing interpretations found in subsequent standards and text books can be traced to a few prominent standards for network security that have been promoted by the computer networking industry. It is our hope that the computer and security industry again can find consensus and converge towards the consistent definition of authorization.

References

1. Department of Finance and Deregulation: National e-Authentication Framework (NeAF). Australian Government Information Management Office, Canberra (2009)
2. Fajardo, V., et al.: RFC 6673 - Diameter Base Protocol. IETF, October (2012). https://tools.ietf.org/html/rfc6733
3. Fraser, B.: RFC 2196 - Site Security Handbook. IETF, Fremont (1997). URL: http://www.ietf.org/rfc/rfc2196.txt (visited 30.01.2017)
4. Harris, S., Maymí, F.: CISSP All-in-One Exam Guide, 7th edn. McGraw-Hill, New York City (2016)
5. Hu, V.C., et al.: Guide to attribute based access control (ABAC) definition and considerations. NIST Special Publication 800-162. Technical report, National Institute of Standards and Technology, January (2014)

6. Hulsebosch, B., Lenzini, G., Eertink, H.: Deliverable D2.3 - STORK quality authenticator scheme. Technical report STORK eID Consortium (2009)
7. ISO: ISO/IEC 29115:2013. Entity authentication assurance framework. ISO, Geneva, Switzerland (2013)
8. ISO: ISO/IEC 27000:2016 - Information technology - security techniques - information security management systems - overview and vocabulary. ISO/IEC (2016)
9. ITU: Recommendation X.800, Security Architecture for Open Systems Interconnection for CCITT Applications. International Telecommunications Union (formerly known as the International Telegraph and Telephone Consultantive Committee), Geneva (1991). (X.800 is a re-edition of IS7498-2)
10. OASIS: eXtensible Access Control Markup Language (XACML) Version 3.0. Organization for the Advancement of Structured Information Standards, 22 January 2013
11. Rigney, C., et al.: RFC 2865 - Remote Authentication Dial in User Service (RADIUS). IETF, Fremont (2000)

Security Vulnerabilities and Protocols

Formal Analysis of V2X Revocation Protocols

Jorden Whitefield[1], Liqun Chen[1], Frank Kargl[2], Andrew Paverd[3],
Steve Schneider[1], Helen Treharne[1(✉)], and Stephan Wesemeyer[1]

[1] Department of Computer Science, University of Surrey, Guildford, UK
{J.Whitefield,Liqun.Chen,S.Schneider,H.Treharne,S.Wesemeyer}@surrey.ac.uk
[2] Ulm University, Ulm, Germany
frank.kargl@uni-ulm.de
[3] Aalto University, Espoo, Finland
andrew.paverd@ieee.org

Abstract. Research on vehicular networking (V2X) security has produced a range of securitymechanisms and protocols tailored for this domain, addressing both security and privacy. Typically, the security analysis of these proposals has largely been informal. However, formal analysis can be used to expose flaws and ultimately provide a higher level of assurance in the protocols. This paper focusses on the formal analysis of a particular element of security mechanisms for V2X found in many proposals, that is the revocation of malicious or misbehaving vehicles from the V2X system by invalidating their credentials. This revocation needs to be performed in an unlinkable way for vehicle privacy even in the context of vehicles regularly changing their pseudonyms. The REWIRE scheme by Förster et al. and its subschemes PLAIN and R-TOKEN aim to solve this challenge by means of cryptographic solutions and trusted hardware. Formal analysis using the TAMARIN prover identifies two flaws: one previously reported in the lierature concerned with functional correctness of the protocol, and one previously unknown flaw concerning an authentication property of the R-TOKEN scheme. In response to these flaws we propose OBSCURE TOKEN (O-TOKEN), an extension of REWIRE to enable revocation in a privacy preserving manner. Our approach addresses the functional and authentication properties by introducing an additional key-pair, which offers a stronger and verifiable guarantee of successful revocation of vehicles without resolving the long-term identity. Moreover O-TOKEN is the first V2X revocation protocol to be co-designed with a formal model.

Keywords: Ad hoc networks · Authentication · Security verification · V2X

1 Introduction

The term Intelligent Transportation Systems (ITS) denotes the on-going trend to include information and communication technologies (ICT) in vehicles and transportation infrastructure in order to enable safer, coordinated, environmentally

© Springer International Publishing AG 2017
G. Livraga and C. Mitchell (Eds.): STM 2017, LNCS 10547, pp. 147–163, 2017.
DOI: 10.1007/978-3-319-68063-7_10

friendly, and smarter transportation networks [35]. Having smarter transportation systems typically involves extending the communication capabilities between the involved entities.

This goes by the term "Vehicle-to-X (V2X)" communication and involves various forms of ad-hoc and cellular networking among vehicles and traffic infrastructure. Security and privacy in V2X have played an important role right from the start [22].

In particular, anonymity is a requirement in a V2X network as various privacy issues arise from the frequent and real-time broadcasting of the position of vehicles in an ITS [31], as otherwise mobility patterns can easily be identified. This makes tracking and profiling of entities possible, which can be used to systematically collect and infer private information. Pseudonym certificates (pseudonyms) [25] are the most commonly applied way to address privacy concerns and are also foreseen in emerging standards.

Schaub et al. [31] discuss various requirements for such a pseudonym system and Petit et al. [25] survey a large body of existing work and from there identify an abstract pseudonym life cycle which is comprised of five main phases: issuance, use, change, resolution and revocation. Within an ITS architecture there are three trusted third parties that support the life cycle of pseudonyms: a certification authority (CA), a provider of pseudonyms (PP), and a revocation authority (RA). The CA issues long-term credentials to vehicles. The PP is responsible for handing out shorter-lived pseudonym certificates. The RA receives and collects information such as reports on misbehaviour, takes decisions to revoke a misbehaving entity, and implement this revocation by whatever means a specific scheme foresees.

Effective revocation has been identified as a challenge [29] due to the decentralised nature of vehicle networks and the ability of vehicles to change their active pseudonyms.

Related Work. Pseudonym revocation techniques have largely been based on the distribution of certificate revocation lists (CRLs) [25,29], such that when a misbehaving vehicle is revoked an updated CRL is broadcast to all vehicles. Several approaches have been taken to optimise the protocols and distribution process of CRL delivery [10,13,15,17,20,24]. However, these approaches often either revoke only one pseudonym of a vehicle – thereby missing the goal of removing a misbehaving vehicle completely – or they create a way of linking pseudonyms – then hurting privacy protection.

Bißmeyer et al. [2] propose the CORPA protocol that allows conditional pseudonym resolution which preserves the privacy.

Raya et al. propose an infrastructure-based revocation protocol [29], which remotely deletes keys in a trusted component. Their protocol requires that a vehicle's identity is known to perform revocation, in combination with a CRL – again a clear drawback with respect to privacy.

Schaub et al. propose *V*-Tokens [30], which introduces embedding vehicle resolution information directly into pseudonyms. A V-Token is a ciphertext field in the pseudonym certificate that is created from a vehicle's identity, the

CA's identity and a randomisation factor r all encrypted with the RA's public key. In this scheme multiple trusted parties need to collaborate to resolve the pseudonym, which then reveals a vehicle's identity that is used for revocation. In case of a revocation, this therefore violates the privacy of vehicles, as resolution of their pseudonym to an identity is required.

Förster et al. propose PUCA [11], a pseudonym scheme based on anonymous credentials where privacy of the vehicle owner has absolute priority and no way exists for resolving pseudonyms. PUCA foresees no way of credential revocation. However, the same authors then also propose REWIRE [12], a modular revocation mechanism within a decentralised network which is not relying on the resolution approach that can be used to introduce revocation in PUCA. Instead, REWIRE assumes on-board Trusted Components (TC) in vehicles to support revocation.

A series of EU research projects, e.g., SeVeCom [23], EVITA [33] and PRE-CIOSA [26] have investigated securing V2X architectures using TCs. The recent project PRESERVE [27] has even prototyped this in an ASIC for secure ITS. Feiri et al. [9] propose to use TCs to store pseudonyms in secure storage and use a physical-unclonable function (PUF) to reduce the need for large amounts of secure storage. Based on such earlier work, it seems a reasonable assumption that hardware security modules (IISMs) are available as trust anchors, as done in the specification of our O-TOKEN approach.

In this paper we explore the two versions of the REWIRE protocols [12], which are referred to as REWIRE PLAIN and R-TOKEN. This protocol represents the current state of the art of those proposed for revocation in V2X architectures. No revocation protocol has been deployed in vehicles as yet.

Contribution. In this paper, we describe the formalisation of the revocation protocols proposed by Förster et al. [12], which was done using multiset rewriting as supported by the TAMARIN prover. These protocols have not previously been formally analysed. We present definitions of functional correctness and authentication as properties of the protocols. Our formal analysis reveals that the PLAIN model does not preserve functional correctness, specifically that a vehicle is not guaranteed to be revoked and therefore could continue to participate in communication messages within an ITS. This formally confirms a flaw that was observed by Förster et al. [12]. Our analysis of the R-TOKEN protocol identifies a hitherto unknown flaw: that it does not guarantee authentication properties, in particular it does not guarantee that the confirmation of revocation actually came from the intended vehicle. This new unknown weakness is acknowledged by the authors of the R-TOKEN protocol as a flaw.

The insights gained from the formal modelling motivated our proposal for a new protocol. We therefore develop a new protocol which proposes improvements to the REWIRE protocols that ensures correct revocation of an entity under any pseudonym without requiring resolution even if its active pseudonym has changed by the time of revocation. In this paper we refer to our new protocol as the OBSCURE TOKEN (O-TOKEN) protocol. Its novelty is the inclusion of an additional asymmetric key pair for signature, used to augment the pseudonyms that are utilised within message exchanges for verifiable revocation. The new protocol is shown to preserve all the desired authentication and functional correctness properties. Our proposed protocol, similar to the previous protocols discussed in this paper, requires a trusted device at the car which will engage in the revocation protocol and on completion can be trusted to erase all of the pseudonyms that the car may have available.

Due to limited space, we will not present the details of the TAMARIN model rules and lemmas in this paper. The models of the three protocols presented in this paper have been made available [34].

Structure. This paper is organised as follows: Section 2 presents a revocation scenario. Section 3 introduces TAMARIN, together with the security notation used throughout the paper and the modelling assumptions made in our symbolic models. Section 4 defines formal models and evaluates the existing REWIRE protocols. Section 5 presents our new enhanced REWIRE protocol and its analysis and Section 6 finally provides conclusions and identifies preservation of privacy properties as an area of future analysis for revocation protocols.

2   System Model and Revocation Scenario

The process of revocation for the existing REWIRE protocols and our O-TOKEN protocol follows the same pattern shown in Fig. 1. Figure 1 illustrates the three main authorities in an ITS, namely the CA, the PP and the RA, and how vehicles interact with them. The purpose of these authorities and vehicles in a revocation scenario is as follows:

- The CA and PP issue long-term certificates and pseudonyms respectively to vehicles and may optionally implement a resolution mechanism to allow linking back pseudonyms to long-term IDs.
- Vehicles in the ITS communicate with other participants. They monitor each others behaviour using misbehaviour detection mechanisms [14] and may issue reports of vehicle misbehaviour to the RA.
- The RA collects misbehaviour reports from participating vehicles in an ITS, and takes a decision to revoke reported pseudonyms. It then creates and broadcasts signed revocation messages to the misbehaving vehicle.
- Vehicles receive and process revocation commands to revoke their pseudonyms, and send confirmations back to the RA.

The REWIRE protocols and our variant has the following steps: In step 1 vehicle V_1 obtains a long-term certificate from the CA enabling it to obtain pseudonyms. In step 2 V_1 obtains pseudonyms from the PP to communicate securely with other vehicles including vehicle V_2. Steps 1 and 2 are not part of a revocation protocol itself, rather they are part of the issuance phase of pseudonyms. During the communication in the ITS, vehicle V_1 will receive messages from V_2 under a pseudonym which could be changed frequently. V_2 will apply misbehaviour detection mechanisms [14] in order to detect indications of faulty or malicious behaviour. Examples of such mechanisms may detect spoofed positions or incorrect speeds reported in messages.

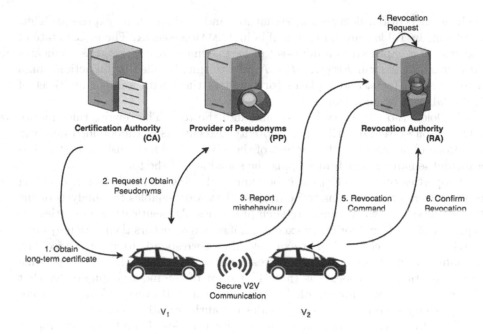

Fig. 1. High-level V2X revocation scenario

In such cases, step 3 is triggered by V_1 submitting a misbehaviour report to the RA accusing V_2 of misbehaviour. Similarly other vehicles may make the same report to the RA against V_2 (omitted from the diagram). The RA takes a decision to have V_2's access to the ITS infrastructure revoked if some threshold is reached. Then the RA crafts a report containing the reason for revocation and V_2's current pseudonym (step 4). Following the receipt, a revocation message is broadcast to all vehicles in step 5. V_2 receives the designated revocation message and its TC will be triggered to delete all of its pseudonyms. Finally, V_2 constructs and sends a confirmation message back to the RA in step 6 to inform the RA all of its pseudonyms were deleted.

3 Background and Assumptions

3.1 TAMARIN

We model and analyse all three protocols, the PLAIN and R-TOKEN protocols and our new O-TOKEN protocol in Sect. 5 using the TAMARIN prover. For this paper we give a general description of what the TAMARIN tool provides. There are several full introductions to the tool [18, 19, 32] for further details.

The TAMARIN prover is a symbolic analysis tool that is based on multi-set rewriting rules and first order logic. It supports the analysis of security protocols, which are described using multi-set rewrite rules to describe actions corresponding to protocol agents taking part in protocol steps. Protocol messages are modelled as terms which enable cryptographic protocol constructions such as encryption, decryption, signatures and hashing to be expressed. Thus the terms in Table 1 are all expressible in TAMARIN syntax. The global state of the system is captured as a multi-set of Facts, which are expressed as predicates on terms, of the form $F(t_1, \ldots, t_n)$. A rewrite rule, labelled by an action, takes a multi-set of facts, and replaces (or rewrites) them with another multi-set of facts, labelled by an action.

A Dolev-Yao adversary is also built into the tool. The rewrite rules induce a transition system describing the potential executions of (unbounded numbers of) protocol instances in the context of the adversary. The transition system has a formal semantics which underpins the soundness of the tool.

Properties on the actions can be expressed using first-order logic, enabling requirements on executions to be defined. TAMARIN enables the analysis of the transition system with respect to such properties. Authentication properties are typically of the form "for every execution, if action a_2 occurs then action a_1 must previously have occurred". For example, if a_2 corresponds to agent A receiving a confirmation message, and a_1 corresponds to B sending that message, then the authentication property is that A's receipt of the message guarantees that B sent it (i.e., it was not spoofed by the adversary). If every execution satisfies this property then the protocol provides the authentication required.

TAMARIN has numerous built-in security theories that abstractly support common cryptographic functions. For example, in this paper we use the *signing* built-in which models a signature scheme. It provides the function symbols `sign` and `verify` such that digital signatures can be verified using the equation: `verify(sign(m, sk), m, pk(sk)) = true`.

3.2 Security Notation and Analysis

The notation defined in Table 1 is used across all models in the paper. The last three entries are specific to our new protocol in Sect. 5. The following seven proof goals are considered in this paper to model our correctness requirements.

G1: Executable ensures the model is executable and demonstrates successful transmission of all core messages. It is a sanity check of the model's correctness.

G2: Weak agreement, defined by Lowe [16], is a form of authentication which guarantees that when an initiator A completes a run of the protocol then it was interacting with another agent B who had also been running the protocol. In the revocation protocols the initiator A is the RA and an agent B is a vehicle.

G3: Non-injective agreement, again defined by Lowe [16], adds a further condition to ensure that the two agents, A and B, agree on the roles they are taking and agree on the data items used in their message exchange. In our protocols *non-injective agreement* guarantees that the RA and vehicle both agree upon the completion of a run with each other and that in those runs the contents of the received messages correspond to the sent messages.

G4: Non-injective synchronisation, defined by Cremers and Mauw [5], is very similar to *non-injective agreement* but additionally requires that the corresponding send and receive messages have to be executed in their expected

Table 1. Security notation

Syntax		Description
V_j		An arbitrary vehicle j
SK_{V_j}	PK_{V_j}	Asymmetric key pair for V_j
$Ps_{i(V_j)}$		i^{th} pseudonym of V_j
$SK_{Ps_i(V_j)}$	$PK_{Ps_i(V_j)}$	Asymmetric pseudonym key pair for V_j's i^{th} pseudonym
SK_{RA}	PK_{RA}	Asymmetric key pair for the RA
$\sigma_{Ps_i(V_j)} := \{|V_j\,\|\,PK_{V_j}\,\|\,r\,|\}_{SK_{V_j}}$		An R-TOKEN of the ith pseudonym of V_j, where r is a nonce
LTK_{V_j}		Long-term symmetric key of a vehicle V_j (replaces asymmetric pair in line 2 above)
$SK_{O_{Ps_i(V_j)}}$	$PK_{O_{Ps_i(V_j)}}$	Asymmetric key pair for an O-TOKEN, belonging to the ith pseudonym of V_j
$\phi_{Ps_i(V_j)} := \{|\,SK_{Ps_i(V_j)}\,|\}_{LTK_{V_j}}$		An O-TOKEN of the ith pseudonym of V_j

order. This means that in the revocation protocols revoke messages are sent later than receive messages. This means that if a protocol preserves a *non-injective synchronisation* property then the corresponding *non-injective agreement* property will also hold.

C5: Revoke after change exists, defined in this paper, states that if a vehicle changes its pseudonym and a previous pseudonym is revoked, it should still be possible for the vehicle to create a message to confirm the Revocation Authority (RA) that it has taken the action for revocation. This is a sanity check that the a vehicle can be revoked even after a change of pseudonym.

G6: Order for self revocation (OSR) request received with change all, defined in this paper, indicates that if a vehicle receives the OSR request, the vehicle will perform the revocation and create a confirmation.

G7: Revoke with change all, defined in this paper, states that if a confirmation of a pseudonym revocation is accepted by the RA from a vehicle then that vehicle will have accepted and processed a revocation request from the RA.

3.3 Modelling Assumptions

In this section we provide a scope for the protocols and identify the modelling abstractions that are used for the analysis. We assume that for each of the protocol models a registration and enrolment phase has executed, resulting in vehicles holding valid pseudonyms. All vehicles in a network have a Trusted Component (TC) and abstractly this means that (1). vehicle keys cannot be leaked, and (2). vehicles cannot ignore revocation messages. We consider the CA, PP and RA to be distinct roles and in the architecture there is one of each. These roles are all trustworthy and therefore, we remove the possibility of their keys leaking from the analysis.

Steps 1 and 2 in Sect. 2 denotes the issuing of pseudonyms to vehicles by the CA and will be abstractly captured as a rule within our models. A revocation protocol focuses on steps 3, 4, 5 and 6 from Fig. 1. Within the TAMARIN model steps 3 and 4 are abstractly represented by a report event which the RA receives. Steps 5 and 6 are described in three rules which focus on the message exchange to revoke a vehicle and a confirmation to affirm the vehicle followed the request. All the formal models in this paper follow this pattern of communication but the format of the messages and the verification that can be performed on the signed messages changes with each protocol.

The Dolev-Yao adversary in our models is in control of the network and other untrusted parts of the system including the vehicles themselves. It is not in control of the TCs of the vehicles and the trusted third parties.

4   REWIRE Protocols

This section describes our modelling and analysis of the PLAIN and R-TOKEN protocols. Our security and functional correctness analysis shows the following *main results* which are weaknesses in the existing protocols:

- If the PLAIN protocol executes a change of pseudonym, then no confirmation guarantee can be communicated to the RA. Hence even though authentication properties may hold, a misbehaving vehicle may avoid revocation by changing its pseudonym, and so functional correctness will not be guaranteed. While the original paper [12] already identified this issue and addressed it in the R-TOKEN version, TAMARIN was independently able to discover this problem.
- Following attempted revocation of a vehicle's pseudonym the RA is unable to verify successful confirmation in the R-TOKEN scheme, thus none of the authentication properties hold. In particular a confirmation can be spoofed by a malicious agent and accepted by the RA, even when the misbehaving vehicle is not revoked. This flaw was not previously recognised.

4.1   REWIRE: PLAIN

Modelling. Section 3.3 informally identified the steps of a revocation protocol based on the behaviour of an RA and a misbehaving vehicle. We model the protocol roles of the RA and an arbitrary vehicle (V_j) in TAMARIN by a set of rewrite rules, which correspond to the steps of the protocol. The PLAIN model has three distinct types of rules to: (1). setup all required key pairs for secure communication, (2). create misbehaviour reports and (3). describe revocation requests and receiving subsequent confirmation.

The heart of the protocol involves an exchange of messages to effect revocation: an Order for Self-Revocation (OSR) request, followed by a confirmation response.

The OSR request message OSR-REQ [12] is the first message sent to a vehicle, which triggers its revocation process. OSR-REQ contains the command to revoke,

Table 2. Summary of results

Goal	Content	PLAIN	R-TOKEN	O-TOKEN
G1	Executable	✓	✓	✓
G2	Weak_agreement	✓	×	✓
G3	Noninjective_agreement	✓	×	✓
G4	Noninjective_synchronisation	✓	×	✓
G5	Revoke_after_change_exists	×	✓	✓
G6	Osr_req_received_with_change_all	N/a	✓	✓
G7	Revoke_with_change_all	N/a	×	✓

the reported misbehaving pseudonym and additional information as to why the revocation occurred. The pseudonym $Ps_{i(V_j)}$ in this protocol is simply $PK_{Ps_{i(V_j)}}$ belonging to V_j. OSR-REQ is signed by the RA, and can be verified by receiving vehicles.

$$\text{OSR-REQ} := \{| \ \text{``revoke''} \ || \ Ps_{i(V_j)} \ || \ reason|\}_{SK_{RA}} \tag{1}$$

The OSR-REQ message is received and verified by a V_j, and the TC in V_j can identify the pseudonym as belonging to V_j. Following this identification the vehicle constructs an OSR-CONF message confirming the command to revoke was followed, and the TC in V_j will flag all available pseudonyms as revoked to prevent their future use in V2X communication. The OSR-CONF message is comprised of two terms: a confirm command and the active reported public pseudonym key.

The message is signed with the corresponding secret pseudonym key.

$$\text{OSR-CONF} := \{| \ \text{``confirm''} \ || \ Ps_{i(V_j)} \ |\}_{SK_{Ps_{i(V_j)}}} \tag{2}$$

We model a well formed OSR-REQ message duly signed by the RA and addressed to its current pseudonym. The vehicle verifies that the message came from the RA and contains the vehicle's active pseudonym, before deleting all its pseudonyms and creating the OSR-CONF message signed under the active secret pseudonym key, which is sent back to the RA. The adversary is able to learn the OSR-REQ message terms and the signature. However the adversary cannot modify the contents of the message as the adversary does not posses the RA's secret key. We also model the incoming OSR-CONF message from a V_j. The RA verifies the OSR-CONF message is signed with the reported pseudonym $PK_{Ps_{i(V_j)}}$.

Proof Goals. We state several proof goals for our model, G1-G7 discussed in Sect. 3.2, that represent authentication and functional correctness properties. The results of whether each of the numbered proof goals hold are summarised in Table 2. All the goals include predicates requiring that the vehicle's long-term key and secret pseudonym keys are not compromised, and so correct behaviour is dependent on these keys not being compromised.

A successful run of the model guarantees that V_j was running the protocol with the RA. Receipt of the OSR-CONF message represents completion of a run for the RA. An OSR-REQ message is represented by facts from both the RA and vehicle's perspective. The model observes that the RA will have completed a run and verified a confirmation from a vehicle. Furthermore, the vehicle must have received the OSR-REQ message before it is possible for the RA to receive the OSR-CONF message, hence the communication order is preserved. The above proof goals are trace authentication properties demonstrating that the attacker cannot construct OSR-REQ or OSR-CONF messages from its observations. Thus no logical attacks are identified for the PLAIN protocol from our symbolic analysis.

4.2   REWIRE: PLAIN with Change of Pseudonym

Modelling. In the PLAIN pseudonym scheme revocation of REWIRE [12], a *change of pseudonym* for a vehicle can occur at any point prior to an OSR-REQ being received. For example, consider a vehicle V_1 and two of its pseudonyms $Ps_{1(V_1)}$ and $Ps_{2(V_1)}$ in the following change of pseudonym scenario. When the RA receives a report to revoke V_1, it broadcasts the OSR-REQ message containing the misbehaving pseudonym $Ps_{1(V_1)}$, as shown in Fig. 2. However, before an OSR-REQ message is ever received by V_1 a change of pseudonym can occur resulting in a new pseudonym now being active. In an naïve implementation, changing to $Ps_{2(V_1)}$ means that the receipt of the OSR-REQ will be ignored as the vehicle has deleted its previous pseudonym. Therefore, no OSR-CONF message will be generated by V_1 as the vehicle has deleted its previous pseudonyms and the revocation process will fail. Consequently V_1 can continue to misbehave under the new pseudonym $Ps_{2(V_1)}$.

We model the changing of pseudonyms in such a way that the model creates a fresh pseudonym key for an arbitrary vehicle V_j. The "can change" fact is included to control when a vehicle can change its current pseudonym. The model concludes by storing the new pseudonym secret key for V_j and outputs the public key of the new pseudonym, which the intruder learns.

Proof Goals. Adding this extra behaviour to the protocol yields another proof goal, G5, discussed in Sect. 3.2. If a vehicle changes its pseudonym and a previous pseudonym is revoked, it should be possible for the vehicle to create an OSR-CONF

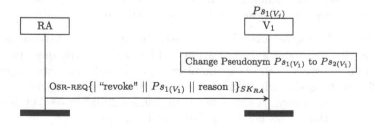

Fig. 2. REWIRE: PLAIN pseudonym scheme incomplete run

message. This model fails for the PLAIN protocol, showing that the protocol does not guarantee a successful revocation of a misbehaving vehicle in the presence of changing pseudonyms, and indeed that if a vehicle changes its pseudonym then it can escape revocation. Therefore, the PLAIN protocol is not functionally correct in the context of changing pseudonyms. To address this shortcoming in [11,12] a variant to the PLAIN protocol is proposed, referred to as the R-TOKEN protocol.

4.3   REWIRE: R-TOKEN

Modelling. The R-TOKEN variant embeds additional information in pseudonym certificates with the aim of allowing revocation even with changing pseudonyms. This additional information is an R-TOKEN, $\sigma_{Ps_i(V_j)}$, which is constructed from a vehicle's public identity, public key and a nonce r, encrypted under a vehicle's secret key. There is a fresh R-TOKEN for each pseudonym. $Ps_{i(V_j)}$ in this protocol is a pseudonym containing $PK_{Ps_i(V_j)}$ and the R-TOKEN $\sigma_{Ps_i(V_j)}$.

It is the purpose of the R-TOKEN to allow a vehicle to later detect whether a revocation request is directed to it, without allowing others to identify the vehicle. By encrypting the R-TOKEN under SK_{V_j}, all vehicles must attempt to decrypt the R-TOKEN. Only the correct vehicle can decrypt the R-TOKEN, meaning the revocation was designated for the vehicle and should be executed.

In PUCA and REWIRE a "cut and choose" approach [28] is used to generate the R-TOKEN, but in the model we have simply abstracted this to a fresh value that is encrypted under the secret key of the vehicle.

The R-TOKEN protocol is represented in Fig. 3. The OSR-REQ message is of the same format as the PLAIN protocol where the pseudonym contains the R-TOKEN. Once a vehicle receives an OSR-REQ it attempts to decrypt the R-TOKEN irrespective of its active pseudonym. Only the designated vehicle can decrypt the R-TOKEN since the decryption uses SK_{V_j}, others will simply ignore

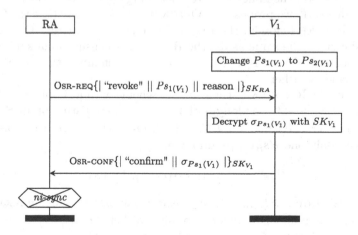

Fig. 3. REWIRE: R-TOKEN scheme

the OSR-REQ. The OSR-CONF message now contains the R-TOKEN and not the pseudonym, and the message is signed with the vehicle's secret key.

$$OSR\text{-}CONF := \{| \ \text{``confirm''} \ || \ \sigma_{Ps_i(V_j)} \ |\}SK_{V_j} \tag{3}$$

The modelling of the rules for the R-TOKEN protocol is almost identical but there are two important changes. Firstly the model includes having to decrypt the R-TOKEN as an additional action. Secondly, the model is weakened to remove the verify step (which checks the correctness of the confirmation $\sigma_{Ps_i(V_j)}$) since the RA is not in possession of the PK_{V_j}.

Proof Goals. For consistency we analysed functional correctness. All the proof goals for the PLAIN protocol remain applicable. Proof goal G5 holds because any vehicle can create a confirmation message. Two additional goals are included to analyse the correct behaviour of the vehicle (G6) and RA (G7) in the context of changing pseudonyms, as shown in Table 2. For each goal we again assume that SK_{V_j} is not compromised. The security analysis yields that neither of the authentication properties hold. The adversary is able to intercept the OSR-REQ message and create a OSR-CONF message containing the inferred R-TOKEN. The adversary then generates a fresh secret key which is used to sign the OSR-CONF message. The created OSR-CONF is sent to the RA. The RA accepts the confirmation but cannot verify its authenticity because the LTK_{V_j} is only known to V_j and CA. Therefore, The RA does not obtain a guarantee that it is communicating with a running vehicle.

This flaw in the protocol was not previously recognised, and has been accepted by the designers of the R-TOKEN protocol.

5   O-TOKEN Protocol

Modelling. To solve the issue of the RA not being able to verify the confirmation message, OSR-CONF, we propose the O-TOKEN protocol. Note that the O-TOKEN mimics the R-TOKEN closely: the reason for generating different O-TOKENS for each pseudonym is the same as for the R-TOKEN, to ensure unlinkability of the vehicle in question. If the R-TOKEN or O-TOKEN remained the same, it would act as a vehicle identifier.

We replace the R-TOKEN in the previous scheme with a simpler construction: an O-TOKEN for the ith pseudonym of V_j, $\phi_{Ps_i(V_j)}$, consisting of an $SK_{O_{Ps_i(V_j)}}$ key which is encrypted under LTK_{V_j}. Each O-TOKEN is fresh and associated with one and only one $Ps_{i(V_j)}$ pseudonym.

$$\phi_{Ps_i(V_j)} := \{| \ SK_{O_{Ps_i(V_j)}} \ |\}LTK_{V_j}$$

The aim of using fresh $SK_{O_{Ps_i(V_j)}}$ keys is to make pseudonyms unlinkable.

The pseudonym also contains one additional field, $PK_{O_{Ps_i(V_j)}}$, which is the corresponding public key for the particular O-TOKEN. Therefore, the pseudonym contains enough information for the RA to verify a received OSR-CONF message and for the vehicle to change its pseudonym.

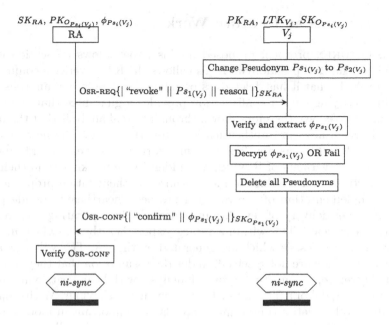

Fig. 4. O-TOKEN revocation

A revocation run which uses O-TOKEN is shown in Fig. 4. The OSR-REQ message is of the same format as the other protocols but the pseudonym contains the O-TOKEN. The OSR-CONF message now contains the O-TOKEN and the message is signed with $SK_{O_{Ps_i(V_j)}}$ instead of signing with LTK_{V_j} which the vehicle extracted earlier:

$$\text{OSR-CONF} := \{|\,\textit{``confirm''}\,||\,\phi_{Ps_i(V_j)}\,|\}SK_{O_{Ps_i(V_j)}} \qquad (4)$$

The subtle change in signing the OSR-CONF message, together with the RA's knowledge of $PK_{O_{Ps_i(V_j)}}$ enables the RA to verify the confirmation message.

The modelling of the other rules for the O-TOKEN protocol is largely similar but there are two further changes. Firstly, the rule for receiving the OSR request includes having to decrypt the O-TOKEN as an additional action, Secondly, changing pseudonym behaviour is supported with a new rule, by creating a fresh pseudonym secret key, a fresh $SK_{O_{Ps_i(V_j)}}$ and the newly encrypted O-TOKEN.

Proof Goals. The results for the formal analysis for the O-TOKEN protocol is presented in Table 2 and achieves all desired guarantees. Notably all the authentication properties hold which means that the RA is communicating with the revoked vehicle and can verify the received confirmation, which was not the case with the R-TOKEN protocol. Therefore, all the desired functional correctness properties hold.

6   Conclusions and Future Work

The new O-TOKEN protocol proposed in this paper allows revocation even if vehicles have changed pseudonym. It also allows the RA to verify a confirmation sent by a vehicle that it has deleted its pseudonyms. The formal analysis establishes that verifying such a confirmation provides a guarantee that the revocation occurred. We have therefore shown through formal analysis that the desired functional correctness and authentication properties hold. The new O-TOKEN protocol for REWIRE was developed by first formally modelling and analysing the two previous variants of REWIRE, then identifying weaknesses in their functional correctness and a failure to meet required authentication properties.

In an implementation of a revocation protocol, heartbeats provide protection against non-delivery of revocation requests by incorporating such requests within the heartbeats. TCs within a vehicle expect heartbeats (which may contain revocation requests), which are generated by the RA. TCs will take appropriate action if they are not received, under the assumption that they have been blocked. Therefore, augmenting a formal analysis with heartbeats will require a more detailed model of a TC and further adversarial behaviour. With respect to the greater level of detail timestamps may also be important in modelling time out behaviour of heartbeats. The inclusion of time may also allow us to model the retention of keys before the deletion of pseudonyms. TC's could also consider storing the last k pseudonyms and the analysis would need to ensure that the adversary could not evade revocation by changing pseudonym at least k times.

Another consideration in an implementation is the handling of cases where no confirmation is sent. If heartbeats are not used then further revocation requests will need to be sent until confirmation is received.

In the analysis, we currently focus on functional correctness and authentication. In future work we will consider generalising the correctness analysis, in particular G5, to include liveness properties such that we could prove a more general property such as "any revocation request must eventually be confirmed". The TAMARIN tool chain has been extended in a recent paper by Backes *et al.* [21] to enable verification of liveness properties. Not considered here are privacy requirements such as unlinkability which could likewise merit a formal analysis.

Delaune and Hirschi [7] and Chadha et al. [4] survey various anonymity and privacy related properties, including anonymity, unlinkability and strong secrecy, which can be proved using equivalence-based reasoning. Behavioural equivalence allows us to determine whether two situations are different, in particular whether the confirmation of a revocation came from one vehicle or another. The use of process equivalences to analyse privacy properties can also be seen in TAMARIN [1] and in other modelling tools, e.g. PROVERIF [3], which has been used successfully to analyse privacy properties [6,8]. Future work will be to explore anonymity and privacy properties of revocation protocols and of other V2X protocols.

Our proposed protocol requires a trusted device at the car which can be trusted to erase all of the pseudonyms that the car may have available. However, it is still under debate whether this is the right trust model for the car. Furthermore, which functions is it reasonable to place within this trusted device, and which cannot be made trustworthy? To answer these questions in a satisfactory way is not straightforward, and to make the vehicle industry reach agreement on a specific trust model is even more demanding. This is an interesting challenge for future work.

Acknowledgements. Jorden Whitefield is funded by EPSRC iCASE studentship 15220193 through Thales UK. Thanks to Cas Cremers for detailed discussions on TAMARIN. Thanks also to François Dupressoir and Adrian Waller for detailed feedback, and to the reviewers for their constructive comments.

References

1. Basin, D.A., Dreier, J., Sasse, R.: Automated symbolic proofs of observational equivalence. In: Proceedings of the 22nd ACM SIGSAC Conference on Computer and Communications Security, Denver, CO, USA, pp. 1144–1155 (2015)
2. Bißmeyer, N., Petit, J., Bayarou, K.M.: CoPRA: conditional pseudonym resolution algorithm in VANETs. In: 2013 10th Annual Conference on Wireless On-demand Network Systems and Services (WONS), pp. 9–16. IEEE (2013)
3. Blanchet, B., Smyth, B., Cheval, V.: Proverif 1.96: automatic cryptographic protocol verifier, user manual and tutorial (2016). http://prosecco.gforge.inria.fr/personal/bblanche/proverif/manual.pdf
4. Chadha, R., Cheval, V., Ciobâcă, Ş., Kremer, S.: Automated verification of equivalence properties of cryptographic protocols. ACM Trans. Comput. Log. **17**(4), 23:1–23:32 (2016)
5. Cremers, C., Mauw, S.: Operational Semantics and Verification of Security Protocols. Information Security and Cryptography. Springer, Heidelberg (2012)
6. Dahl, M., Delaune, S., Steel, G.: Formal analysis of privacy for vehicular mix-zones. In: Gritzalis, D., Preneel, B., Theoharidou, M. (eds.) ESORICS 2010. LNCS, vol. 6345, pp. 55–70. Springer, Heidelberg (2010). doi:10.1007/978-3-642-15497-3_4
7. Delaune, S., Hirschi, L.: A survey of symbolic methods for establishing equivalence-based properties in cryptographic protocols. J. Log. Algebraic Methods Program. **87**, 127–144 (2017)
8. Fazouane, M., Kopp, H., van der Heijden, R.W., Métayer, D., Kargl, F.: Formal verification of privacy properties in electric vehicle charging. In: Piessens, F., Caballero, J., Bielova, N. (eds.) ESSoS 2015. LNCS, vol. 8978, pp. 17–33. Springer, Cham (2015). doi:10.1007/978-3-319-15618-7_2
9. Feiri, M., Petit, J., Kargl, F.: Formal model of certificate omission schemes in VANET. In: 2014 IEEE Vehicular Networking Conference, VNC 2014, Paderborn, Germany, 3–5 December 2014, pp. 41–44 (2014)
10. Fischer, L., Aijaz, A., Eckert, C., Vogt, D.: Secure revocable anonymous authenticated inter-vehicle communication (SRAAC). In: 4th Conference on Embedded Security in Cars (ESCAR 2006), Berlin, Germany (2006)
11. Förster, D., Kargl, F., Löhr, H.: PUCA: a pseudonym scheme with strong privacy guarantees for vehicular ad-hoc networks. Ad Hoc Netw. **37**(Part 1), 122–132 (2016). Special Issue on Advances in Vehicular Networks

12. Förster, D., Löhr, H., Zibuschka, J., Kargl, F.: REWIRE - revocation without resolution: a privacy-friendly revocation mechanism for vehicular ad-hoc networks. In: Trust and Trustworthy Computing - 8th International Conference, TRUST 2015, Heraklion, Greece, 24–26 August 2015, Proceedings, pp. 193–208 (2015)
13. Haas, J.J., Hu, Y.C., Laberteaux, K.P.: Efficient certificate revocation list organization and distribution. IEEE J. Sel. Areas Commun. **29**(3), 595–604 (2011)
14. van der Heijden, R.W., Dietzel, S., Leinmüller, T., Kargl, F.: Survey on misbehavior detection in cooperative intelligent transportation systems. CoRR abs/1610.06810 (2016). http://arxiv.org/abs/1610.06810
15. Kondareddy, Y., Di Crescenzo, G., Agrawal, P.: Analysis of certificate revocation list distribution protocols for vehicular networks. In: Global Telecommunications Conference (GLOBECOM 2010), pp. 1–5, IEEE (2010)
16. Lowe, G.: A hierarchy of authentication specifications. In: 10th Computer Security Foundations Workshop, pp. 31–44. IEEE Computer Society (1997)
17. Ma, Z., Kargl, F., Weber, M.: Pseudonym-on-demand: a new pseudonym refill strategy for vehicular communications. In: IEEE 68th Vehicular Technology Conference, 2008. VTC 2008-Fall, pp. 1–5. IEEE (2008)
18. Meier, S., Schmidt, B.: Tamarin prover - information security group — eth zurich (2016). http://www.infsec.ethz.ch/research/software/tamarin.html. Accessed 18 Jan 2017
19. Meier, S., Schmidt, B., Cremers, C., Basin, D.: The TAMARIN prover for the symbolic analysis of security protocols. In: Sharygina, N., Veith, H. (eds.) CAV 2013. LNCS, vol. 8044, pp. 696–701. Springer, Heidelberg (2013). doi:10.1007/978-3-642-39799-8_48
20. Michael, E.N., Henry, L.O.: Scalable certificate revocation list distribution in vehicular ad hoc networks. In: GLOBECOM Workshops (GC Wkshps), pp. 54–58. IEEE (2010)
21. Backes, M., Jannik Dreier, S.K., Künnemann, R.: A novel approach for reasoning about liveness in cryptographic protocols and its application to fair exchange. In: 2nd IEEE European Symposium on Security and Privacy (2017)
22. Papadimitratos, P., Buttyan, L., Holczer, T., Schoch, E., Freudiger, J., Raya, M., Ma, Z., Kargl, F., Kung, A., Hubaux, J.P.: Secure vehicular communication systems: design and architecture. IEEE Commun. Mag. **46**(11), 100–109 (2008)
23. Papadimitratos, P., Buttyan, L., Hubaux, J.P., Kargl, F., Kung, A., Raya, M.: Architecture for secure and private vehicular communications. In: 2007 7th International Conference on ITS Telecommunications, pp. 1–6. IEEE (2007)
24. Papadimitratos, P.P., Mezzour, G., Hubaux, J.P.: Certificate revocation list distribution in vehicular communication systems. In: Proceedings of the Fifth ACM International Workshop on VehiculAr Inter-NETworking, pp. 86–87. ACM (2008)
25. Petit, J., Schaub, F., Feiri, M., Kargl, F.: Pseudonym schemes in vehicular networks: a survey. IEEE Commun. Surv. Tutor. **17**(1), 228–255 (2015)
26. PRECIOSA: European commission : Cordis : Projects and results service : Privacy enabled capability in co-operative systems and safety applications (2010). http://cordis.europa.eu/project/rcn/86606_en.html. Accessed 31 Jan 2017
27. PRESERVE: www.preserve-project.eu — preparing secure V2X communication systems (2011). https://preserve-project.eu/. Accessed 31 Jan 2017
28. Rabin, M.O.: Digitalized signatures and public-key functions as intractable as factorization. In: Foundations of Secure Computation, pp. 155–168 (1978)
29. Raya, M., Papadimitratos, P., Aad, I., Jungels, D., Hubaux, J.P.: Eviction of misbehaving and faulty nodes in vehicular networks. IEEE J. Sel. A. Commun. **25**(8), 1557–1568 (2007)

30. Schaub, F., Kargl, F., Ma, Z., Weber, M.: V-Tokens for conditional pseudonymity in VANETs. In: 2010 IEEE Wireless Communications and Networking Conference, WCNC 2010, Proceedings, Sydney, Australia, 18–21 April 2010, pp. 1–6 (2010)
31. Schaub, F., Ma, Z., Kargl, F.: Privacy requirements in vehicular communication systems. In: Computational Science and Engineering, CSE 2009, vol. 3, pp. 139–145, IEEE (2009)
32. Schmidt, B., Meier, S., Cremers, C.J.F., Basin, D.A.: Automated analysis of Diffie-Hellman protocols and advanced security properties. In: 25th IEEE Computer Security Foundations Symposium, CSF 2012, Cambridge, MA, USA, 25–27 June 2012, pp. 78–94 (2012)
33. Weyl, B., Henniger, O., Ruddle, A., Seudie, H., Wolf, M., Wollinger, T.: Securing vehicular on-board IT systems: the EVITA project. In: 25th Joint VDI/VW Automotive Security Conference, Ingolstadt, Germany (2009). http://www.evita-project.org/Publications/HRSW09.pdf
34. Whitefield, J., Chen, L., Kargl, F., Schneider, S., Treharne, H., Wesemeyer, S.: Formal analysis of V2X revocation protocols (2017). http://www.computing.surrey.ac.uk/personal/st/H.Treharne/papers/2017/rewire.html
35. Willke, T.L., Tientrakool, P., Maxemchuk, N.F.: A survey of inter-vehicle communication protocols and their applications. IEEE Commun. Surv. Tutor. 11(2), 3–20 (2009)

Refinement-Aware Generation of Attack Trees

Olga Gadyatskaya[1], Ravi Jhawar[1,2], Sjouke Mauw[1],
Rolando Trujillo-Rasua[1(✉)], and Tim A.C. Willemse[3]

[1] SnT and University of Luxembourg, Esch-sur-Alzette, Luxembourg
{olga.gadyatskaya,sjouke.mauw,rolando.trujillo}@uni.lu
[2] ILNAS, Esch-sur-Alzette, Luxembourg
ravi.jhawar@ilnas.etat.lu
[3] Eindhoven University of Technology, Eindhoven, The Netherlands
t.a.c.willemse@tue.nl

Abstract. Attack trees allow a security analyst to obtain an overview of the potential vulnerabilities of a system. Due to their refinement structure, attack trees support the analyst in understanding the system vulnerabilities at various levels of abstraction. However, contrary to manually synthesized attack trees, automatically generated attack trees are often not refinement-aware, making subsequent human processing much harder. The generation of attack trees in which the refined nodes correspond to semantically relevant levels of abstraction is still an open question. In this paper, we formulate the attack-tree generation problem and propose a methodology to, given a system model, generate attack trees with meaningful levels of abstraction.

1 Introduction

Attack trees are a well-known graphical security model [Sch99,MO05,RKT12, KMRS14]. They are widely used in industry and academia for handling threat modeling and security risk assessment [Sho14], as they help the analysts to structure the reasoning, facilitate communications across the board, and can store succinctly very complex threat scenarios [FFG+16]. Yet, the process of creating an attack tree is quite lengthy, tedious, and error-prone [FFG+16,Sho14]. It can be facilitated by applying industry threat catalogues [FFG+16] and security knowledge bases [GLPS14], but these information sources may be unavailable for particular organizations or too generic to be useful. This is why recently researchers started to develop techniques for generating attack trees automatically [VNN14,IPHK15,HKT13,PAV15,Gad15].

Automatic generation of attack trees can be interpreted as model transformation. The initial model is typically a domain-specific language specifying the system components, their interactions, and the attacker's goal as an undesired state of the system, and formalizing attack paths towards the goal. In that regard, the attack-tree generation problem consists in encoding all attacks achieving a common goal into an attack tree model. However, this problem formulation overlooks one of the strengths of attack trees: its *refinement structure*.

© Springer International Publishing AG 2017
G. Livraga and C. Mitchell (Eds.): STM 2017, LNCS 10547, pp. 164–179, 2017.
DOI: 10.1007/978-3-319-68063-7_11

Refining a goal into subgoals is an intuitive process for humans, used in attack trees and other visual languages, e.g., mind maps. That makes attack trees easily readable and comprehensible by a simple top-down inspection, as it allows the analyst to understand the attack potential at various levels of abstraction. This dimension, however, almost completely escapes in the literature on attack-tree generation, as we discuss in the following short overview of relevant approaches.

Vigo et al. [VNN14] generate trees from a process calculus system model by translating algebraic specifications into formulae and backward-chaining these formulae into a formula for the attacker's goal success. Reachability-based approaches, such as [IPHK15, Gad15, HKT13], transform system models into attack trees using information about connected elements in the model. In essence, these approaches reason that the attacker can reach the desired location from any system location adjacent to it. This reasoning is applied recursively to traverse complete attack paths. The main drawback of the techniques proposed in [VNN14, IPHK15, HKT13, Gad15] is that they do not leverage the refinement structure of attack trees, when parent nodes are more abstract than child nodes. In fact, [VNN14] does not provide any meaning to intermediate nodes, which only serve to express how child nodes are combined, while [IPHK15, Gad15, HKT13] have intermediate nodes at the same level of abstraction as child nodes, representing actions in the system model.

The attack traces-based approaches rely on a set of successful traces that capture transitions from the initial state to the state in the system in which the attacker has achieved the goal. The basic idea of generating successful attack paths has been explored in, e.g., [RA00, SHJ+02], where the authors applied model-checking to network system models. Dawkins and Hale [DH04] have generated attack trees from network attack graphs (a formalism different from attack trees [SHJ+02]) by finding minimum cut sets for successful attack paths (traces). This approach also does not offer a refinement structure, and each branch in a generated attack tree corresponds to a sequence of vulnerability exploitations.

The ATSyRA approach [PAV14, PAV15] synthesizes attack trees from attack graphs. It requires that the analyst first defines a set of actions at several abstraction levels in the system model, and a set of rules for refinement of higher level actions into combinations of lower-level ones. This action hierarchy allows to transform successful attack paths in the attack graph (generated by model-checking) into an attack tree, containing precise actions as leaf nodes, while intermediate nodes represent more abstract actions. This tree enjoys a refinement structure that is more familiar to the human analyst, but the analyst still has to define the refinement relation herself; it is not created automatically.

We conclude that there exists a gap between manual and automatic generation of attack trees that has not been covered in literature yet. Automatic generation approaches work with concrete attacks, while manual creation of attack trees focuses on the refinement of goals into subgoals. In this paper, we address this gap by formalising the attack-tree generation problem that connects both properties, namely that of encoding a set of attacks and that of respecting a given refinement structure. Further, we develop a methodology to, given a system model, generate attack trees with meaningful abstraction levels.

Our Contributions. This paper presents the following main results:

– We formally define the attack-tree generation problem as a task to generate a tree with an expected meaning that respects a given refinement structure.
– We propose an approach for generating attack trees from traces of successful attacks in a system model. Our approach utilizes a heuristic for encoding and decomposing attack traces that is based on the edge biclique problem [Pee03]. Furthermore, we derive the refinement structure from an abstraction relation on system predicates.
– We demonstrate the feasibility of our approach with a running example of a network security scenario.

2   The Attack-Tree Generation Problem

In this section we first formally introduce attack trees and the notion of a refinement specification. Next, we define what it means for an attack tree to satisfy a refinement specification and we formulate the *attack-tree generation problem.* Informally, this problem requires the derivation of a tree with a given semantics, that satisfies a given refinement specification.

Intuitively, an attack tree defines how higher (parent) nodes are interpreted through lower (child) nodes. The interpretations are defined by the refinement operators: OR specifies that if any of the child nodes is achieved, then the immediate parent node is also achieved; and AND defines that all child nodes need to be achieved to achieve the parent node's goal [MO05]. We will consider also the sequential AND operator, or SAND, that demands that the goals of the child nodes are to be achieved in a particular order for achieving the parent node [JKM+15].

Formally, let $\mathbb{B}$ denote a set of *actions,* OR and AND be two unranked associative and commutative operators, and SAND be an unranked associative but non-commutative operator. A SAND attack tree t is an expression over the signature $\mathbb{B} \cup \{OR, AND, SAND\}$, generated by the following grammar (for $b \in \mathbb{B}$):

$$t ::= b \mid b \lhd OR(t, \ldots, t) \mid b \lhd AND(t, \ldots, t) \mid b \lhd SAND(t, \ldots, t).$$

We use $\mathbb{T}_{SAND}$ to denote all SAND attack trees generated by the grammar above. Different to the definition of SAND trees given in [JKM+15], we require every node in the tree to be annotated with an action. An action in a node typically provides a generic (sometimes vague) description of the type of attack, e.g. *get a user's credentials* or *impersonate a security guard,* which is helpful to a top-down interpretation of the tree. An expression like $b \lhd SAND(t_1, \ldots, t_n)$ denotes an attack tree of which the top node is labelled with action b, and which has n children $t_1, \ldots, t_n$ that have to be executed sequentially.

Example 1. Figure 1 illustrates a simple SAND attack tree in which the goal of the attacker is to gain unauthorized access to a server. To achieve this goal, the attacker must first get a suitable credential for the server, and then, use this credential to log in remotely. A suitable credential can be obtained by eavesdropping on communications of an honest user, who knows the server password.

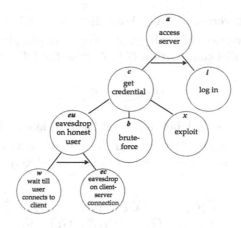

Fig. 1. A human-designed attack tree representing possible threat scenarios

Alternatively, the attacker can bruteforce the password on the server, or use an exploit to create a new password.

Using shorthands for the action names, this tree can be represented by the following expression: $a \triangleleft \mathsf{SAND}(c \triangleleft \mathsf{OR}(eu \triangleleft \mathsf{SAND}(w, ec), b, x), l)$.

We define the auxiliary function *top* to obtain the action at the root node as follows (for $\Delta \in \{\mathsf{OR}, \mathsf{AND}, \mathsf{SAND}\}$):

$$top(b) = top(b \triangleleft \Delta(t, \ldots, t)) = b.$$

We say that t' is a subtree of t, denoted $t' \in t$, if $t = t'$ or $t = \Delta(b, t_1, \ldots, t_n)$ and $t' \in t_i$ for some $i \in \{1, \ldots, n\}$, where $\Delta \in \{\mathsf{OR}, \mathsf{AND}, \mathsf{SAND}\}$.

Given a semantical domain D, an attack-tree semantics S defines a function $[\cdot]_S \colon \mathbb{T}_{\mathsf{SAND}} \to D$. We denote semantic equivalence of two trees $t, t' \in \mathbb{T}_{\mathsf{SAND}}$ by $t =_S t'$, which means $[t]_S = [t']_S$. In the next section we will provide an example of a semantics for SAND attack trees, which is called the SP semantics [JKM+15].

In this article we use the SP semantics [JKM+15] as the semantic domain for SAND attack trees. Note that our attack-tree generation problem formulation abstracts away from any concrete interpretation of the attack tree semantics.

The SP semantics encodes an attack tree as a set of *Series-Parallel graphs* (SP graphs). An SP graph is an edge-labeled directed graph with a *source* vertex and a *sink* vertex. The simplest SP graph has the form $u \xrightarrow{b} v$, where b is an edge label, u is the *source* vertex because it has no incoming edges, and v is the *sink* vertex because it has no outgoing edges. Any other SP graph is obtained as the composition of single-edge SP graphs.

Two composition operators are used to build SP graphs: the sequential composition operator ($\cdot$) and the parallel composition operator ($\parallel$). A sequential composition joins the sink vertex of a graph with the source vertex of the other graph. For example, given $G = u \xrightarrow{b} v$ and $G' = x \xrightarrow{z} y$, we obtain that $G \cdot G' = u \xrightarrow{b} v \xrightarrow{z} y$. Note that the source vertex of G' has been replaced in $G \cdot G'$ by the sink vertex v of G. A parallel composition, instead, joins the source and the sink vertices of both graphs. For example, given $G = u \xrightarrow{b} v$ and $G' = x \xrightarrow{z} y$, the parallel composition $G \parallel G'$ gives the following SP graph.

$$u \underset{z}{\overset{b}{\rightleftarrows}} v$$

In the SP semantics, edge labels represent basic actions in $\mathbb{B}$, and vertex labels are ignored. Hence a graph of the type $u \xrightarrow{b} v \xrightarrow{z} y$ is read as $\xrightarrow{b}\xrightarrow{z}$. Moreover, both composition operators are extended to sets of SP graphs as follows: given sets of SP graphs $\mathcal{G}_1, \ldots, \mathcal{G}_k$,

$$\mathcal{G}_1 \parallel \mathcal{G}_2 \parallel \ldots \parallel \mathcal{G}_k = \{G_1 \parallel \ldots \parallel G_k \mid (G_1, \ldots, G_k) \in \mathcal{G}_1 \times \ldots \times \mathcal{G}_k\}$$
$$\mathcal{G}_1 \cdot \mathcal{G}_2 \cdot \ldots \cdot \mathcal{G}_k = \{G_1 \cdot \ldots \cdot G_k \mid (G_1, \ldots, G_k) \in \mathcal{G}_1 \times \ldots \times \mathcal{G}_k\}.$$

Definition 1. *Let $\mathbb{G}_{SP}$ denote the set of SP graphs labeled with the elements of $\mathbb{B}$. The SP semantics for SAND attack trees is given by the function $[\![\cdot]\!]_{SP} : \mathbb{T}_{SAND} \to \mathcal{P}(\mathbb{G}_{SP})$, which is defined recursively as follows: for $b \in \mathbb{B}, t_i \in \mathbb{T}_{SAND}, 1 \leqslant i \leqslant k$,*

$$[\![b]\!]_{SP} = \{\xrightarrow{b}\}$$
$$[\![OR(t_1, \ldots, t_k)]\!]_{SP} = \bigcup_{i=1}^{k} [\![t_i]\!]_{SP}$$
$$[\![AND(t_1, \ldots, t_k)]\!]_{SP} = [\![t_1]\!]_{SP} \parallel \ldots \parallel [\![t_k]\!]_{SP}$$
$$[\![SAND(t_1, \ldots, t_k)]\!]_{SP} = [\![t_1]\!]_{SP} \cdot \ldots \cdot [\![t_k]\!]_{SP}.$$

We kindly refer the reader to [JKM+15] for more details on the SP semantics.

Example 2. The SAND attack tree in Fig. 1 has the following SP semantics: $\{\xrightarrow{w}\xrightarrow{ec}\xrightarrow{l}, \xrightarrow{b}\xrightarrow{l}, \xrightarrow{x}\xrightarrow{l}\}$. Note that the labels of the internal nodes are not represented in the SP semantics. Further note that the SP graphs occurring in this example are linear traces because the tree has no AND nodes.

Refinement Specification. The transition from one level in an attack tree to the next level defines a *refinement*. More precisely, a refinement is an expression of the form $b \triangleleft \Delta(b_1, \ldots, b_n)$, where $b, b_1, \ldots, b_n \in \mathbb{B}$ and $\Delta \in \{OR, AND, SAND\}$. That is to say, a refinement corresponds to a tree of depth one. It follows that the set of refinements, denoted R, is a subset of the set of attack trees $\mathbb{T}_{SAND}$. In particular, the refinement of the root node of an attack tree is determined by the partial function $ref \colon \mathbb{T}_{SAND} \to R$, defined by

$$ref(b \triangleleft \Delta(t_1, \ldots, t_n)) = b \triangleleft \Delta(top(t_1), \ldots, top(t_n)).$$

This is a partial function, since the refinement of an attack tree that consists of a single node is not defined. This function can be generalized to non-root nodes, allowing us to determine the set of all refinements that occur in an attack tree. Therefore, we define the function $refs \colon \mathbb{T}_{SAND} \to \mathcal{P}(R)$, as follows:

$$refs(t) = \{ref(t') \mid t' \in t \wedge \neg \exists b \in \mathbb{B} \colon t' = b\}.$$

A *refinement specification* specifies which refinements should be satisfied by an attack tree. A refinement specification is simply defined as a set of refinements. Given an attack tree $t \in \mathbb{T}_{\mathsf{SAND}}$ and a refinement specification $\rho \subseteq R$, we use $t \vdash \rho$ to denote that t *satisfies* ρ. We define satisfaction by $t \vdash \rho \iff \mathit{refs}(t) \subseteq \rho$. That is, a tree satisfies a refinement specification, if all refined actions in the tree also occur as refined actions in the specification.

Attack Tree Generation Problem. Given an attack tree semantics and a refinement specification, the challenge is to design or derive an attack tree with this semantics that satisfies the refinement specification. We call this problem *the attack-tree generation problem*.

Definition 2 (The attack-tree generation problem). *Let S be an attack-tree semantics with semantic domain D. The* attack-tree generation problem *consists in, given a semantical element $d \in D$ and a refinement specification $\rho \subseteq R$, finding an attack tree $t \in \mathbb{T}_{SAND}$, such that $[t]_S = d$ and $t \vdash \rho$. Such a tree is called* correct *with respect to a semantics and refinement specification (d, ρ).*

Example 3. Given required semantics $\{\xrightarrow{w}\xrightarrow{ec}\xrightarrow{l}, \xrightarrow{b}\xrightarrow{l}, \xrightarrow{x}\xrightarrow{l}\}$ and refinement specification $\{a \lhd \mathsf{SAND}(c, l), c \lhd \mathsf{OR}(eu, b, x), eu \lhd \mathsf{SAND}(w, ec), c \lhd \mathsf{SAND}(p, q)\}$, a possible solution to the attack-tree generation problem is given in Fig. 1. Note that the last refinement does not occur in the tree.

Clearly, an instance of the attack-tree generation problem may not have a solution. If it has a solution, the solution may not be unique. Depending on the purpose of the tree, the application domain, or even the taste of the designer, one could have a preference for a certain type of tree, aiming at, e.g., trees with minimal width, balanced trees or trees with a minimum number of leaf nodes.

The remainder of this paper is devoted to addressing the attack-tree generation problem.

3   Generating Correct Attack Trees

In this section we will specialize the attack-tree generation problem by focusing only on OR and SAND nodes, and considering the semantic domain for attack trees to be the SP semantics [JKM+15]. Given this restriction, we develop an algorithm to generate correct attack trees using a greedy heuristic based on the *edge biclique* problem.

The motivation for omitting the AND operator is the following. One of the inputs to the attack-tree generation problem is the intended semantics of the tree. We assume that the intended semantics is given by a set of traces, where each trace is an ordered sequence of actions. Such a set of traces could, e.g., be generated by a model checker that aims to reach the goal of the attacker [LMO15]. As traces are totally ordered, we can use the SAND operator to represent a trace and the OR operator to represent the choice between the alternative traces. Hence, starting from a set of traces, there is no need for the AND operator. An example of a trace model based on labelled transition systems is given in Sect. 4.

Properties of Correct Attack Trees. Next we provide necessary and sufficient conditions for a tree to be correct. For the sake of simplicity, we focus on binary instances of the attack tree operators only. This simplifies the analysis and generalizes easily due to associativity of all operators.

Theorem 1. *Let $\mathcal{G}$ be a set of SP graphs with labels in $\mathbb{B}$, ρ a refinement specification, and t an attack tree of the form $b \triangleleft SAND(t_l, t_r)$ (resp. $b \triangleleft OR(t_l, t_r)$) where t_l and t_r are attack trees. The attack tree t is correct w.r.t. $(\mathcal{G}, \rho)$ if and only if there exist sets of SP graphs $\mathcal{G}_l$ and $\mathcal{G}_r$ such that all the following conditions are satisfied:*

1. *t_l is correct with respect to $(\mathcal{G}_l, \rho)$,*
2. *t_r is correct with respect to $(\mathcal{G}_r, \rho)$,*
3. *$\mathcal{G} = \mathcal{G}_l \cdot \mathcal{G}_r$ (resp. $\mathcal{G} = \mathcal{G}_l \cup \mathcal{G}_r$),*
4. *$b \triangleleft SAND(top(t_l), top(t_r)) \in \rho$ (resp. $b \triangleleft OR(top(t_l), top(t_r)) \in \rho$).*

Proof. ($\Rightarrow$) Let t be a correct tree w.r.t. $(\mathcal{G}, \rho)$ of the form $b \triangleleft SAND(t_l, t_r)$ (resp. $OR(t_l, t_r)$). Condition 1 holds by definition given that $t \vdash \rho$. Similarly we obtain that t_l and t_r must satisfy that $t_l \vdash \rho$ and $t_r \vdash \rho$, otherwise $t \nvdash \rho$. Condition 1 holds by definition of the SP semantics, where $[\![t]\!]_{SP} = [\![t_l]\!]_{SP} \cdot [\![t_r]\!]_{SP}$ if t is of the form $b \triangleleft SAND(t_l, t_r)$, $[\![t]\!]_{SP} = [\![t_l]\!]_{SP} \cup [\![t_r]\!]_{SP}$ otherwise. Therefore, t_l and t_r are correct w.r.t. $([\![t_l]\!]_{SP}, \rho)$ and $([\![t_r]\!]_{SP}, \rho)$, respectively.

($\Leftarrow$) Now, let us assume that the four conditions above are satisfied. On the one hand, because t_l and t_r are correct w.r.t. $(\mathcal{G}_l, \rho)$ and $(\mathcal{G}_r, \rho)$, respectively, it follows that $\mathcal{G}_l = [\![t_l]\!]_{SP}$ and $\mathcal{G}_r = [\![t_r]\!]_{SP}$. Therefore, an attack tree t of the form $b \triangleleft SAND(t_l, t_r)$ (resp. $b \triangleleft OR(t_l, t_r)$) satisfies that $[\![t]\!]_{SP} = \mathcal{G}_l \cdot \mathcal{G}_r = \mathcal{G}$ (resp. $[\![t]\!]_{SP} = \mathcal{G}_l \cup \mathcal{G}_r = \mathcal{G}$). On the other hand, because $b \triangleleft SAND(top(t_1), top(t_2)) \in \rho$ (resp. $b \triangleleft OR(top(t_1), top(t_2)) \in \rho$) and t_1 and t_2 both satisfy ρ, we obtain that t satisfies ρ as well. This gives that t is correct w.r.t. $(\mathcal{G}, \rho)$. $\qquad\square$

According to Theorem 1, a disjunctive refinement requires finding two subsets $\mathcal{G}_l$ and $\mathcal{G}_r$ that cover $\mathcal{G}$, i.e. $\mathcal{G}_l \cup \mathcal{G}_r = \mathcal{G}$. This is a fairly trivial task as, for example, a partition of a set is also a covering. However, a sequential conjunctive refinement requires finding a sequential decomposition of $\mathcal{G}$ in two sets $\mathcal{G}_l$ and $\mathcal{G}_r$ such that $\mathcal{G}_l \cdot \mathcal{G}_r = \mathcal{G}$. Clearly, such a decomposition is not always possible. Therefore, we focus on the problem of finding two sets $\mathcal{G}_l$ and $\mathcal{G}_r$ such that $\mathcal{G}_l \cdot \mathcal{G}_r \subseteq \mathcal{G}$ and $|\mathcal{G}_l \cdot \mathcal{G}_r|$ is maximum, which we call the *set decomposition problem*.

In this article we tackle the set decomposition problem by reducing it to the *edge biclique problem* [Pee03], which benefits from well-known efficient algorithms [GG14] in the graph theory field. For the sake of comprehensibility, we next introduce in detail the edge biclique problem and how it can be approximated by a greedy heuristic. Afterwards we show our reduction.

The edge biclique problem consists in finding, given a bipartite graph G, a biclique in G with maximum number of edges. A graph G is *bipartite* if its set of vertices can be partitioned into subsets V_1 and V_2 such that every edge in G connects a vertex in V_1 with a vertex in V_2. And G is said to be a *biclique* if every $(u, v) \in V_1 \times V_2$ is an edge in G. We usually write $G = (V_1 \cup V_2, E)$ to denote that G is bipartite with partite sets V_1 and V_2.

Theorem 2. *The set decomposition problem is polynomial-time reducible to the edge biclique problem, and vice-versa.*

Proof. ($\Rightarrow$) Let $\mathcal{G}$ be a non-empty set of SP graphs. Given an SP graph $\alpha = \xrightarrow{b_1}$ $\dots \xrightarrow{b_n}$, let α_i^l and α_i^r denote the SP graphs $\xrightarrow{b_1} \dots \xrightarrow{b_i}$ and $\xrightarrow{b_{i+1}} \dots \xrightarrow{b_n}$, respectively. Let $G = (V, E)$ be a simple graph with set of vertices $V = \{\alpha_i^l | \alpha \in \mathcal{G} \wedge i < |\alpha|\} \cup \{\alpha_i^r | \alpha \in \mathcal{G} \wedge i < |\alpha|\}$ and set of edges $E = \{(\alpha_i^l, \beta_j^r) | \alpha_i^l \cdot \beta_j^r \in \mathcal{G}\}$. Now, let $G' = (U' \cup V', E')$ be a biclique in G. By construction of G we obtain the following two results. First, for every $(u, v) \in U' \times V'$ it holds that $u \cdot v \in \mathcal{G}$. Hence $U' \cdot V' \subseteq \mathcal{G}$. Second, for every pair of sets $\mathcal{G}_l$ and $\mathcal{G}_r$ such that $\mathcal{G}_l \cdot \mathcal{G}_r \subseteq \mathcal{G}$ it holds that $\mathcal{G}_l \subseteq U$ and $\mathcal{G}_r \subseteq V$. Hence the subgraph of G induced by the vertices $\mathcal{G}_l \cup \mathcal{G}_r$ is a biclique. Therefore, $G' = (U' \cup V', E')$ is a maximum biclique if and only if (U', V') is an optimal solution to the set decomposition problem.

($\Leftarrow$) Let $G = (U \cup V, E)$ be a bipartite graph and $\mathcal{G} = \{u \cdot v | u \in U \wedge v \in V \wedge (u, v) \in E\}$. Let $\mathcal{G}_l$ and $\mathcal{G}_r$ be a decomposition (not necessarily optimal) of $\mathcal{G}$, i.e. $\mathcal{G}_l \cup \mathcal{G}_r \subseteq \mathcal{G}$. As before, we obtain by construction the following two results. First, because $\mathcal{G}_l \subseteq U$ and $\mathcal{G}_r \subseteq V$, it follows that the subgraph in G induced by $\mathcal{G}_l \cup \mathcal{G}_r$ is a biclique. Second, for every biclique $G' = (U' \cup V', E')$ in G it holds that $U' \cdot V' \subseteq \mathcal{G}$. Therefore, $\mathcal{G}_l$ and $\mathcal{G}_r$ form an optimal decomposition of $\mathcal{G}$ if and only if the subgraph in G induced by $\mathcal{G}_l \cup \mathcal{G}_r$ is a maximum biclique. $\square$

From Theorem 2 we extract two conclusions. First, the set decomposition problem is NP-complete, given that the edge biclique problem is NP-complete [Pee03]. Second, we can use well-known approximation algorithms for the edge biclique problem to find approximate solutions for the set decomposition problem. Due its simplicity, in this article we use the greedy heuristic proposed by Gillis and Glineur [GG14]. A pseudocode description of such a heuristic is given in Fig. 2.

Example 4. To illustrate the procedure of decomposing a set of SP graphs in two sets of SP graphs, let us consider the following set $\mathcal{G} = \{\xrightarrow{a}\xrightarrow{a}, \xrightarrow{b}\xrightarrow{a}\xrightarrow{a}, \xrightarrow{b}\xrightarrow{a}\xrightarrow{c}, \xrightarrow{a}, \xrightarrow{c}\}$. We first transform $\mathcal{G}$ into a graph G as indicated in Theorem 2. The resulting graph is depicted in Fig. 3. Note that, for the sake of simplicity, we have omitted the arrow ($\rightarrow$) representing single-edge SP graphs in the vertex labels in G. By running the BICLIQUE algorithm depicted in Fig. 2, we obtain a subgraph of G that is a biclique. The obtained complete bipartite graph (see Fig. 3) is then transformed into two sets of SP graphs by considering the vertex set partition. In the example, the two sets are $\mathcal{G}_l = \{\xrightarrow{a}, \xrightarrow{b}\xrightarrow{a}\}$ and $\mathcal{G}_r = \{\xrightarrow{a}, \xrightarrow{c}\}$. The pair of sets satisfies that $\mathcal{G}_l \times \mathcal{G}_r = \mathcal{G}$, because the biclique found by BICLIQUE is optimal. If the biclique is not optimal, then $\mathcal{G}_l \times \mathcal{G}_r \subsetneq \mathcal{G}$.

Binary Attack Trees. We use the DECOMPOSITION procedure on a set of SP graphs to generate correct attack trees, with the peculiarity that the resulting tree is binary, until, possibly, the last refinement (i.e., parents of the leaf nodes may be decomposed in more than 2 nodes). The algorithm is given in Fig. 4.

procedure BICLIQUE($G = (X \cup Y, E)$)
    Let Z be an empty set of vertices
    while G is *not* bipartite **do**
        Let u be any vertex in G with maximum degree that is not contained in Z
        Let $W = X$ if $u \notin X$, $W = Y$ otherwise
        for all $v \in W$ such that $(u, v) \notin E$ **do**
            Remove u from G and the corresponding edges from E
        Remove isolated vertices from G
        Add u to Z
    return G

Fig. 2. BICLIQUE is a greedy heuristic that approximates the edge biclique problem.

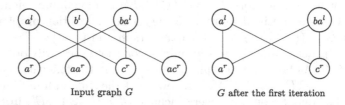

Input graph G G after the first iteration

Fig. 3. An example of the execution of BICLIQUE on graph G. The vertex with maximum degree chosen in this execution is a^l. The resulting graph is already a biclique.

The procedure GEN-BIN-TREE focuses on creating an attack tree t such that $[\![t]\!]_{SP} = \mathcal{G}$, where $\mathcal{G}$ is a set of SP graphs given as input. For example, if $\mathcal{G}$ contains a single SP graph $\xrightarrow{b_1} \cdots \cdots \xrightarrow{b_n}$, then it outputs the tree $b \triangleleft \mathsf{SAND}(b_1, \ldots, b_n)$, where $b \in \mathbb{B}$ satisfies that $b \triangleleft \mathsf{SAND}(b_1, \ldots, b_n) \in \rho$. Moreover, GEN-BIN-TREE guarantees that all refinements in the generated tree are in the refinement specification ρ, otherwise the algorithm aborts. Therefore, it follows that GEN-BIN-TREE either generates a correct tree or aborts.

It is worth remarking that GEN-BIN-TREE favours SAND refinements over OR refinements. The reason is that a SAND refinement requires solving the edge biclique problem. Thus, whenever a sequential decomposition of $\mathcal{G}$ is found, a SAND refinement is created.

Example 5. To illustrate the attack-tree generation approach, consider the SAND attack tree in Fig. 1, whose SP semantics is $\mathcal{G} = \{\xrightarrow{w}\xrightarrow{ec}\xrightarrow{l}, \xrightarrow{b}\xrightarrow{l}, \xrightarrow{x}\xrightarrow{l}\}$. For the sake of simplicity, let us also consider the existence of a special action $\epsilon \in \mathbb{B}$ and a refinement specification ρ defined as the minimum set satisfying that $\epsilon \triangleleft \mathsf{OR}(b_1, b_2) \in \rho$ and $\epsilon \triangleleft \mathsf{AND}(b_1, b_2) \in \rho$ for every $b_1, b_2 \in \mathbb{B}$. This is for the moment an oversimplification of the role of the refinement specification. We defer the task of providing a tree with meaningful refinements to the next section.

By using the BICLIQUE procedure we obtain that $\mathcal{G}$ can be decomposed by $\mathcal{G}_l = \{\xrightarrow{w}\xrightarrow{ec}, \xrightarrow{b}, \xrightarrow{x}\}$ and $\mathcal{G}_r = \{\xrightarrow{l}\}$. The application of the GEN-BIN-TREE algorithm on input $\mathcal{G}_l$ gives the tree displayed in Fig. 5. The same figure depicts the tree obtained on input $\mathcal{G}_r$. The sequential composition of the two trees is finally the output of GEN-BIN-TREE on input $\mathcal{G}$.

procedure GEN-BIN-TREE$((\mathcal{G}, \rho))$

   if $\mathcal{G} = \{\xrightarrow{b_1} \dots \xrightarrow{b_n}\}$ **then**   ▷ $\mathcal{G}$ contains a single SP graph
      Let $b \in \mathbb{B}$ such that $b \lhd \mathtt{SAND}(b_1, \dots, b_n) \in \rho$
      if b exists **then**
         return $b \lhd \mathtt{SAND}(b_1, \dots, b_n)$
   else if $\xrightarrow{b_1} \in \mathcal{G}$ for some $b_1 \in \mathbb{B}$ **then**   ▷ A single-edge SP graph exists in $\mathcal{G}$
      Let t_2 be the output of BICLIQUE$(\mathcal{G} - \{\xrightarrow{b_1}\}, \rho)$
      Let $b \in \mathbb{B}$ such that $b \lhd \mathtt{OR}(b_1, top(t_2)) \in \rho$
      if b exists **then**
         return $b \lhd \mathtt{OR}(\xrightarrow{b_1}, t_2)$
   else
      Transform $\mathcal{G}$ into a graph G as indicated in Theorem 2
      Find a maximum biclique, and translate the biclique into two sets $\mathcal{G}_l$ and $\mathcal{G}_r$
      if $\mathcal{G}_l \times \mathcal{G}_r = \mathcal{G}$ **then**
         Let t_1 be the output of BICLIQUE$(\mathcal{G}_l, \rho)$
         Let t_2 be the output of BICLIQUE$(\mathcal{G}_r, \rho)$
         Let $b \in \mathbb{B}$ such that $b \lhd \mathtt{SAND}(top(t_1), top(t_2)) \in \rho$
         if b exists **then**
            return $b \lhd \mathtt{SAND}(t_1, t_2)$

      else
         Let t_1 be the output of BICLIQUE$(\mathcal{G}_l \times \mathcal{G}_r, \rho)$
         Let t_2 be the output of BICLIQUE$(\mathcal{G} - \mathcal{G}_l \times \mathcal{G}_r, \rho)$
         Let $b \subset \mathbb{B}$ such that $b \lhd \mathtt{OR}(top(t_1), top(t_2)) \subset \rho$
         if b exists **then**
            return $b \lhd \mathtt{OR}(t_1, t_2)$
   return fail

Fig. 1. GEN-BIN-TREE generates correct and binary attack trees.

We observe that Algorithm GEN-BIN-TREE generates trees that, although correct, use a rather artificial binary branching structure. We thus use semantics-preserving transformation rules to optimize the structure of the tree. A semantics-preserving transformation rule is a total function $r\colon \mathbb{T}_{\mathtt{SAND}} \to \mathbb{T}_{\mathtt{SAND}}$ such that $\forall t \in \mathbb{T}_{\mathtt{SAND}}\colon [\![t]\!]_{S\!P} = [\![r(t)]\!]_{S\!P}$. In our approach we use the following rule: for every $\Delta \in \{\mathtt{OR}, \mathtt{SAND}\}$ and every $t = b \lhd \Delta(t_1, \dots, t_k)$,

$$r(t) = \begin{cases} b \lhd \Delta(t_1^1, \dots, t_{k(1)}^1, \dots, t_1^k, \dots, t_{k(k)}^k) & \text{If } t_i = b_i \lhd \Delta(t_1^i, \dots, t_{k(i)}^i), \forall i \in \{1, \dots, k\} \\ t & \text{otherwise.} \end{cases}$$

This simply amounts to aggregating nodes whenever allowed by associativity of the operator. Figure 5 shows the result of the application of this rule to the binary tree obtained by GEN-BIN-TREE algorithm. Note that the semantics-preserving transformation rule does not take into account the refinement specification ρ. Thus, if ρ is an arbitrary set of refinements and it is not closed under the SP-semantics equivalence relation, the optimized tree may not be correct, while being semantically-equivalent to the original tree.

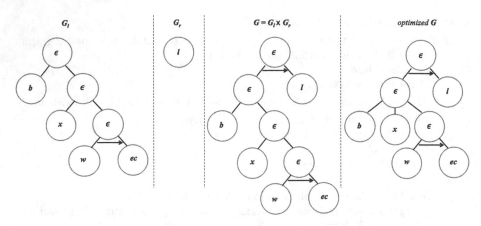

Fig. 5. The attack-tree generation process for the SP-semantics given in Example 2.

4   Specifying a System and Refinement Relation

The attack-tree generation problem is based on two inputs: an intended semantics and a refinement specification. In this section we show how both can be obtained from an LTS-based system model. Finally, we illustrate our methodology through a simple example.

System Specification. Labelled transition systems are used to describe the behaviour of a system by defining the transitions that bring a system from one state into another. Formally, a *Labelled Transition System* (LTS) is a quadruple $(\mathcal{S}, \Sigma, \rightarrow, s_0)$, where $\mathcal{S}$ is a set of *states*; Σ is a set of *labels*; $\rightarrow \colon \mathcal{S} \times \Sigma \times \mathcal{S}$ is a *transition relation*; $s_0 \in \mathcal{S}$ is the *initial state*.

We define a state as a set of predicates. A predicate defines a mutable property of the system, such as $knows(Alice, psw)$, which means that *Alice* knows password psw. States are denoted by $[p_1, \ldots, p_n]$, where $p_1, \ldots, p_n$ are the predicates that determine the state. If s is a state, then by $s[p_1, \ldots, p_n]$ we mean the state s augmented with predicates $p_1, \ldots, p_n$. If a predicate is preceded by a $\neg$ symbol it means that the predicate is removed from the state. For instance, if $s_0 = [p_1, p_2]$, then $s_0[p_3, \neg p_1] = [p_2, p_3]$.

The states will be used to label the nodes of the attack tree that will be generated, so we will equate the set of states and the set of actions in the attack tree, $\mathbb{B} = \mathcal{S}$.

The transition relation is defined through *transition rules*. Figure 6 shows some example transition rules. Every transition rule contains a condition (above the horizontal line) and a conclusion (below the line). The name of a transition rule is given left of the line. The condition consists of a number of predicates that must be present in the current state to enable the transition rule. The conclusion describes the state change when the transition occurs. The old state is described left of the transition arrow and the new state right of the arrow. The arrow is

$$if\ b \sqsubseteq b_1 \wedge \ldots \wedge b \sqsubseteq b_n\ then\ b \vartriangleleft \mathtt{OR}(b_1 \cdots b_n) \in \rho_\sqsubseteq,\ and$$
$$if\ b \sqsubseteq b_n\ then\ b \vartriangleleft \mathtt{SAND}(b_1 \cdots b_n) \in \rho_\sqsubseteq.$$

$$[startTerm]\ \frac{}{s \xrightarrow{\ startTerm(a,t)\ } s[located(a,t)]}$$

$$[loggingInRem]\ \frac{located(a,m), connected(m,m_1), stores(m_1,r), knows(a,r)}{s \xrightarrow{\ loggingInRem(a,m,m_1,r)\ } s[located(a,m_1)]}$$

$$[loggingOut]\ \frac{located(a,m),}{s \xrightarrow{\ loggingOut(a,m)\ } s[\neg located(a,m)]}$$

$$[exploiting]\ \frac{located(a,m), connected(m,m_1),}{s \xrightarrow{\ exploiting(a,m,m_1,r)\ } s[stores(m_1,r), knows(a,r)]}$$

$$[bruteforcingPsw]\ \frac{located(a,m), connected(m,m_1) stores(m_1,r)}{s \xrightarrow{\ bruteforcingPsw(a,m,m_1,r)\ } s[knows(a,r)]}$$

$$[eavesdropping]\ \frac{located(a,m), located(a_1,m), connected(m,m_1), knows(a,r), stores(m_1,r)}{s \xrightarrow{\ eavesdropping(a,a_1,m,m_1,r)\ } s[knows(a_1,r)]}$$

Fig. 6. Transition rules for the example $(a, a_1 \in A, m, m_1 \in M, t \in T$ and $r \in R)$.

labeled with the event that describes the transition. The predicates may contain variables, which are implicitly universally quantified.

Refinement Specification. The second input to our algorithms is the refinement relation. We first define a partial order $\sqsubseteq$ on $\mathbb{B}$, which we call an *abstraction relation*. Given that states are sets of predicates, we can define this abstraction relation as set inclusion, $s \sqsubseteq s' \iff s \subseteq s'$. If $s \sqsubseteq s'$, we say that s is *more abstract* than s'. From this abstraction relation we can derive a refinement specification, as follows.

Definition 3 (Abstraction-based refinement specification). *Let $\mathbb{B}$ be a set of actions with abstraction relation $\sqsubseteq$. The abstraction-based refinement relation is the smallest refinement relation $\rho_\sqsubseteq$ that satisfies (for $\forall b, b_1, \ldots, b_n \in \mathbb{B}$):*

$$if\ b \sqsubseteq b_1 \wedge \ldots \wedge b \sqsubseteq b_n\ then\ b \vartriangleleft OR(b_1 \cdots b_n) \in \rho_\sqsubseteq,\ and$$
$$if\ b \sqsubseteq b_n\ then\ b \vartriangleleft SAND(b_1 \cdots b_n) \in \rho_\sqsubseteq.$$

This definition expresses that the attacker's goal of an OR node must be more abstract than the attacker's goals of its children, and that the attacker's goal of a SAND node must be more abstract than the goal of its right-most child.

Note that for more elaborated definitions of the system state, the abstraction relation can be modified accordingly. We could, for instance, consider a state consisting of two sets of predicates describing desired and undesired properties.

Network Security Example. We consider a set of machines M on a simple network and a set of human actors A that can use these machines. We also consider a set of credential records R, and a set of user terminals $T \subseteq M$.

Further, we consider the following set of predicates:

- *located*: $A \times M$ determines to which machines actors are connected;
- *connected*: $M \times M$ defines directly connected machines;
- *stores*: $M \times R$ identifies credentials accepted by a machine.
- *knows*: $A \times R$ determines which credentials are known to actors.

Figure 6 presents a set of transition rules for this system. The first three rules define the behaviour of legitimate users, and the other three rules introduce actions for attackers.

As an example system we consider the set M consisting of just two machines, client C and server S, and the set of terminals T to contain only C. We consider two actors *Alice* and *Mallory*, and two credentials *psw* and psw_1.

Initial state:
$s_0 = [located(Mallory, C), connected(C, S), stores(S, psw), knows(Alice, psw)]$.

Final state: Any state s_f that contains $located(Mallory, S)$.

Traces: We consider the following three traces that lead to a successful attack.
Trace T^1:

$$s_0 \xrightarrow{exploiting(Mallory,C,S,psw_1)} s_0[stores(S, psw_1), knows(Mallory, psw_1)]$$

$$\xrightarrow{loggingInRem(Mallory,C,S,psw_1)} s_0[stores(S, psw_1), knows(Mallory, psw_1),$$
$$located(Mallory, S)]$$

Trace T^2:

$$s_0 \xrightarrow{bruteforcingPsw(Mallory,C,S,psw)} s_0[knows(Mallory, psw)]$$

$$\xrightarrow{loggingInRem(Mallory,C,S,psw)} s_0[knows(Mallory, psw), located(Mallory, S)]$$

Trace T^3:

$$s_0 \xrightarrow{startTerm(Alice,C)} s_0[located(Alice, C)]$$

$$\xrightarrow{eavesdropping(Alice,Mallory,C,S,psw)} s_0[located(Alice, C), knows(Mallory, psw)]$$

$$\xrightarrow{loggingInRem(Mallory,C,S,psw)} s_0[located(Alice, C), knows(Mallory, psw),$$
$$located(Mallory, S)]$$

Intuitively, the tree for *Mallory* accessing the server S would be as presented in Fig. 1: *Mallory* can attempt to eavesdrop on *Alice* to learn *psw* or to bruteforce *psw*; or he can exploit S to create a new credential psw_1. Next we show the tree obtained by using our approach for automated attack-tree generation.

- The path in T^1 is characterised by $b_1^1 b_2^1$, where
  $b_1^1 = (\varnothing, \{stores(S, psw_1), knows(Mallory, psw_1)\}$ and $b_2^1 = (\{\varnothing, \{located (Mallory, S)\}$.
- The path in T^2 is characterised by $b_1^2 b_2^2$, where $b_1^2 = (\varnothing, \{knows(Mallory, psw)\}, b_2^2 = (\varnothing, \{located(Mallory, S)\})$.
- The path in T^3 is characterised by $b_1^3 b_2^3 b_3^3$, where $b_1^3 = (\varnothing, \{located(Alice, C)\})$, $b_2^3 = (\varnothing, \{knows(Mallory, psw)\})$, and $b_3^3 = (\varnothing, \{located(Mallory, S)\})$.

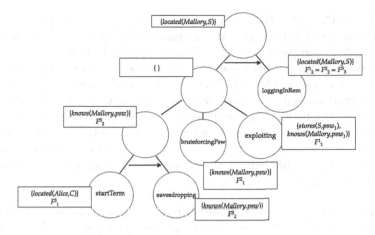

Fig. 7. Generated attack tree for the network example. (Color figure online)

Based on these runs, our approach generates the tree presented in Fig. 7. In this figure, the node labels identified by our approach are in boxes. Furthermore, note that we have also labelled leaf nodes in a more meaningful way (labels in the red circles) by using the corresponding actions (labels in the LTS) of the system transitions. At the same time, most of the labels for the intermediate nodes in the generated tree are also informative, as they specify only the facts relevant for achieving the attack's success in a particular subtree.

Note that one intermediate node has a label that represents an empty set of facts, as there are no common facts for its children. This node has to be interpreted by the analyst as a combination of its children nodes. Yet, our approach can be extended to be able to suggest meaningful labels also for such nodes. This can be realized, e.g., through supporting first-order logic facts with quantifiers, such as $\{\exists r \in R : knows(Mallory, r), stores(S, r)\}$.

It is worth remarking that the generated tree is identical in structure to the human-designed tree (Fig. 1). However, this is not guaranteed for other scenarios.

5 Conclusions

In this paper we have introduced the attack-tree generation problem as a task of constructing a correct attack tree that both has some expected meaning and respects a pre-defined refinement relation. This problem definition supports a more uniform treatment of the issues arising in both manual creation of attack trees and automatic generation from system models. Furthermore, we have developed a solution for this problem that utilizes an abstraction-based refinement specification derived from a system model and a set of traces representing successful attack scenarios in the model to generate a correct attack tree.

The trees we generate are refinement-aware, and thus provide more insight to the analyst than attack trees generated by previously proposed approaches, such as [IPHK15, Gad15, HKT13, VNN14]. Furthermore, our approach derives the refinement relation from the system model itself, and so it reduces the load on the analyst in comparison to the ATSyRA approach [PAV15].

The novelty of our approach consists also in the labelling technique for intermediate and leaf nodes. Our labelling is based on the facts about the system state that the attacker wants to achieve or avoid in order to realize the attack. Our running example of the network security case has shown that the proposed generation and labelling technique is practical and yields meaningful attack trees.

To continue this work, we plan to integrate a model checker for obtaining system traces, and to implement the generation algorithm in the open-source attack tree software ADTool [GJK+16].

Acknowledgements. The research leading to these results has received funding from the European Union Seventh Framework Programme under grant agreement number 318003 (TREsPASS) and from the Fonds National de la Recherche Luxembourg under grant C13/IS/5809105 (ADT2P).

References

[DH04]   Dawkins, J., Hale, J.: A systematic approach to multi-stage network attack analysis. In: Proceedings of the Information Assurance Workshop. IEEE (2004)

[FFG+16] Fraile, M., Ford, M., Gadyatskaya, O., Kumar, R., Stoelinga, M., Trujillo-Rasua, R.: Using attack-defense trees to analyze threats and countermeasures in an ATM: a case study. In: Horkoff, J., Jeusfeld, M.A., Persson, A. (eds.) PoEM 2016. LNBIP, vol. 267, pp. 326–334. Springer, Cham (2016). doi:10.1007/978-3-319-48393-1_24

[Gad15]   Gadyatskaya, O.: How to generate security cameras: towards defence generation for socio-technical systems. In: Mauw, S., Kordy, B., Jajodia, S. (eds.) GraMSec 2015. LNCS, vol. 9390, pp. 50–65. Springer, Cham (2016). doi:10.1007/978-3-319-29968-6_4

[GG14]   Gillis, N., Glineur, F.: A continuous characterization of the maximum-edge biclique problem. J. Global Optim. **58**(3), 439–464 (2014)

[GJK+16] Gadyatskaya, O., Jhawar, R., Kordy, P., Lounis, K., Mauw, S., Trujillo-Rasua, R.: Attack trees for practical security assessment: ranking of attack scenarios with ADTool 2.0. In: Agha, G., Van Houdt, B. (eds.) QEST 2016. LNCS, vol. 9826, pp. 159–162. Springer, Cham (2016). doi:10.1007/978-3-319-43425-4_10

[GLPS14] Ghani, H., Luna Garcia, J., Petkov, I., Suri, N.: User-centric security assessment of software configurations: a case study. In: Jürjens, J., Piessens, F., Bielova, N. (eds.) ESSoS 2014. LNCS, vol. 8364, pp. 196–212. Springer, Cham (2014). doi:10.1007/978-3-319-04897-0_13

[HKT13]   Hong, J.B., Kim, D.S., Takaoka, T.: Scalable attack representation model using logic reduction techniques. In: Proceedings of the TrustCom. IEEE (2013)

[IPHK15] Ivanova, M.G., Probst, C.W., Hansen, R.R., Kammüller, F.: Transforming graphical system models to graphical attack models. In: Mauw, S., Kordy, B., Jajodia, S. (eds.) GraMSec 2015. LNCS, vol. 9390, pp. 82–96. Springer, Cham (2016). doi:10.1007/978-3-319-29968-6_6

[JKM+15] Jhawar, R., Kordy, B., Mauw, S., Radomirović, S., Trujillo-Rasua, R.: Attack trees with sequential conjunction. In: Federrath, H., Gollmann, D. (eds.) SEC 2015. IAICT, vol. 455, pp. 339–353. Springer, Cham (2015). doi:10.1007/978-3-319-18467-8_23

[KMRS14] Kordy, B., Mauw, S., Radomirovic, S., Schweitzer, P.: Attack-defense trees. Oxford Univ. Press J. Logic Comput. **24**(1), 55–87 (2014)

[LMO15] Lenzini, G., Mauw, S., Ouchani, S.: Security analysis of socio-technical physical systems. Elsevier Comput. Electr. Eng. **47**, 258–274 (2015)

[MO05] Mauw, S., Oostdijk, M.: Foundations of attack trees. In: Won, D.H., Kim, S. (eds.) ICISC 2005. LNCS, vol. 3935, pp. 186–198. Springer, Heidelberg (2006). doi:10.1007/11734727_17

[PAV14] Pinchinat, S., Acher, M., Vojtisek, D.: Towards synthesis of attack trees for supporting computer-aided risk analysis. In: Canal, C., Idani, A. (eds.) SEFM 2014. LNCS, vol. 8938, pp. 363–375. Springer, Cham (2015). doi:10.1007/978-3-319-15201-1_24

[PAV15] Pinchinat, S., Acher, M., Vojtisek, D.: ATSyRa: an integrated environment for synthesizing attack trees. In: Mauw, S., Kordy, B., Jajodia, S. (eds.) GraMSec 2015. LNCS, vol. 9390, pp. 97–101. Springer, Cham (2016). doi:10.1007/978-3-319-29968-6_7

[Pee03] Peeters, R.: The maximum edge biclique problem is NP-complete. Discrete Appl. Math. **131**(3), 651–654 (2003)

[RA00] Ritchey, R.W., Ammann, P.: Using model checking to analyze network vulnerabilities. In: Proceedings of the S&P Symposium, pp. 156–165. IEEE (2000)

[RKT12] Roy, A., Kim, D.S., Trivedi, K.: Attack countermeasure trees (ACT): towards unifying the constructs of attack and defense trees. Secur. Commun. Netw. **5**(8), 929–943 (2012)

[Sch99] Schneier, B.: Attack trees: modeling security threats. Dr. Dobb's J. Softw. Tools **24**(12), 21–29 (1999)

[SHJ+02] Sheyner, O., Haines, J., Jha, S., Lippmann, R., Wing, J.M.: Automated generation and analysis of attack graphs. In: Proceedings of the S&P Symposium, pp. 273–284. IEEE (2002)

[Sho14] Shostack, A.: Threat Modeling: Designing for Security. Wiley, Hoboken (2014)

[VNN14] Vigo, R., Nielsen, F., Nielson, H.R.: Automated generation of attack trees. In: Proceedings of the CSF, pp. 337–350. IEEE (2014)

Exploit Prevention, Quo Vadis?

László Erdődi(✉) and Audun Jøsang

University of Oslo, Oslo, Norway
{laszloe,josang}@ifi.uio.no

Abstract. Exploits are advanced threats that take advantage of vulnerabilities in IT infrastructures. The technological background of the exploits has been changed during the years. Several significant protections have been introduced (e.g. Data Execution Prevention, Enhanced Mitigation Experience Toolkit, etc.), but attackers have always found effective ways to bypass any protection. This study gives a summary on the main software vulnerability exploitation methods including protections. Furthermore the study analyzes the capabilities and the predicted future of software exploitation in the light of the new protection technologies.

Keywords: Exploits · Prevention · Vulnerability · Control-flow · Protection

1 Introduction

According to a common definition, an exploit is a piece of software, a chunk of data, or a sequence of commands that takes advantage of a bug or vulnerability in order to cause unintended or unanticipated behavior to occur in computer software [35]. From the vulnerability point of view two major categories can be distinguished: the configuration error based and the software error based exploits. The object of this paper is to analyze the case when the software code contains vulnerability both from the attack and the protection point of view. Within this the emphasis is laid on the lower level type of vulnerabilities where the exploitation is carried out directly in the virtual memory.

Exploits are usually categorized from different aspects such as the capability (e.g. remote code execution, DOS), the way of execution (local, remote) or the platform it can be applied for (Windows, Linux, Ios, etc.). The exploit database [25] is a website where users can submit ready to use exploits. Even if this site obviously does not contain all the existing exploits it is nevertheless interesting to observe the evolution in the number of the available exploits throughout the years. The number of new exploits was on the top around December 2009. After this a significant decrease can be observed. The reason for the decline can be both the use of new protections such as the Data Execution Prevention (DEP) [18] or the Address Space Layout Randomization (ASLR) [17] and other new possibilities such as the dark web that appeared for exploit writers. An additional

© Springer International Publishing AG 2017
G. Livraga and C. Mitchell (Eds.): STM 2017, LNCS 10547, pp. 180–190, 2017.
DOI: 10.1007/978-3-319-68063-7_12

exploit database is the Metasploit framework [32] which makes exploits available in a unified form providing an easy–to–use framework for the exploits.

The Common Vulnerabilities and Exposures database [6] is an alternative source of information about available exploits. It is important to consider the dark web communities which offer exploits for virtual currencies. An exploit is usually connected to one particular vulnerability on a particular software, but there are some exceptions. Several exploitation and attacking techniques exist and considering the protection the main focus is to stop the exploitation without significant resource usage overhead. Hardware based techniques as protection are usually more preferable since they hardly slow down the normal execution speed. Section 2 focuses on the different exploitation and protection techniques, while in Sect. 3 the current situation and future predictions are analyzed. In Sect. 4 the latest potential exploitation techniques are analyzed.

2   Exploitation and Protection Techniques

2.1   Early Vulnerability Exploitations

In the early years of exploitations the attacker did not have to focus on bypassing any protection that was provided either by the compiler or the operating system. In the virtual memory everything was allocated and applied for the sake of the fast and efficient code execution. The program code is loaded into the virtual memory as well as the shared libraries with the operating system API. Each thread has its own stack segment where the methods data are placed by stack frames. The whole process has some common heaps, where the dynamically allocated objects are stored. The objects have virtual method tables where the actual addresses of the virtual methods are placed. The heap is organized as series of linked list chunks because of the effective and fast memory allocation and free in runtime. Figure 1, shows the arrangement of the virtual memory.

In the early stages the security of the software is based only on the code security. Unfortunately with a single coding error the attacker can simply misuse the software to execute malicious code. This is possible with several well-known techniques such as the stack overflow [16], the heap overflow [14], the format string vulnerability [24] or the use–after–free bug [8], etc. In the case of stack overflow [16] a local variable (e.g. a string or an array) is overwritten in the stack frame. As the stack frame contains the method return pointer the attacker can redirect the execution to an arbitrary place by providing a new return pointer. By placing the attack payload in the corrupted local variable on the stack the attacker redirects the execution to the stack itself and the payload is executed there. In case of heap overflow [14] the overwritten variable is in the heap. By overrunning the current heap chunk the attacker is able to modify the next heap chunk header data such as the addresses pointing to the next and previous chunk. When the attacker-modified chunk is freed the modified header pointers are used for merging the current chunk with other chunks. In that process the header pointers are used for writing data, so the attacker can write an arbitrary data to an arbitrary place. That is how the control flow is modified to execute

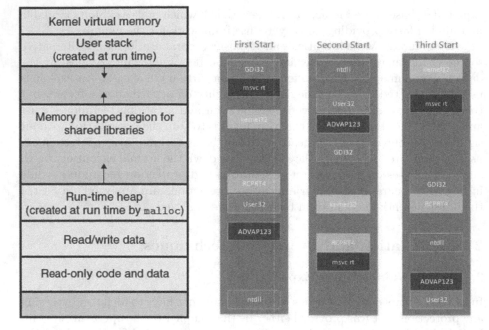

Fig. 1. Virtual address space layout

Fig. 2. Address Space Layout Randomization [17]

the malicious code. In case of format string vulnerability [24] the attacker can write an almost arbitrary data to an arbitrary place by providing special invalid string formatting parameters. By overwriting a stack method return pointer or modifying a virtual address table pointer the execution is redirected to the attacker controlled place where the malicious payload is executed. The use–after–free exploitation [8] is based on the virtual method table modification. If an object is used after being freed then the attacker can allocate a fake object to the same place where the original object was. The objects contain a pointer to its own virtual address table. In the case of the fake object that value is pointing to an attacker-created virtual address table with pointers to the malicious code (Fig. 2).

2.2   Early Defenses

The early protections focused on protecting the critical data from the right program-flow point of view. Stack cookie [34] is an example technique to protect the method return address from being overwritten. Since the stack cookie is placed between the method local variables and the return pointer, any modification outside the local variables results in the change of the stack cookie. This modification signs the stack frame corruption for the operating system. Although this protection is quite good to filter the stack frame corruption, it

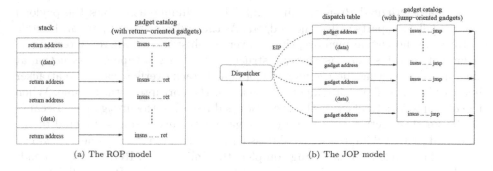

(a) The ROP model

(b) The JOP model

Fig. 3. Return Oriented and Jump Oriented Programming [17]

comes with a significant performance penalty. The heap chunk header modification is prevented by the secure unlink process [10] that validates the chunk header pointers before it is merged with another chunk. Another protection is the secure structured exception handling [19] which validates the exception handler pointer before it is executed. Several robust protections appeared in the middle of the 2000s. These protections such as the Data Execution Prevention (DEP) [18] and the Address Space Layout Randomization (ASLR) [17] do not aim to prevent only one typical exploitation, but the aim was to make the exploitation more difficult in general. Data execution prevention enforces memory page rights for the different types of pages. Reading the page data, writing the page data or executing the page data are all different types of operations. DEP ensures that a memory page cannot be written and executed at the same time. Using this protection several previously mentioned exploitation methods are disabled since the payload can be written to a writable memory place but it cannot be executed. Address Space Layout Randomization [17] is about to prevent malicious code reuse. If the place of the virtual memory pages are randomized every time when the program is launched (Fig. 3) then the attacker cannot rely on the known memory addresses. In the early protection stage of the ASLR the randomization entropy was insufficient to protect the software against address guessing.

2.3   Advanced Exploitations

After Data Execution Prevention [18] had been widely implemented, exploit writers had to turn to new techniques. Since the attacker could no longer place the payload to execute it because of the DEP, the main idea became to execute the already existing code parts that have the right to be executed. The first technique was the return to libc [28] type of exploitations where the corrupted method is redirected to an operating system API method such as the WinExec or Execve methods. In this case the attacker only provides the method parameters (e.g. the name of the software that has to be executed). However this technique is only capable to execute only one method, but choosing the right method with right parameters it can be sufficient. A huge break-through was the invention of the Return Oriented Programming [26]. This technique assembles the payload from small code parts called the gadgets. As the gadgets are the part of the code libraries in the virtual memory, this is a very sophisticated code reuse technique. A gadget contains some assembly instructions with a `ret` type of instruction at the end. Considering the previously mentioned stack overflow case, the attacker has to place the series of gadget addresses on the corrupted stack frame. When the corrupted method exits, the execution is directed to the first gadget. Because of the `ret` instruction at the end of the gadget the execution is directed to the next gadget by taking the next address on the corrupted stackframe by the `ret` instruction. Since ROP is Turing complete the limitation of ROP highly depends on the gadget catalog provided by the virtual address space. Practically there is no limitation, the attacker can always have enough gadgets to turn off the DEP and continue the payload execution in the traditional way. A generalization of ROP is the Jump Oriented Programming (JOP) [3]. Similarly to ROP, JOP executes the payload step by step by using small code parts called functional gadgets. Each functional gadget has an indirect jump instruction at the end to redirect the instruction pointer to a special code part called the dispatcher gadget. The dispatcher gadget maintains a table pointer to execute the functional gadgets after each other in the right order. Instead of building upon the stack and the `ret` instruction, JOP realizes its own stack like structure the dispatcher table and the concatenation of the gadgets are ensured by the dispatcher gadget and not the `ret` like instructions.

Several other forms of scattered code reuse technique exist such as the Sigreturn Oriented Programming (SROP) [4] or the Call Proceeded Return Oriented Programming (CPROP) [5]. In the first case the exploitation is based on the kernel context switching which saves the current execution context in a frame on the stack. Unlike ROP, SROP exploits are usually portable across different binaries and can bypass ASLR in some cases. Call Proceeded Return Oriented Programming uses whole functions as a gadget in order to bypass the control flow protections. Bypassing ASLR in code reuse attacks is always a challenge. Special techniques such as the Blind Return Oriented Programming (BROP) [2] and Just in Time Return Oriented Programming [7] can bypass ASLR by guessing the randomization offset or with just in time payload customization. In some cases ASLR can be bypassed by simple guessing the randomization offset [27] or by taking advantage on another vulnerability that expose the randomization offset [22].

2.4   Enhanced Protections

Due to the continuously improving exploitation techniques, protection methods have to keep up with the new challenges. Increasing the entropy of the Address Space Layout Randomization [13] decreases the chance to successfully bruteforce the randomization offsets. Forcing ASLR is another technique to achieve better protection. Microsoft aimed to prevent the exploitation with the Enhanced Mitigation Experienced Toolkit (EMET) [20] that provides special protections such as the anti-ROP technique. In 2016 Microsoft admitted that EMET is not proper for preventing 0 day exploits and stopped the development of it. Microsoft has also introduced some new protections for the Edge browser [36] such as the separated heap for the html objects or the delayed free to prevent the exploitation of use-after-free bugs. Other software such as the Palo Alto exploit prevention [21] provides wide choice of different protections e.g. detection of heap spraying, detection of ROP, etc. Several other ideas exist to maintain and verify the correct control flow of a software [29]. One of the main questions of the protection is the performance. It is unfavorable if the exploit detection slows down the execution speed significantly. Hardware based protection ideas such as the Intel's Control Flow Enforcement (CFE) [12] are very promising technologies. According to CFE the protection is provided by two components: the shadow stack and the indirect jump verifier. CFE maintains two separate stacks: the data stack for the normal operation, but also a shadow stack which is not accessible for the code. Whenever a method returns both the data stack and the return stack pointers are popped and compared as a control. This technique should prevent the execution of small gadgets with not intended `ret` instructions. The indirect jump verifier is a method which controls the indirect jumps with a `nop-like` special instruction. Whenever an indirect jump is executed this special `nop-like` instruction must follow it. This measure should stop the unintended indirect jumps through the code libraries.

3 Current Exploits

Although several protections exist, exploits still represent a real danger for IT systems. Nowadays attackers have to consider the DEP and the ASLR as a basic feature of the modern operating systems, so bypassing them is essential from the successful exploitation point of view. Some browser exploits turned into light in the late 2016 and the favorite exploitation technology was the Just in time Return Oriented Programming. At the end of 2016 a Firefox/Tor exploit (CVE-2016-9079) is revealed [31] which attacked Tor browser users. The exploit maps the Windows PE structure in runtime to find appropriate ROP gadgets. The ROP code turns off the DEP with the `kernel32.VirtualAlloc` method then the rest of the payload is executed in the conventional way. Another DEP and ASLR bypassing exploit is related to the chakra JavaScript [22]. This exploit uses two different vulnerabilities. CVE 2016-7200 is used for the ASLR bypass, the mshtml.dll randomization offset is obtained with that bug, while CVE 2016-7201 is used to execute a short ROP code to turn off the DEP. This case belongs to the Just in Time Return Oriented Programming category as well as well as the case of the Tor exploit. ROP based exploits are deployed against network devices too. A vulnerability (CVE 2017-3881) [15] in the Cisco Cluster Management Protocol (CMP) processing code in Cisco Software could allow an unauthenticated, remote attacker to execute code with elevated privileges. The exploit for this vulnerability uses ROP to bypass the DEP protection as well.

Considering other cases too, it is clear that the main technique of the current exploits is still the Return Oriented Programming. DEP and ASLR thought to be a very strong protection together, but current examples show that they can be bypassed routinely in several cases. That is the reason why the current direction of the protection strengthening is to enforce the right control-flow in order to disable ROP. For example, Intel's Control Flow Enforcement is a promising plan that should stop Return Oriented Programming without any speed decrease. The question is, if the software bug exploitation will be stopped or significantly decreased by making ROP totally impossible with some countermeasures or is it just a step of the exploitation-protection fight that makes exploitation techniques more sophisticated. Currently it is very difficult to predict what is going to happen after the protection against ROP is completely solved. There are several ongoing research projects on new exploitation methods such as for example the Loop Oriented Programming [1] or the Data Oriented Programming (DOP) [11] and also the Counterfeit Object-oriented Programming (COOP) [23]. The following chapter focuses on these types of exploitations these can be one of the next milestones of the modern software exploitation.

4   Bypassing the Control Flow Enforcement - The New Direction

Current protections and tendencies indicate that code reuse will be the main technology in the future too. Bypassing ASLR is possible with brute-forcing and through information leakage today, but more sophisticated ASLR bypass techniques [9, 33] are already presented. Considering a successful ASLR bypass, Loop Oriented Programming [1] looks like a possible option against control flow enforcement. The most important part of the LOP is the loop gadget. The loop gadget executes legitimate shared library methods after each other to carry out the malicious task. Similarly to JOP, the loop gadget is like a dispatcher. It concatenates the functional gadgets, so the payload is executed step-by-step. Contrary to ROP and JOP the LOP gadgets are not only small code parts. Each functional gadget is a legitimate method, so the shadow stack protection is useless against it, because exiting from a method does not violate the regular method exit rules. Since Control Flow Integrity also has the protection against indirect jumps, each functional gadget must contain the indirect jump marker nop like instruction at the very beginning of the gadget. This can decrease the gadget catalogue significantly, which is a challenge for exploit writers. Figure 4, shows the LOP execution process [1].

According to our analysis the following conditions have to be satisfied in order to carry out a successful LOP exploitation: 1. Bypassing ASLR in order to use accurate memory addresses; 2. Having an attacker controlled memory region that contains the gadget method addresses that have to be executed in the right order; 3. Having the appropriate loop gadget that implements the loop for the execution while reading the address table and directing the execution to the appropriate method; 4. Initializing the attack successfully by directing the execution to the loop gadget with the appropriate register values; 5. Having sufficient method catalog to turn off the DEP and continue the payload execution in the conventional way.

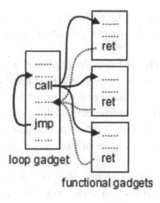

Fig. 4. Loop Oriented Programming

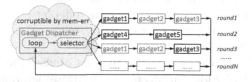

Fig. 5. Data Oriented Programming [11]

Since there are already existing options to bypass ASLR and there is no predictable solution to prevent ASLR bypass by information leakage, we consider that the first condition can be satisfied. Having of an attacker controlled method address table can be satisfied easily too since attackers can easily write data to the virtual memory e.g. with heap spraying [30]. According to some previous analyses [1], finding appropriate loop gadgets is also possible. Having a sufficient method catalog (condition 4) is a question as well as the successful initialization of the attack (condition 5). Since processors with hardware supported Control Flow Enforcement do not exist yet, there is nothing that can be stated related to the LOP gadget catalog. With Intel's proposed Control Flow Enforcement the libraries should be rewritten with the indirect jump protection instructions. So condition 5 will depend on the new CFE supported libraries. Condition 4 is significantly influenced by the type of the vulnerability. As the exploitation has to direct the instruction pointer to the loop gadget with the appropriate register settings, if the loop gadget exists and the attacker can set the method table index of the loop gadget, so can the initialization be successful. It is clear that conventional stack overflow cannot be used with CFE anymore with the return address modification, but if the vulnerable method contains an indirect call where the address is read from the corrupted stack then the exploitation can be successful. In the case of heap related vulnerabilities e.g. in use–after–free, the initialization can be successful if the attacker can control at least two registers: the one that contains the loop gadget method address and another one with the method table addresses.

Data Oriented Programming [11] seems to be another option to bypass Control Flow Enforcement. Similarly to JOP and LOP the code execution is controlled by one special code part, in this case this is the gadget dispatcher (Fig. 5). The gadget dispatcher has a loop which is controlled by the attacker. The loop contains different type of data oriented gadget invocations such as assignment, store, load and jump. As the attacker controls the local variables of the corrupted function he can set how many times the loop is executed and also the loop parameters in every step (which data oriented gadget should be invoked with which parameters). With the loop the appropriate data oriented gadgets are chained.

In case of COOP [23], virtual functions exist in the vulnerable application are repeatedly invoked on special C++ objects carefully arranged by the attacker. These special C++ objects are injected by the attacker and contain an attacker-chosen virtual pointer and a few attacker-chosen data fields. Similarly to other code reuse attacks chaining different code parts are directed by a special gadget: COOP program essentially relies on a special main loop containing a virtual function call.

From the protection point of view the most promising technology is the Control Flow Enforcement. Hardware supported CFE does not exist yet, but it is clearly visible that operating systems has to apply new libraries to support hardware assisted control flow enforcement. Our analysis concluded that the control flow enforcement solutions will make the successful exploitation more difficult: 1. In all of the existing control flow bypassing techniques the attacker has to control more parameters (registers, local variables) than in the case of an average exploitation today; In all of the existing control flow bypassing techniques the attacker has to identify a special code part (loop gadget, gadget dispatcher, etc.) which is responsible for chaining the payload parts from small code blocks. According to our investigations the possible control flow bypassing techniques must be considered when overwriting the operating system libraries. This should be done by identifying dangerous code parts (loop gadget candidates, gadget dispatcher candidates) and remove them with the introduction of hardware assisted control flow enforcement libraries.

5 Summary

Based on previous experiences we cannot simply let system security be based on perfect software without vulnerabilities to avoid software vulnerability exploitations. Additional advanced protections are necessary. From performance point of view hardware based solutions are preferred such as the DEP. However the ROP which is the favorite technique of todays exploitations can bypass DEP. ASLR is an efficient protection against ROP, but information leakage can reveal the randomization offset, which makes the code reuse type of exploitations still possible. Anyhow, the trend in protection innovation indicates that sooner or later ROP based exploits will be disabled with some protection technique. CFE aims to prevent ROP, for example. New exploit ideas such as the LOP, DOP and COOP are being published continuously to bypass the new protections. Right now it is not clear whether there exists any protection that is capable of stopping the exploitation of unknown software bugs or that the only thing that can be done on the protection side is to mitigate the percentage of successful exploitations. In this paper we summarized the main exploitation and protection techniques and in addition we analyzed the latest code reuse exploitations. These might be the most relevant exploitations of the future that underlines the question: Exploit prevention - Quo Vadis?

References

1. Li, Y., Lan, B., Sun, H., Su, C., Liu, Y., Zeng, Q.: Loop-oriented programming: a new code reuse attack to bypass modern defenses. In: 2015 IEEE Trustcom/BigDataSE/ISPA, pp. 91–97. IEEE Computer Society (2015)
2. Bittau, A., Belay, A., Mashtizadeh, A., Mazieres, D., Boneh, D.: Hacking blind (2015). http://www.scs.stanford.edu/sorbo/brop/bittau-brop.pdf
3. Bletsch, T., Jiang, X., Freeh, V.: Jump-oriented programming: a new class of code-reuse attack. In: 17th ACM Computer and Communications Security (2010)
4. Bosman, E., Bos, H.: Framing signalsa return to portable shellcode. In: SP 2014 Proceedings of the IEEE Symposium on Security and Privacy, pp. 243–258 (2014)
5. Carlini, N., Wagner, D.: ROP is still dangerous: breaking modern defenses (2014). https://people.eecs.berkeley.edu/daw/papers/rop-usenix14.pdf
6. cvedetails.com. CVE details - the ultimate security vulnerability datasourse. http://cvedetails.com
7. Davi, L., Liebchen, C., Snow, K.Z., Monrose, F.: Isomeron: code randomization resilient to (just-in-time) return-oriented programming. In: NDSS Symposium 2015 (2015)
8. CWE Common Weakness Enumeration. CWE-416: use after free (2012). https://cwe.mitre.org/data/definitions/416.html
9. Evtyushkin, D., Ponomarev, D., Abu-Ghazaleh, N.: Jump over ASLR: attacking branch predictors to bypass ASLR (2016). http://www.cs.ucr.edu/nael/pubs/micro16.pdf
10. Ferguson, J.N.: Understanding the heap by breaking it (2007). http://www.black hat.com/presentations/bh-usa-07/Ferguson/Whitepaper/bh-usa-07-ferguson-WP.pdf
11. Hu, H., Shinde, S., Adrian, S., Chua, Z.L., Saxena, P., Liang, Z.: Data-oriented programming: on the expressiveness of non-control data attacks (2016). http://ieeexplore.ieee.org/iel7/7528194/7546461/07546545.pdf
12. Intel. Control-flow enforcement technology preview (2016). https://software.intel.com/sites/default/files/managed/4d/2a/control-flow-enforcement-technology-preview.pdf
13. Johnson, K., Miller, M.: Exploit mitigation improvements in Windows 8 (2012). http://media.blackhat.com/bh-us-12/Briefings/M_Miller/BH_US_12_Miller_Exploit_Mitigation_Slides.pdf
14. Kaempf, M.: Smashing the heap for fun and profit. Phrack Mag. **57**(11), 8 (2001)
15. Kondratenko, A.: CVE-2017-3881 Cisco Catalyst RCE Proof-of-Concept (2017). https://artkond.com/2017/04/10/cisco-catalyst-remote-code-execution/
16. Levy, E.: Smashing the stack for fun and profit. Phrack Mag. **49**(14), 8 (1996)
17. Seka, R., Li, L., Just, J.E.: Address-space randomization for windows systems (2012). http://seclab.cs.sunysb.edu/seclab/pubs/acsac06.pdf
18. Microsoft: A detailed description of the data execution prevention (DEP) feature in windows XP service pack 2, windows XP tablet pc edition 2005, and windows server 2003 (2006). https://support.microsoft.com/en-us/help/875352/a-detailed-description-of-the-data-execution-prevention-dep-feature-in-windows-xp-service-pack-2-windows-xp-tablet-pc-edition-2005-and-windows-server-2003
19. Microsoft: Preventing the exploitation of structured exception handler (SEH) overwrites with sehop (2009). https://blogs.technet.microsoft.com/srd/2009/02/02/preventing-the-exploitation-of-structured-exception-handler-seh-overwrites-with-sehop/

20. Microsoft: The enhanced mitigation experience toolkit (2012). https://support. microsoft.com/en-us/help/2458544/the-enhanced-mitigation-experience-toolkit

21. Paloalto Networks. Traps administrators guide (2017). https://www.paloaltone tworks.com/content/dam/pan/en_US/assets/pdf/framemaker/32/endpoint/endpo int-admin-guide/section_1.pdf

22. Pak, B.: Microsoft edge (Windows 10) - 'chakra.dll' info leak/type confusion remote code execution (2017). https://www.exploit-db.com/exploits/40990/

23. Schuster, F., Tendyck, T., Liebcheny, C., Daviy, L., Sadeghiy, A.-R., Holz, T.: Counterfeit object-oriented programming - on the difficulty of preventing code reuse attacks in C++ applications (2015). http://syssec.rub.de/media/emma/ veroeffentlichungen/2015/03/28/COOP-Oakland15.pdf

24. scut/team teso. Exploiting format string vulnerabilities (2001). https://crypto. stanford.edu/cs155/papers/formatstring-1.2.pdf

25. Offensive Security. Offensive securitys exploit database archive. https://www. exploit-db.com/

26. Shacham, H., Buchanan, E., Roemer, R., Savage, S.: Return-oriented program- ming: exploitation without code injection (2008). https://www.blackhat.com/ presentations/bh-usa-08/Shacham/BH_US_08_Shacham_Return_Oriented_Program ming.pdf

27. Shacham, H., Page, M., Pfaff, B., Goh, E.-J., Modadugu, N., Boneh, D.: On the effectiveness of address-space randomization (2004). http://benpfaff.org/papers/ asrandom.pdf

28. El Sherei, S.: Return to libc. https://www.exploit-db.com/docs/28553.pdf

29. Tang, J.: Exploring control flow guard in Windows 10 (2016). http://sjc1-te-ftp. trendmicro.com/assets/wp/exploring-control-flow-guard-in-windows10.pdf

30. Corelan Team: Exploit writing tutorial part 11: heap spraying demystified (2011). https://www.corelan.be/index.php/2011/12/31/exploit-writing-tutorial-part-11-heap-spraying-demystified/

31. Ars Technica: Firefox 0-day in the wild is being used to attack tor users (2016). https://arstechnica.com/security/2016/11/firefox-0day-used-against-tor-users-al most-identical-to-one-fbi-used-in-2013/

32. Blogger technology: Metasploit. https://blgtechn.blogspot.no/2012/08/metasplo it.html

33. van Schaik, S., Razavi, K., Gras, B., Bos, H., Giuffrida, C.: Reverse engineering hardware page table caches using side-channel attacks on the MMU (2017). http:// www.cs.vu.nl/herbertb/download/papers/revanc_ir-cs-77.pdf

34. Wagle, P.M.: Stackguard: simple buffer overflow protection for GCC. In: Proceed- ings of the GCC Developers Summit, pp. 243–256 (2003)

35. Wikipedia. Exploit (computer security) (2010). https://en.wikipedia.org/wiki/ Exploit_(computer_security)

36. Yason, M.V.: Understanding the attack surface and attack resilience of project spartans (edge) new edgehtml rendering engine (2015). https://www.blackhat.co m/docs/us-15/materials/us-15-Yason-Understanding-The-Attack-Surface-And-A ttack-Resilience-Of-Project-Spartans-New-EdgeHTML-Rendering-Engine-wp.pdf

Secure Systems

Estimating Software Obfuscation Potency
with Artificial Neural Networks

Daniele Canavese[✉], Leonardo Regano, Cataldo Basile,
and Alessio Viticchié

Politecnico di Torino, Torino, Italy
{daniele.canavese,leonardo.regano,cataldo.basile,
alessio.viticchie}@polito.it

Abstract. This paper presents an approach to estimate the potency of obfuscation techniques. Our approach uses neural networks to accurately predict the value of complexity metrics – which are used to compute the potency – after an obfuscation transformation is applied to a code region. This work is the first step towards a decision support to optimally protect software applications.

Keywords: Software protection · Code obfuscation · Potency · Neural networks

1 Introduction

Obfuscation is one of the most effective and used solution to protect the software against reverse engineering and tampering. Several obfuscation techniques are available in literature [5] that can be driven by different protection/performance degradation parameters. While some results proved that it is impossible to create a perfect obfuscator [2], empirical results showed that obfuscation works well in practice [3, 21]. Several tools are also prominent at industrial level[1].

Nevertheless, the strength of obfuscation in mitigating the attacks cannot be formally defined. Collberg et al. have proposed to compute an effectiveness index, named *potency*, by measuring the changes in complexity metrics induced by the obfuscation transformations [5]. This value can only be measured *a posteriori*, after the actual application of the transformation. As it is impractical to apply and measure all the possible ways to apply obfuscation, protection experts are asked to (1) use their intuition and past knowledge to select the parts to protect and the most promising techniques to apply on each of them, then to (2) apply the protections, and to (3) actually measure the effects. This practice conflicts with the need that several companies have to protect different versions of one or more applications in a very short time.

This paper proposes to estimate *a priori* the potency of obfuscation techniques, before they are applied on a specific code region. We used Artificial

---

[1] Two examples of commercial obfuscators are Stunnix (http://stunnix.com) and Proguard (https://www.guardsquare.com/en/proguard).

© Springer International Publishing AG 2017
G. Livraga and C. Mitchell (Eds.): STM 2017, LNCS 10547, pp. 193–202, 2017.
DOI: 10.1007/978-3-319-68063-7_13

Neural Networks (ANNs) to predict the changes that obfuscation techniques cause on a set of metrics. Then, the predicted metrics have been used to estimate the *predicted potency* of the protection. Finally, the predicted potency has been used to make decisions about the best way to protect the application. Our assessment has proved that the estimated potency allows making nearly optimal decisions in a very limited time. Our ANNs predict very well the metric changes when a single protection is applied on each asset. However, the prediction ability decreases when ANNs are serially connected to estimate the changes created by the subsequent application of more protections, because of the error propagation. Nonetheless, this paper discusses how to improve the prediction abilities and extend this approach to be used to build a decision support system.

This paper is structured as follows. Section 2 contains the background of our approach, Sect. 3 introduces our methodology with a simple motivating example. Sections 4 and 5 discuss how we gathered our training/test data and detail the achieved results. Finally, Sects. 6 and 7 list the related works, draw our conclusions and sketch the future work.

2   Background

Software protection has been a crucial research topic since the last decades [7]. One of the most enduring technique is obfuscation [12,15], a set of transformations that can be applied both on data and code and at different levels: source, byte, or binary level. These transformations aim at making the software less intelligible thus hardening any attack that implies software understanding.

Obfuscation is not provably secure, as it has been demonstrated that it can be reverted, even automatically [19]. Moreover, a general obfuscator able to protect an application in untrusted environments cannot be created [2]. Although obfuscation is actually a kind of *security through obscurity*, it enhances the level of protections of the applications, as it delays attacks (rather than preventing them at all), as empirically assessed by Ceccato et al. for code obfuscation [3], and by Viticchié et al. for data obfuscation [21].

Collberg et al. have proposed several measures to evaluate the effectiveness of an obfuscation [5]. The *potency* aims at evaluating the complexity introduced by the transformation and gives an index of how hard would be to understand the obfuscated code. Given the transformation $T : P \xrightarrow{T} P'$ that transforms the original program P into the obfuscated program P', the potency of T with respect to the program P can be obtained with the following formula (from [5]):

$$T_{POT}(P) = \frac{E(P')}{E(P) - 1}$$

where $E(\cdot)$ is a complexity metric of a program. Therefore, the potency can only be computed after the transformation has been applied, or, as proposed by this work, by predicting the values of the metrics in the transformed program.

A *code region* is a portion of well-formed code, that is, a slice of syntactically valid code if parsed in isolation. A code region is unequivocally determined by the containing source file, its starting and ending line numbers. Code regions are hierarchical, i.e. one can contain another. Therefore, a program (or one of its portions) can be seen as a tree where each node is a code region containing all its descendant nodes.

A *protection* is a technique that applies a transformation on the application source or binary code. The transformation applied by a protection can be fixed or depending on a set of parameters. We will use the definition *Protection Instance (PI)* to identify a selection of the parameters of a protection. In other words, a PI is a precise way to use a protection. For example, the Diablo binary code obfuscator [20], allows the selection of various obfuscation types (e.g. opaque predicates or control flow flattening), and the (expected) level of obfuscation effectiveness (passed as an integer). Hence, a Diablo protection instance includes one obfuscation technique and an integer for the expected effectiveness. The PIs of a protection are determined by the combinations of the allowed values of the parameters. Since some parameters can be unbounded, the cardinality of the PIs set may be infinite. However, the bare combination of the parameters domain sets may produce PIs that are meaningless or do not significantly differ one from another. Carefully selecting a set of PIs may reduce the decision space.

A *metric* is a measurement of a software feature. In this work, we only use binary level complexity metrics. Indeed, metrics computed at source level can be altered, thus invalidated, by the compiler (e.g. for optimisation purposes). Software metrics can be defined depending on several aspects of the software structure [4,10,16]. We concentrated on the the seven metrics that Collberg et al. proposed to use to compute the potency [5], however, the tool that we choose to work with, Diablo, is only able to compute the cyclomatic complexity and Halstead length. The *cyclomatic complexity* measures the complexity as the number of linearly independent paths in the program's control flow graph [16], an index of the nesting level easily computed on binary code. The cyclomatic complexity v of a control flow graph G is $v(G) = e - n + p$, where e is the number of edges, n is the number of nodes and p is the number of connected components of the graph. The *Halstead length* considers a program implementation as a sequence of *operators* and their relative *operands* [10]. The length N of a program, according to Halstead, is calculated as $N = N_1 + N_2$, where N_1 is the total number of operators and N_2 is the total number of operands.

3   Motivating Example

In this section we show how our approach can positively impact the process of protecting, by means of binary code obfuscation, the intellectual property of the algorithms underlying a test application. Our test application is *Sumatra*[2], an open-source command line tool written in C that compares DNA sequences. Sumatra provides two functionalities: comparing among all the DNA sequences in a single dataset, or (pairwise) comparing DNA sequences from two datasets.

---

[2] https://git.metabarcoding.org/obitools/sumatra/wikis/home.

We will behave like it was a proprietary software that must be protected against reverse engineering, to preserve the IP of the comparison algorithms.

Sumatra performs the DNA comparison in four consecutive phases. The first phase evaluates the command line arguments and calls the proper comparison functions. During the second phase, Sumatra parses the DNA datasets and stores them in several internal data structures. The third phase is the core of the program as it performs the actual comparison of the DNA sequences, so it should be obfuscated in a thorough way. The fourth and last phase presents the results to the user. These algorithm should be also strongly protected since they access the internal data structures, thus revealing information about the core algorithms.

We have classified the phases with a sensitivity value on a two level scale (i.e. high, low), as high sensitive assets should be protected with highly effective obfuscation techniques. Namely, the first, second and forth phases have a low sensitivity (and contains respectively one, five and three assets), and the third phase has a high sensitivity (and contains ten assets).

Mitigation is performed by applying on every asset a tuple of PIs, as applying them in different orders may lead to different results. Ideally, we must aim at reaching the best level of protection, by exploring the whole space of the possible ways to protect each asset. Thus, the solution space of the best protection becomes the set of all the PI combinations. As some PIs can be applied to the same code region several times, the number of PI combinations is theoretically unbounded. Therefore, we fixed the maximum length of PI sequences to l, so that the number of the sequences to consider is $c \geq \text{COMB}(l, n_p)$, where $\text{COMB}(l, n_p)$ is the number of l-combinations with repetition of n_p PIs.

To measure the overall effectiveness of a sequence of PIs σ on the asset a we introduced the *combined potency P*:

$$P_{\sigma,a} = \sum_{m \in M} w_m \cdot \pi_{\sigma,m,a} \tag{1}$$

where $\pi_{\sigma,m,a}$ is the potency of σ on a for the metric m (which uses the value of m before and after the protection has been applied [5]), M is the set of all the metrics m where the values $\pi_{\sigma,m,a}$ are computed and w_m are arbitrary weights.

Deciding the best protection would need the computation of the potency of all the possible σ sequences on each asset. Since we can protect all the assets with the same sequence of PIs, the number of times the target program needs to be obfuscated equals the number of the possible sequences[3].

Instead of computing the metrics *a posteriori*, we use ANNs to predict, from the value of the metrics of the unprotected application, the value of the metrics after the application of a PI. A single ANN predicts the changes of the metric m induced by the application of a single PI. Hence, we have trained an ANN for each pair (PI, m). The changes in the metric m when a sequence σ of PIs is estimated by using ANNs serially, i.e. by using the output of an ANN as input

---

[3] We do not take into account the case of nested assets, i.e. when an asset contains other asset. With nested assets, the number of compilation needed increases, since all the compilations should be repeated separately for each nesting level.

of the next one. Evaluating the potency of all possible PI sequences on all the n_a assets requires $b = n_a \cdot n_m \cdot (\text{COMB}(l, n_p) - 1)$ ANN simulations, where n_m is the number of metrics needed to compute the combined potency.

We experimentally demonstrated that our approach is faster, by testing it on Sumatra (see Sect. 5). We need more ANN interrogations than the protection applications required by the current approach, however, a ANN interrogation is typically completed in a few milliseconds, while the time needed for obfuscating assets (and often also compiling the whole application) may be in the order of seconds. Moreover, n_m is a small value and, from our experience in the ASPIRE project[4], increasing the application's lines of code slightly increases the number of assets n_a, but greatly increases the obfuscation (and compilation) time.

4 Data Set Acquisition

We trained the ANNs with a set of pre- and post-transformation metrics' values on a sufficiently large set of code regions. The Diablo linker [20] has been used to compute the complexity metrics on a set of code regions and to apply branch functions [12], function flattening [22] and opaque predicates [6] obfuscations. Diablo takes as input the object files and a JSON file, which allow the selection of the code regions of interest, then it maps these regions to the corresponding assembler instructions via the debugging information.

We selected 21 open source packages from the Debian repository. They encompass different areas such as scientific computations (e.g. the libstarlink-pal astrophysical library), security (e.g. the ccrypt cryptographic tool), network management (e.g. the qmail mail server) and utilities (e.g. the bc calculator).

For each application, our work flow consisted of the following steps:

1. automatically divide the application in code regions (i.e. potential assets);
2. for each optimization flag -Os, -O2 and -O0 do:
   (a) compile the application without any obfuscation and extract the metrics;
   (b) for each PI, compile the application, apply the current PI to all the code regions in Step 1, and extract the post-PI metrics.

To implement the Step 1, we created a simple tool that parses the source files and automatically generates the JSON file with the code regions. The tool selects as valid code regions every function body and, recursively, each nested loop, if statement, or curly brackets block (see Fig. 1 for an example). With this tool, we identified 35510 code regions.

We have defined 2 PIs for each of the three supported Diablo obfuscations types. One PI has been defined (using an effectiveness parameter) to have a low protection/overhead obfuscation, for the other one, we required a high protection/overhead obfuscation. Figure 2 shows the graphs of the cyclomatic complexity (CC) and Halstead length (HL) before and after applying the PI

---

[4] https://aspire-fp7.eu/.

```
int function(int a, int b) {
    int c = 0, d = a;
    while (d > 0) {
        if (function2(b, d) % 2 == 0) {
            function3(TRUE);
            --c;
        }
        else {
            function3(FALSE);
            ++c;
        }
        --d;
    }
    return c;}
```

Fig. 1. Example of function splitting.

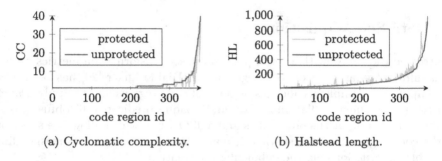

(a) Cyclomatic complexity.   (b) Halstead length.

Fig. 2. Code region metrics for the "branch functions, high overhead" PI.

"high overhead, branch functions" to a 1% random selection of the data set[5]. The plots clearly show that the relationship between the pre- and post-PI metrics cannot be easily modelled since it is a complex non-linear multivariate transformation.

5 Experimental Results

We tested our ANNs to estimate the potency of protected versions of the Sumatra application (Sect. 3). We used Diablo 2.82, GCC 4.9.2 and MathWorks MATLAB R2017a on an Intel i7-4980HQ CPU @ 2.80 GHz with 16 GiB RAM under Debian GNU/Linux testing with kernel 4.9.0.

We randomly selected 10% of our data set as the test set (3551 samples) and the remaining observations formed the training set (31959 samples). Then, we trained 36 feed-forward neural networks (6 PIs × 6 metrics) by using a multi-loop approach to iteratively try different parameters (i.e. training and activation functions, number of neurons) and find the ideal architectural structure. We selected the parameters that minimized the Root Mean Square Error (RMSE), which was computed using a k-fold cross-validation approach with $k = 10$ where we averaged the errors of each validation fold [11].

---

[5] For the sake of readability, we limited the y-axis to about one quarter of the maximum metric value in Figs. 2, 3, and 4.

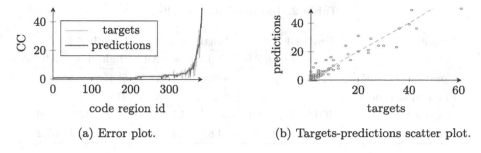

(a) Error plot.   (b) Targets-predictions scatter plot.

Fig. 3. CC predictions for "branch functions, high overhead" PI.

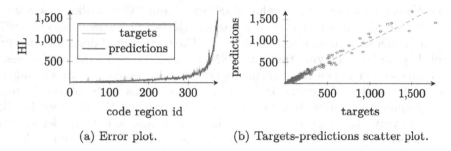

(a) Error plot.   (b) Targets-predictions scatter plot.

Fig. 4. HL predictions for "branch functions, high overhead" PI.

Table 1. Neural networks performance.

PI	CC			HL		
	RMSE	MAE	R^2 [%]	RMSE	MAE	R^2 [%]
Branch functions, low overhead	2.4	0.7	97.3	160.5	32.9	97.8
Branch functions, high overhead	3.2	0.9	96.9	142.6	33.9	97.8
Function flattening, low overhead	3.2	0.7	96.1	86.4	24.8	99.1
Function flattening, high overhead	4.5	0.9	92.8	74.2	26.4	98.7
Opaque predicates, low overhead	2.6	0.7	97.6	110.1	37.8	98.2
Opaque predicates, high overhead	3.3	0.8	96.4	94.9	34.5	98.8

Each network receives as inputs six metrics (i.e. cyclomatic complexity, Halstead length, the number of input/output operands, instructions and edges in the control flow graph). These values are normalized in the $[-1, +1]$ range and then processed by the ANNs, having one hidden layer with three neurons. We used the Levenberg-Marquardt back-propagation training with early stopping to avoid overfitting (the `trainlm` function). The hidden layer activation function is the hyperbolic tangent sigmoid, while the single neuron output layer function is a simple linear transfer (the `tansig` and `purelin` functions).

Table 1 reports the RMSE, the Mean Absolute Error (MAE) and the coefficient of determination (R^2) of the ANNs used to predict the cyclomatic complexity (CC) and the Halstead length (HL). The average cyclomatic complexity in our

Table 2. Test application results.

Priority	Length 1			Length ≤ 2			Length ≤ 3		
	High	Low	All	High	Low	All	High	Low	All
Compilation time [s]	156.1			949.6			5535.9		
Simulation time [s]	1.6			9.2			31.6		
Accuracy [%]	100.0	77.8	89.5	50.0	66.7	57.9	12.1	37.0	21.9
Proximity [%]	100.0	87.0	93.9	84.6	75.4	80.2	64.2	70.4	67.2

data set is 5.1 with a maximum value of 187 and all our CC networks show a MAE less than one. On the other hand, the average HL is 206.2 with a peak at 6887 and our HL networks have a MAE of about 30. The coefficient of determination R^2 is well beyond 90%, proving that our ANNs accurately predict metric changes.

Figures 3a and 4a plot the targets (i.e. actual) and predicted metrics (random selection of the 10% of the test set). The ANN predictions easily follows the real data, grasping the general trend of the metrics. Note that the Halstead length curves are very close together, so that the ANN is also able to model several spikes in the graph. Figures 3b and 4b sketch the scatter plots of the predicted-target ratios. Each point represents a sample, the closer the point to the dashed line the better. The cyclomatic complexity prediction shows more dispersion, but the overall trend is still close the ideal line.

Assessing how the estimated metrics can be used to select the best PI sequence for each asset is more complex, as this prediction requires to serially connect multiple ANNs, thus propagating the errors. For the 10 high priority Sumatra assets we use the high overhead PIs, and for the 9 low priority ones the low overhead PIs. We fixed the maximum length of the PI sequences to $l = 3$, giving us a grand total of 760 sequences. We computed the combined potency of each sequence (Eq. 1) using both the real and predicted metrics, as shown in Table 2, which also reports the compilation and the simulation times (the time to estimate all the metrics with our ANNs). As expected, the time exponentially increases as the length of PI sequences grows. However, actually applying the protections required 1.5 h, while the prediction was completed in 31.6 s.

To assess how good are our predictions, we introduced the *accuracy*, a percentage that reports how often the estimated potency allowed the selection of the same protections using the measured potency. For sequences of length 1, we yield nearly a perfect score, which decreases as the depth increases. We also introduced the notion of *proximity*, as accuracy does not report how close a solution is to the optimum. The function $\text{ORD}(\sigma_i, a_i)$ returns the position of σ_i in the list of PIs for the asset a_i sorted in descending order of measured potency. Let's take one PI sequence for each asset, $\Pi = (\sigma_1, \ldots, \sigma_{n_a})$, the proximity of Π with maximum length l and with n_p PIs is defined as:

$$\text{PROX}(\Pi) = \frac{1}{n_a} \sum_{i=1}^{n_a} \frac{\text{COMB}(l, n_p) - \text{ORD}(\sigma_i, a_i)}{\text{COMB}(l, n_p) - 1}$$

A proximity of 100% indicates that the optimum was reached and a 0% means that the worst solution was chosen. At length 1, the proximity of our solution is 93.9%, very close to the optimality. When the length increases to 2 and 3, it decreases to 80.2% and 67.2%, still being relatively close to the best value.

6   Related Works

To our knowledge, the only work that leverages ANNs for software security assessment, by identifying security flaws in software design, is a paper of Adebiyi et al. [1]. They manually converted 715 attack scenarios gathered from various vulnerability databases into regular expressed attack patterns [9], and used the latter to train a back-propagation neural network to classify the attacks.

On the other hand, several works used ANN to assess the security of computer networks. Liu et al. proposed a message security scheme to encrypt messages with a Real-time Recurrent Neural Network-based (RRNN) cipher [14]. Fu et al. leveraged a back-propagation ANN to assess the security of wireless networks against risk assessment models defined by the authors [8]. Turčaník designed a packet filter that uses ANNs to greatly reduce the time needed to perform the filtering [18]. Finally, several intrusion detection systems makes use of ANNs to classify access logs (e.g. firewall logs) in normal and anomalous [13,17].

7   Conclusions and Future Work

This paper presented an approach to estimate the potency of obfuscation techniques with neural networks that are able to accurately predict the value of several software metrics. To improve the precision of the technique and achieve a higher lever of accuracy, we will enlarge the data set used to train the ANNs, allowing them to be more accurate on a single protection. Moreover, we will train ANNs that predict changes created by sequences of protections.

In addition, we are also considering other obfuscators and protection techniques that alter software metrics. Finally, by also taking into account the dynamic metrics, we will exploit machine learning to predict protection overheads introduced on execution performance, memory allocation and network usage.

References

1. Adebiyi, A., Arreymbi, J., Imafidon, C.: Applicability of neural networks to software security. In: 14th International Conference on Computer Modelling and Simulation, pp. 19–24 (2012)
2. Barak, B., Goldreich, O., Impagliazzo, R., Rudich, S., Sahai, A., Vadhan, S., Yang, K.: On the (im)possibility of obfuscating programs. In: Kilian, J. (ed.) CRYPTO 2001. LNCS, vol. 2139, pp. 1–18. Springer, Heidelberg (2001). doi:10.1007/3-540-44647-8_1

3. Ceccato, M., Penta, M.D., Nagra, J., Falcarin, P., Ricca, F., Torchiano, M., Tonella, P.: The effectiveness of source code obfuscation: an experimental assessment. In: IEEE 17th International Conference on Program Comprehension, pp. 178–187 (2009)
4. Chidamber, S.R., Kemerer, C.F.: A metrics suite for object oriented design. IEEE Trans. Softw. Eng. **20**(6), 476–493 (1994)
5. Collberg, C., Thomborson, C., Low, D.: A taxonomy of obfuscating transformations. Technical report, University of Auckland, July 1997
6. Collberg, C., Thomborson, C., Low, D.: Manufacturing cheap, resilient, and stealthy opaque constructs. In: 25th ACM SIGPLAN Symposium on Principles of Programming Languages, pp. 184–196 (1998)
7. Collberg, C.S., Thomborson, C.: Watermarking, tamper-proofing, and obfuscation-tools for software protection. IEEE Trans. Softw. Eng. **28**(8), 735–746 (2002)
8. Fu, J., Huang, L., Yao, Y.: Application of BP neural network in wireless network security evaluation. In: 2010 IEEE International Conference on Wireless Communications, Networking and Information Security, pp. 592–596 (2010)
9. Gegick, M., Williams, L.: On the design of more secure software-intensive systems by use of attack patterns. Inf. Softw. Technol. **49**(4), 381–397 (2007)
10. Halstead, M.H.: Elements of Software Science. Operating and Programming Systems Series. Elsevier Science Inc., New York (1977)
11. Kohavi, R.: A study of cross-validation and bootstrap for accuracy estimation and model selection. In: 14th International Joint Conference on Artificial Intelligence, pp. 1137–1143 (1995)
12. Linn, C., Debray, S.: Obfuscation of executable code to improve resistance to static disassembly. In: 10th ACM conference on Computer and Communications Security, pp. 290–299 (2003)
13. Lippmann, R.P., Cunningham, R.K.: Improving intrusion detection performance using keyword selection and neural networks. Comput. Netw. **34**(4), 597–603 (2000)
14. Liu, C.Y., Woungang, I., Chao, H.C., Dhurandher, S.K., Chi, T.Y., Obaidat, M.S.: Message security in multi-path ad hoc networks using a neural network-based cipher. In: 2011 IEEE Global Telecommunications Conference, pp. 1–5 (2011)
15. Low, D.: Protecting Java code via code obfuscation. Crossroads - Spec. Issue Robot. **4**(3), 21–23 (1998)
16. McCabe, T.J.: A complexity measure. IEEE Trans. Softw. Eng. **2**(4), 308–320 (1976)
17. Mukkamala, S., Janoski, G., Sung, A.: Intrusion detection using neural networks and support vector machines. In: Proceedings of the 2002 International Joint Conference on Neural Networks, vol. 2, pp. 1702–1707 (2002)
18. Turčaník, M.: Packet filtering by artificial neural network. In: 2015 International Conference on Military Technologies, pp. 1–4 (2015)
19. Udupa, S.K., Debray, S.K., Madou, M.: Deobfuscation: reverse engineering obfuscated code. In: 12th Working Conference on Reverse Engineering, pp. 45–54 (2005)
20. Van Put, L., Chanet, D., De Bus, B., De Sutter, B., De Bosschere, K.: Diablo: a reliable, retargetable and extensible link-time rewriting framework. In: 5th IEEE International Symposium on Signal Processing and Information Technology, pp. 7–12 (2005)
21. Viticchié, A., Regano, L., Torchiano, M., Basile, C., Ceccato, M., Tonella, P., Tiella, R.: Assessment of source code obfuscation techniques. In: IEEE 16th International Working Conference on Source Code Analysis and Manipulation, pp. 11–20 (2016)
22. Wang, C., Davidson, J., Hill, J., Knight, J.: Protection of software-based survivability mechanisms. In: 2001 International Conference on Dependable Systems and Networks, pp. 193–202 (2001)

EigenTrust for Hierarchically Structured Chord

Kalonji Kalala$^{(\boxtimes)}$, Tao Feng, and Iluju Kiringa

School of Electrical Engineering and Computer Science, University of Ottawa,
800 King Edward Avenue, Ottawa, ON K1N 6N5, Canada
{hkalo081,tfeng038,iluju.kiringa}@uottawa.ca
http://engineering.uottawa.ca/eecs/

Abstract. The paper proposes Hierarchical EigenTrust, an extension of EigenTrust, a trust and reputation algorithm that was proposed for flat peer-to-peer networks. The paper introduces the components of the hierarchical model architecture based on Chord, a scalable P2P (Peer-to-Peer) lookup service for Internet applications. The paper also extends the EigenTrust scheme to the hierarchically structured Chord P2P network. The proposed algorithm handles a huge number of nodes disseminated in different Chord rings, which improves complexity and reduces the number of malicious nodes. The experiments verify and compare the reduction of downloads from malicious peers, load distribution as well as convergence speed between a flat structured network and a hierarchically structured network. Results of the experiments show that hierarchical EigenTrust outperforms the flat EigenTrust in a P2P network that uses only one big ring.

Keywords: Hierarchical P2P network · Hierarchical Chord · Trust · Reputation · DHT · Overlay network · EigenTrust

1 Introduction

1.1 Motivation

A P2P system is defined as a group of organized autonomous peers in which peers share distributed resources (files, computing and services) without any centralized coordinating entity. Chord [14] has long emerged as an efficient structured P2P architecture and system. With the growing interest in P2P networks, combined with the emergence of new computing paradigms such as Big Data and the Internet of things (IoT), a hierarchical design is desired to overcome disadvantages associated with pure P2P networks. These disadvantages include the challenge of managing a network when the number of nodes increases exponentially and thus deteriorates the performance of the entire network, as well the challenge of handling the exponential increase in the number of things in a IoT environment. More specifically, consider an IoT fleet management scenario where a large number of vehicles must be managed. The involved vehicles can be considered as the leaf nodes of a tree-like structure that is formed by Chord ring of

© Springer International Publishing AG 2017
G. Livraga and C. Mitchell (Eds.): STM 2017, LNCS 10547, pp. 203–212, 2017.
DOI: 10.1007/978-3-319-68063-7_14

further Chord rings and be organized around local rings with super-peers that can function as the points at which data can be merged on the local ring and then be passed to a hierarchically higher ring. The hierarchical model reduces the network traffic, decreases the workload and the lookup path length because the number of hops is significantly reduced in addition to the lookup latency. The goal of trust and reputation systems is to evaluate the trustworthiness of peers, provide value to any transaction made among peers, and distinguish good peers from bad peers based on previous interactions and feedbacks from peer transactions. So far, there has been no a serious investigation or study undertaken to implement trust and reputation in hierarchically structured P2P networks. Specifically, this paper proposes a hierarchical redesign of Chord as an efficient solution for managing the complexity of P2P networks amenable for IoT applications and a hierarchical EigenTrust, an extension of EigenTrust.

1.2 Problems

We are confronted to the problem of adequately structuring P2P networks in the presence of a gigantic number of peers. Henceforth there is a need to redesign trust and reputation algorithms that were designed in the context of flat structured P2P network to make those algorithms amenable for the hierarchically structured P2P network context. Due to its popularity in the last ten years, we have considered Chord rings as the existing P2P network to further restructure in order to master the complexity of gigantic P2P networks. We will focus on the design, analysis, and implementation (via simulation) of a trust and reputation algorithm for hierarchically structured Chord systems. Our choice was based EigenTrust because it is one of the earlier and mostly cited trust and reputation algorithms for structured P2P, also many recent algorithms are just trying to improve EigenTrust.

2 Related Work

Many structured P2P systems like Chord, CAN [11], Pastry [12] are P2P overlay networks that implement a key-based and deterministic algorithm for the routing of messages to the destination key that holds the searched content. These overlay networks support storage and search interfaces such as Distributed Hash tables (DHT), a lookup strategy to route and specify the location of objects in the P2P network. This allows them to perform lookup service in $O(log\ N)$. In NodeRanking [10] the reputation value of a node i is evaluated by the number of references (emails, personal web pages) provided by other nodes in the network. PowerTrust [16] carefully and dynamically chooses a small number of power peers with hight reputation value. PowerTrust ameliorates global reputation accuracy as well as the rate of aggregation speed. Absolute Trust [1] is a algorithm for aggregation trust in P2P networks for peers that only exchange files. The algorithm and the metric used determine the true past behavior of peers. This algorithm does not need a normalization of trust, pre-trusted peers or any centralized authority.

3   Hierarchically Structured Chord

3.1   Chord

Chord organizes all peers in a ring (or circle) that maintains all keys in the range
from $2^m - 1$. It maps keys with corresponding content nodes. Each node maintains
a routing table called finger table that maintains the successors, predecessors
and fingers of the node. Every finger table contains up to m entries, m being
the number of bits in the hash key. Each node only possesses knowledge of
its successors on the identifier circle in order to execute look up operations and
knows little about distant nodes. Thus, each node can only maintain information
for a small number of nodes, i.e. a total of $O(\log N)$ fingers [8]. In the finger table
of a node n, the identifier of the first node s (at i^{th} entry) that comes after n
is determined by $s = successor(n + 2^{i-1})$. Node s is what is called the finger
of n. When a query is sent to a node, the node first needs to inspect its own
local storage to ensure if it carries the desired data item. If it holds the desired
data item, it simply sends the result to the requester. Otherwise, it redirects the
query to its nearest successor node according to its finger table.

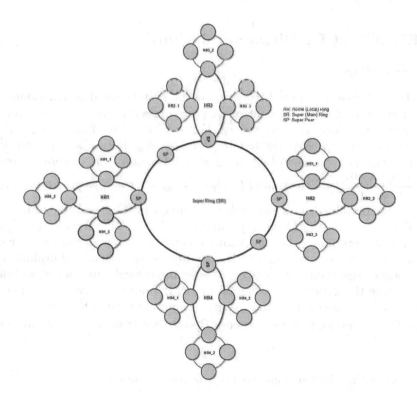

Fig. 1. Hierarchical Chord model

3.2 Extending Chord to a Hierarchical Structure

Each group in Figure 1 has a unique designated group *id*. The directed graph U, X, with $X = \{g_1, \ldots, g_I\}$ = Set of all groups and $U = set\ of\ virtual\ edges$ *among nodes (groups in this case)*. Each group contains at least one superpeer [3]. The lookup service is performed in two steps; first it locates the group that is in charge of the key, and inside the group it locates the peer that is in charge of the key. For N-tiers DHT, the lookup service should go deeper in the hierarchy, by passing through groups until it reaches the group that is in charge of the key. For two-tier DHT, operations are executed in the following orders: A superpeer of group S_j of superpeers of group j receives the query and can then transfer it to the peer p_j belonging to group G_j that is in charge of the key k. When p_j responds back to the query, the response can be transmitted using the reverse path used by the query message, or can be transmitted directly from peer j to the peer i. The lookup system at the top-level administers an overlay of groups. When a new peer p joins a group, it is provided with the *id* of the group to be recognized, such as the name of the group. Then p contacts a node p' already participating in the group to request the IP address of the group's superpeer(s)for the group key g.

4 EigenTrust for Hierarchical Chord

4.1 EigenTrust

EigenTrust [7] is a distributed trust reputation system based on individual reputation and uses distributed control. A peer conserves a record of all previous transactions in a local trust vector $\overrightarrow{c_i}$. Vector $\overrightarrow{c_i}$ consists of all local trust values c_{ij} that peer i has attributed to other peers j. It can be represented as $\overrightarrow{c_i} = (c_{i1}, c_{i2}, c_{i3}, \ldots, c_{in})$. All c_{ij} are positives because there are normalized as $c_{ij} = \dfrac{max(s_{ij}, 0)}{\sum(s_{ij}, 0)}$, and the sum of $(c_{i1} + c_{i2} + c_{i3} + \ldots + c_{in}) = 1$. All local trust values are represented in a matrix $[(c_{ij})]$ defined by C. A gossiping algorithm is used to assemble the global reputation t_i of the P2P network. The global trust value t_i determines the trust that the entire system places in the peer i. $\overrightarrow{t}$ determines the global trust vector of the entire system. EigenTrust evaluates the left principal eigenvector of a matrix of normalized local trust values, so that it can calculate the global trust value of a peer. It computes local reputation and global reputation and it uses transitivity to measure trust. This system needs a group of honest peers, pre-trusted peers $\overrightarrow{P}$ as start vectors to eliminate malicious peers.

4.2 Extending EigenTrust to Hierarchical Chord

Algorithm 1 represents the extended secure EigenTrust to hierarchical Chord. In this algorithm, some important information about group G_j, RRM_j and pre-trusted peers (superpeers) P_j is added to improve the lookup process in the

Algorithm 1. (EigenTrust for Hierarchical Chord)

A_s^i = Set of peers (from local and remote HR (Home Ring)) which have downloaded files from peer i .

B_s^i = Set of peers (from local and remote HR) from which peer i has download files

G_j = Group id

P_j = : Pre-trusted Superpeers

RRM_j : Pre-trusted Superpeer (gateway).

$hops_j$: Number of hops from ring to ring

. $Rpeer_j$: Number of remote peers to send scores

```
 1: for each (Gⱼ) do
 2:     Pⱼ ← const
 3:     hopsⱼ ← const
 4:     Rpeerⱼ ← const
 5: end for
 6: for each peer i in a (Gⱼ) do
 7:     do
 8:        Submit Local trust values cᵢ to all score managers at positions hₘ(posᵢ), m = 1, 2, ...M − 1

 9:        if Local trust value of peers ∈ other HR's then
10:           Transfer their scores to the local RRM
11:           determine the id of the remote HR
12:           Local RRM sends value to remote RRM of the HR, to the score managers
13:        end if
14:        Collect all Local trust values c_d and set of B_d^i
15:        Submit daughter d's Local trust values c_dⱼ to score managers hₘ(posᵢ), m = 1, 2, ...M − 1
                with j ∈ B_d^i
16:        Collect acquaintances A_d^i of daughter peers
17:        Communicate with other HR to collect acquaintances A_d^i of daughter peers
18:        for each daughter peer d ∈ Dᵢ do
19:           query all peers j ∈ A_d^i for c_jd P_j
20:           if peers j ∈ to another HR then
21:              send queries to RRM to transfer them to indicated HR.
22:           end if
23:           repeat
24:              Compute
```

$$t_d^{k+1} = (1 - u)(c_{1s}t_1^k) + (c_{2s}t_2^k) + ... + (c_{ns}t_n^k) + aP_j;$$

```
                 send (o_dⱼt_s^{k+1}) to all peers j ⊂ B_d^i
25:              sent to RRM all (c_dⱼt_s^{k+1}) for other HR's.
26:              wait for all peers j ∈ A_i^d to return (c_jd t_s^{k+1});
27:              wait for all peers j ∈ A_i^d from other HR's to return (c_jd t_s^{k+1});
28:           until |t_s^{k+1} − t_s^k| < ε
29:        end for
30: end for
```

---

hierarchical structure [5]. Thus, at each level, pre-trusted peers are assumed to be involved in the computation of trust and reputation. The algorithm computes the local trust of peers by using score managers of each peer to keep the score, and then aggregating all trust scores of a peer to determine its global reputation in the network. Because this algorithm works in a hierarchical environment, transactions made outside a home ring, are used to bring the scores of all peers from other home rings to local ring in order to compute the global reputation of a local peer.

The number of local trust values reported by a peer i is limited because a network may have a huge number of peers. The algorithm adds a variable $Rpeer_j$ to limit the number of remote peers that can send scores of a peer i located in a local ring. This algorithm allows a peer to have its score managers only locally to optimize the algorithm and to reduce traffic in the network. Peers outside of a local ring can report scores of peers in another ring to their superpeers, which will then transfer scores to score managers of peers into their corresponding HR's. We also assume that a group can only interact with a limited number of other groups. The number of hops from one ring to another rings for lookup purpose is determined and limited by the variable $hops_j$. Small rings (home rings) will execute the algorithm faster than one large flat ring; this allows the algorithm to converge faster. To compute the complexity of the algorithm, we need to take into account the local and remote computation of node scores. Essentially, local computation involves many peers than the remote computation due to restriction of the number of hops and remote peers that can send feedback for a peer in a local HR. Also, the system allows the use of cache to keep results of queries. When the algorithm is run for the first time, it determines pre-trusted peers, the number of hops it is permitted to use while sending a query out-site of a local ring. The algorithm is executed in $O(n^2)$. The idea in a hierarchical structure is to keep queries in the local ring. Finally, we assume that in the computation of the reputation of a node i, the number of HR's from which peers will send feedback after having performed transactions with node i must be limited to increase the performance of the algorithm, and the number of remote peers from other HR's to a local ring is limited to improve the performance of the algorithm.

5   Simulating Hierarchical Chord

In these experiments, we evaluate the performance of the redesigned EigenTrust in an hierarchical structured P2P network using Chord lookup service. We use existing experiment of flat EigenTrust and extend it to a hierarchical structured P2P. We also consider that a main ring is composed of superpeers that connect other nodes to form a ring, and that an m-bit *identifier* is attributed to each peer and each *key*. The model we use is based on a cloud service provider (CSP) that is made up of many data centre disseminated around the globe. Thus, each continent can be connected to the super ring by using a Superpeer called "*remote resource manager (RRM)*", a superpeer that connects two consecutive rings. We assume that when a flat network has 100 nodes, the entire hierarchical network will have 100 nodes. Then, we increase the number of nodes to 500, 1000 and 5000 respectively in both networks, and compare results. For the sake of clarity and fair comparison, we assume that both flat and hierarchical networks have the same number of nodes and that all rings in the hierarchical network have the same number of nodes. In the Hierarchical Chord simulation, we compare the fraction of download, the convergence speed and malicious collective for both flat and hierarchical EigenTrust. To capture the heterogeneity of the peers, we suppose that there are two categories of peers: Stable peers (for node 1 to node 10); Unstable peers for the other nodes. For the hierarchical organization, we select super-peers from a set of stable peers and we suppose that there is at least one stable peer in each group. For the organization, we choose nodes from the two categories randomly. Convergence is another aspect of concern since nonlinearity may result in a large number of iterations and render the system inefficient. We choose to have the same fraction of malicious peers in both hierarchical and at Chord, in order to readily compare the fraction of download from peers.

6   Simulation Results

6.1   Setup

we used an open-source simulator called PeerfactSim [13]. PeerfactSim does not currently support hierarchical Chord. One of the tasks was to modify the source code with an implementation of the flat Chord P2P system structure and extend it to hierarchical Chord. A user can specify the length of the tree and the number of nodes.

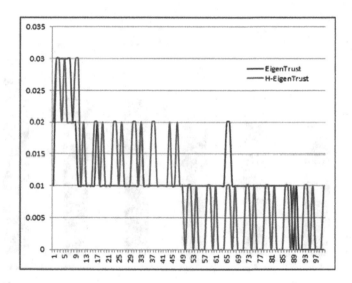

Fig. 2. Results of Fraction of downloads in Flat and Hierarchical EigenTrust for 100 nodes

We use a standalone computer with Intel(R) Core(TM) i5-3320M CPU @2.60 GHz, 64 bits, using 8.00 GB. For coding we use Eclipse IDE for Java Developers, Version: Mars.1 Release(4.5.1) and jdk1.8.0_91. The Windows 7 Professional operating system was used. For the experiments, we want to compare simulation results from a flat chord P2P system(with only one ring) to that of a hierarchical Chord P2P system. Then We compare and analyze experimental results.

6.2   Results

Figure 2 represents the load distribution results of the simulation when the network has 100 nodes. We can see that load distribution for the Hierarchical Chord network is concentrated on nodes with higher stability in each level of the hierarchy. Conversely, in the flat EigenTrust network, load distribution is selecting data sources with more scattered patterns. We increase the number of nodes to 500 and 1000, to simulate malicious collectives in both algorithms. For 100 and 500 nodes, malicious peers represents 43% of nodes, while for 1000 nodes the number of malicious nodes represents 50% of the all nodes in the network. We limit the number of nodes to 16 in each ring. Figure 3 shows that, with more nodes, we can see that the percentage of inauthentic downloads increases very slightly compared to 100 nodes for EigenTrust. This proves that the hierarchical EigenTrust improved significantly in the hierarchical network. The hierarchical EigenTrust presents better performance that the flat EigenTrust, even when the percentage of malicious peers constitutes the half of the total number of peers in the network. EigenTrust downloads more files from malicious peers than hierarchical EigenTrust.

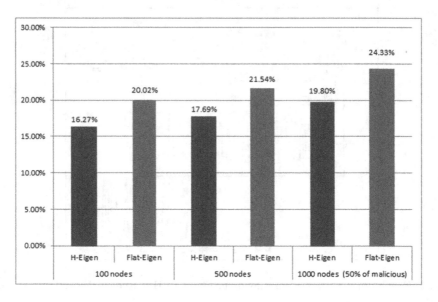

Fig. 3. Trust-based reduction of inauthentic downloads in hierarchical network with 100, 500 and 1000 nodes where a fraction of peers forms a malicious collective

Figure 4 represents the convergence speed of both algorithms for 100, 500, 1000 nodes. Results show that even hierarchical network has many rings, the convergence speed is close to that of flat network. With 1000 nodes, we can see that the flat EigenTrust converges after at most 5 iterations, while the hierarchical EigenTrust converges at most 6 iterations in the network with many rings. Even when the number of nodes changes, the converge still close.

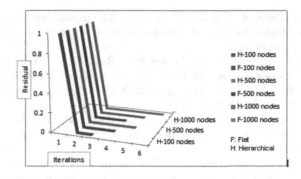

Fig. 4. Convergence speed of algorithms in hierarchical network

7 Conclusion

We have redesigned the EigenTrust trust and reputation algorithm that was designed for flat-structured P2P networks to be used in hierarchically structured P2P networks. We chose Chord to this end and we extended its DHT mechanism to a hierarchical structure where peers are assembled in groups recognized by a unique identifier. We simulated the new algorithm as well as the old algorithm, and we evaluated them in terms of load distribution, residual curl, and malicious collective downloads. We compared the measures obtained for both EigenTrust and its hierarchical version. The results revealed that the hierarchical trust and reputation algorithm achieved better performance than the flat algorithm and converged faster and proportionally to the number of rings. We can therefore conclude that the reduced number of nodes per ring and their organization in hierarchies helped to improve the performance of the Chord P2P system. In the future, as our simulation have been performed on a hierarchically structured Chord P2P network limited to a three levels, we intend to extend our results to a Chord structure with an arbitrary number of levels. Furthermore, we will look into how to extend this research to other trust and reputation systems found in the literature and which were designed around different trust and reputation models such as PowerTrust [16], NodeRanking [10] or Absolute trust [1]. The results of simulations using our simulator will then be compared to determine which algorithm outperformed all others in a hierarchical network environment. We can also apply this research to IoT settings, such as the fleet management setting used in the introduction to this paper as motivation, by building an IoT fleet management network where nodes are hierarchically organized. Further future work can be focused on the extension of EigenTrust to lookup services based on other existing hierarchical overlay structures such as BATON [6], and HD Trees [4].

References

1. Awasthi, S.K., Singh, Y.N.: Absolute trust: algorithm for aggregation of trust in peer-to-peer networks. IEEE Commun. Lett. **20**(7), 1345–1348 (2016)

2. Foster, I., Kesselman, C., Nick, J., Tuecke, S.: The physiology of the grid: an open grid services architecture for distributed systems integration. Technical report, Global Grid Forum (2002)

3. Garcés-Erice, L., Biersack, E.W., Felber, P.A., Ross, K.W., Urvoy-Keller, G.: Hierarchical peer-to-peer systems. In: Kosch, H., Böszörményi, L., Hellwagner, H. (eds.) Euro-Par 2003. LNCS, vol. 2790, pp. 1230–1239. Springer, Heidelberg (2003). doi:10.1007/978-3-540-45209-6_166

4. Gu, Y., Boukerche, A.: HD tree: a novel data structure to support multidimensional range query for P2P networks. J. Parallel Distrib. Comput. **71**(8), 1111–1124 (2011)

5. Hofstatter, Q., Zols, S., Michel, M., Despotovic, Z., Kellerer, W.: Chordella - a hierarchical peer-to-peer overlay implementation for heterogeneous, mobile environments. In: 2008 Eighth International Conference on Peer-to-Peer Computing, pp. 75–76 (2008)

6. Jagadish, H.V., Ooi, B.C., Vu, Q.H.: BATON: a balanced tree structure for peer-to-peer networks. In: Proceedings of the 31st International Conference on Very Large Data Bases, pp. 149–160 (2005)

7. Kamvar, S.D., Schlosser, M.T., Garcia-Molina, H.: The EigenTrust algorithm for reputation management in P2P networks. In: 12th International Conference on World Wide Web (WWW), p. 640 (2003)

8. Maenpaa, J., Camarillo, G.: Study on maintenance operations in a chord-based Peer-to-Peer session initiation protocol overlay network. In: IEEE International Symposium on Parallel Distributed Processing (IPDPS 2009), p. 19 (2009)

9. Montresor, A., Jelasity, M., Babaoglu, O.: Chord on demand. In: Proceedings - Fifth IEEE International Conference on Peer-to-Peer Computing, P2P 2005, vol. 2005, pp. 87–94 (2005)

10. Pujol, J.M., Sangesa, R., Delgado, J.: Extracting reputation in multi agent systems by means of social network topology. In: Proceedings of the First International Joint Conference on Autonomous Agents Multiagent Systems Part 1, pp. 467–474 (2002)

11. Ratnasamy, S., Francis, P., Handley, M., Karp, R., Shenker, S.: A scalable content addressable network. In: Proceedings of the ACM SIGCOMM, vol. TR-00-010, pp. 161–172 (2000)

12. Rowstron, A., Druschel, P.: Pastry: scalable, decentralized object location, and routing for large-scale peer-to-peer systems. In: Guerraoui, R. (ed.) Middleware 2001. LNCS, vol. 2218, pp. 329–350. Springer, Heidelberg (2001). doi:10.1007/3-540-45518-3_18

13. Stingl, D., Gross, C., Ruckert, J., Nobach, L., Kovacevic, A., Steinmetz, R.: PeerfactSim.KOM: a simulation framework for peer-to-peer systems. In: Proceedings of the 2011 International Conference on High Performance Computing and Simulation, HPCS 2011, pp. 577–584 (2011)

14. Stoica, I., Morris, R., Karger, D., Kaashoek, M.F., Balakrishnan, H.: Chord: a scalable peer-to-peer lookup service for internet applications. In: Proceedings of the 2001 Conference on Applications, Technologies, Architectures, and Protocols for Computer Communications, pp. 149–160 (2001)

15. Xiong, L., Liu, L.: PeerTrust: supporting reputation-based trust for peer-to-peer electronic communities. IEEE Trans. Knowl. Data Eng. **16**(7), 843–857 (2004)

16. Zhou, R., Hwang, K.: PowerTrust: a robust and scalable reputation system for trusted peer-to-peer computing. IEEE Trans. Parallel Distrib. Syst. **18**(4), 460–473 (2007)

Cover Traffic: A Trade of Anonymity and Efficiency

Tim Grube[(✉)], Markus Thummerer, Jörg Daubert, and Max Mühlhäuser

Telecooperation Group, Technische Universität Darmstadt, Darmstadt, Germany
{grube,daubert,max}@tk.tu-darmstadt.de, markus.thummerer@gmail.com

Abstract. Communication is ubiquitous in today's societies; more and more devices participate in communication processes, as in for example the Internet of Things. With this omnipresent communication, the process of communication is sensitive itself as it already can disclose information about the content. Anonymous communication is desirable in many scenarios, e.g., the IoT, allowing to communicate without someone being able to attribute the communication to its senders and recipients. Sender anonymity is a hard goal; the only viable option to achieve it is cover traffic which blends communication into noise. In turn, this noise degrades the system's efficiency rendering it unrealizable eventually. Moreover, cover traffic as a technique is hardly understood and analyzed. We perform a parameter study to analyze the influence of varying participation, utilization, and timing properties on anonymity and efficiency. Our results indicate that cover traffic can be generated more efficiently while anonymity is still on a reasonable level. Nonetheless, randomization of cover traffic allows performing intersection attacks to diminish anonymity in the long run.

1 Introduction

Communication is ubiquitous and an essential part of today's societies. With the emergence of the (IoT), communication is no longer bound to humans; it becomes a ubiquitous property of our environment, e.g., our connected homes and offices. Nowadays, even the communication itself leaks data, e.g., work patterns in the case of smart heatings. In such an environment, it is important to obfuscate the communication to provide anonymity as this information are interesting to various parties, e.g., burglars and the organized crime.

Anonymous communication systems, e.g., Tor [4], are usually distributed systems, following a (P2P) implementation. This way, the system gets rid of the central entity, which is a single point of access, allowing to access all data and aim to obfuscate the communication relationships by relaying messages. However, these anonymous communication systems are vulnerable to (near-) global adversaries being able to trace messages [6,8].

One of the goals of anonymous communication is to hide the communication's participants; thus, the act of sending and receiving a message is to be hidden, as well as the communication itself. In particular, sender anonymity tries to

© Springer International Publishing AG 2017
G. Livraga and C. Mitchell (Eds.): STM 2017, LNCS 10547, pp. 213–223, 2017.
DOI: 10.1007/978-3-319-68063-7_15

obfuscate the sender of a communication. Cover traffic (CT) is the only viable solution to achieve sender anonymity so far—all systems around, claiming to achieve sender anonymity [1,5,7], can be boiled down to a kind of CT. CT blends communication traffic in random messages ("noise"). For communication to be hidden from global adversaries, CT has to be pervasive, and all connections have to be utilized at all times. This utilization increases the communication cost, rendering these systems often unrealizable. In a worst case, $2 * (|E| - 1)$ cover messages are sent at each time step with E being the connections in the system.

With increasing connectivity of "smart" and heterogeneous devices, e.g., in the IoT, efficiency gains importance as the communication itself is expensive and accruing costs can render anonymous communication systems unrealizable. Nonetheless, simply removing parts of CT can have a strong impact on anonymity.

We aim to provide a general model for CT to improve understanding. For that, we identify four parameters for fine-grained adjustment of the CT generation. Using these, we control the participation of users and their connection's utilization, as well as their time-wise behavior. In an extensive simulation study, we evaluate the impact of changes in the CT generation behavior on the protection of anonymity and efficiency—and try to bring different CT settings up for discussion in the research community. The probability of participants generating CT has the largest influence on the trade-off between anonymity and efficiency. Time-wise behavior emphasizes the importance of node participation and helps to drastically improve efficiency, however, this comes with the drawback of adding a communication delay according to the time-wise configuration.

The remainder of this paper is structured as follows: we present background information and related work in Sect. 2. In Sect. 3, we introduce and discuss the four tuning parameters of cover traffic. In Sect. 4, we present insights in our simulation study and discuss our findings. Finally, we conclude our contributions and suggest directions for future research in Sect. 5.

2   Background and Related Work

In this section, we introduce the model of our communication system based on an overlay network. Overlay networks are a prime technology to facility large-scale many-to-many communication. The messaging paradigm publish/subscribe (pub/sub) can establish such overlays based on the message content; pub/sub is, therefore, well suited for IoT scenarios.

After that, we introduce the basic concept of CT and present relevant related work considering CT to protect anonymity.

2.1   Anonymous P2P-based Publish/Subscribe

The communication system can be formally represented by a graph $G = (V, E)$. The participants of the communication system are modeled by nodes $v_i \in V$, the participants' interconnectivity is represented by edges $E \subseteq V \times V$. In P2P publish/subscribe (pub/sub) systems, the participants take different roles. Information *sender* take the role of publishers $p \in \mathcal{P}$ and information *recipients* take the role of subscribers $s \in \mathcal{S}$. Additionally, all participants may relay messages to establish the communication, if participants are not directly connected to each other; these participants are brokers $b \in \mathcal{B}$. Roles are always taken over w.r.t. to a topic $t_m \in T$, that is, for example, a common interest, and comprise a communication *overlay* O_t. Thus, the overlay O_t can be modeled as subgraph $O_t = (V_t, E_t)$ of G, with $V_t = \mathcal{P}_t \cup \mathcal{S}_t \cup \mathcal{B}_t$ and E_t the induced set of connections.

Communication messages ("notifications") m_{not} are delivered using the established overlay O_t. Figure 1 visualizes a system with one overlay O_t (one publisher, node 4; four subscribers, nodes 1, 5, 8, and 9; two forwarders, nodes 2 and 6).

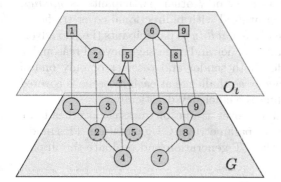

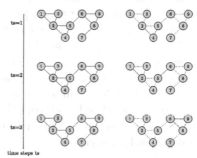

Fig. 1. P2P pub/sub system G with one overlay O_t, formed by one publisher (4), four subscribers (1, 5, 8, and 9), and two brokers (2 and 6)

Fig. 2. Application of CT (left) in comparison to a plain communication (right): idle connections (dotted) and utilized connections (red: comm. messages; blue: cover traffic) (Color figure online).

We present the time continuous system as enumerable snapshots in which a message travels one hop, i.e., from one neighbor to the next, in a single time step.

2.2 Cover Traffic

By definition, CT is designed to hide communication messages among random noise. An external adversary able to observe the message flow should not be able to discriminate communication messages from random noise messages m_{cover}.

For that, participants generate random-looking messages and send them over all their connections. In such a system, all communication messages are encrypted; thus, an adversary cannot distinguish between encrypted communication messages and a random cover message. We visualize this concept in Fig. 2:

a sender (4) disseminates a message to the recipients (1, 5, 8, and 9). On the left, the system is covering the dissemination with CT, on the right is no CT applied.

Two major systems using CT are Dai's PipeNet 1.1 [2] and Freedman's and Morris' Tarzan [5], however, both are implementing CT differently.

PipeNet is a conceptual system that establishes circuits, similar to onion routing, applying multi-layered encryption to provide anonymity for the communication source and intermediate brokers. To protect the anonymity in the system, all participants are utilizing all established connections at a constant rate. Intermediate nodes relay incoming messages in random order, stripping a layer of encryption, thwarting message tracing attacks.

Tarzan protects anonymity in a similar fashion, but participants do not emit cover traffic via all their neighbors; effectively reducing the overhead due to cover traffic. Each participant selects a set of k other participants as *mimics*, connections to these mimics are then utilized with bidirectional cover traffic.

CT-based systems provide *plausable deniability* to participants (i.e., no adversary is able to collect evidence to link a sender and a message beyond reasonable doubt), depending on the design for both sender and receiver or only one of them. Implementing CT raises efficiency as challenge as each message is covered by multiple cover messages, degrading the efficiency drastically.

To fully understand the impact of cover traffic on message overhead, we propose a generalized model of CT with parametrized CT generation. This model allows us to systematically variate the CT generation and evaluate the impact on costs and anonymity.

3　Parametrized Cover Traffic Model

CT protects anonymity by hiding communication messages in a continuous flow of cover messages m_{cover}. This setup also produces a possibly prohibitive amount of overhead. Each message is chaperoned by up to $2 * |E| - 1$ cover messages m_{cover}. Especially when considering large-scale communication with heterogeneous devices, e.g., WSNs, IoT, etc., CT can render the system unusable or even unrealizable. Simply removing *some* cover messages can have a negative or even disastrous impact on the anonymity of participants.

We propose a model for parametrized cover traffic handling that permits the reduction of cover traffic to understand the impact on efficiency and anonymity. For that, we derive four parameters controlling the creation of cover messages.

Node Participation Probability (npp). The intuition of *npp* enables the communication system to produce spotty CT, resembling actual communication happening in different groups within the system. Minimizing the *npp* parameter has a significant impact on the CT-load as less nodes are generating any cover messages. In each round, each node draws a random number to decide her involvement in CT.

Edge Participation Probability (epp). The intuition regarding *epp* is to enable the participants to partially utilize their connections instead of utilizing all incident connections with cover messages m_{cover}. This behavior relieves the message load on the nodes, especially highly connected ones, as they do not need to keep all connections utilized at all times. Note that this probability is only necessary if the participant decided to generate CT based on the above mentioned *npp*.

Time-wise Behavior (tb) and Relaying Probability (rp). Using the time-wise behavior parameter *tb*, the communication system introduces interval-based CT generation. Instead of generating CT with every time step, nodes employ CT only every n_{th} *time step* or even only *upon request*. Hereby, the overhead can be reduced additionally. Nonetheless, when CT is not generated with every time step, relayed messages are no longer covered—allowing an adversary to reduce the set of potential senders to the nodes with incident connection to the relaying node. Thus, we either need to delay the relaying of communication messages until the next batch of CT is generated or relay cover messages m_{cover} as well. The relaying behavior is controlled by the relay probability *rp*, allowing to forward cover messages m_{cover} to avoid additional time delay.

In request-based generation of CT, the requests have to be distributed in advance to allow nodes to generate appropriate cover. This distribution has to be hidden as well, e.g., by utilizing regular maintenance messages, otherwise, can the adversary track down the information sender by following the CT requests.

Adaption of Edge Participation Probabilities. When a node receives a communication message and forwards it while also generating CT, the activity of this node is (noticeably) larger as the activity of other nodes as she relays the "additional" message. To compensate this additional (forced) activity, we adapt the *epp* dynamically with $epp_{modified} = epp * e_i - /e_{i,t}e_i$ where e_i denotes incident connections of node v_i in the *system* and $e_{i,t}$ the incident connections in the *overlay* O_t (i.e., the connections being utilized with communication messages).

4   Evaluation

In this section, we first describe our parameter study providing the parameters and design decisions, the adversary models and discuss the scope and limitations of our evaluation. Next, we discuss our findings of the conducted parameter study with varied node and edge participation probabilities, timing behavior settings and relaying probabilities.

4.1   Parameter Study Setup

Parameter Study. We conducted a parameter study to gain insights into the "behavior" of CT under the influence of varying participation and timely behaviors.

Target systems of CT are P2P-based communication systems, thus revealing topologies with social structures according to the ties of the participants. Barabasi-Albert networks resemble those social structures. We generate 50 Barabasi-Albert networks with 1000 participants each. One information sender is randomly selected, 1.5% of participants are randomly selected to be information recipients.

We perform one simulation run on each of the 50 networks with 1,050 time steps, after 50 time steps we assume the communication overlay to be established. The communication overlays are established based on shortest paths; thus, the overlay is established in a worst case scenario with two times the diameter (10.265). After initialization, the information sender emits a message every 50 ± 3 time steps. The probabilities of CT generation, namely npp, epp, and rp are varied from $[0.0, 1.0]$ in steps of 0.1, the tb parameter is varied between 1, 10, and $request$. We summarize the complete parameter settings of our study in Table 1.

Table 1. Simulation details

Parameter	Instantiation	Parameter	Instantiation
Network	Barabasi-Albert	Node participation probability npp	$[0.0, 1.0]$ in 0.1 steps
Number of participants	1,000	Edge participation probability epp	$[0.0, 1.0]$ in 0.1 steps
Communication overlay	Avg. 15 recipients, 1 sender	Time-wise behavior tb	1, 10, request
Overlay establishment	Shortest path tree	Relay probability rp	$[0.0, 1.0]$ in 0.1 steps
Waiting time between publications	50 ± 3 time steps		

Adversary Model. We assume an adversary with the goal of identifying the information sender, i.e., an adversary that attempts to link a communication message to its initial sender. For that, the adversary is assumed to be *passive* and *global*, i.e., the adversary traces every message and tries to identify the sender of a message without interacting with the system. Moreover, the adversary can evaluate message flows over time, thus, can perform intersection attacks [9] evaluating the active nodes in multiple time steps trying to determine the sender.

Scope and Limits of our Evaluation. In our evaluation, we compute the number of *remaining cover nodes* at the end of our simulation, i.e., after 19 messages being sent; the second measure is the efficiency where we present the *noise to content ratio*, i.e., the number of cover messages m_{cover} over one content message. Additionally, we also analyze the *activity* of the sender, i.e., we count the number of sent messages and compare it remaining nodes in the system.

We are aware of more sophisticated adversaries, e.g., adversaries that can interact with the system by controlling one or multiple participants, and attack strategies, e.g., statistical disclosure attacks [3]. Nonetheless, we aim to provide basic understanding of CT, enabling subsequent analyses.

4.2 CT with Randomized Participation

In this section, we analyze CT with randomized participation in generating CT of system participants (node participation probability; npp) and randomized utilization of connections (edge participation probability; epp).

In this experiment, we performed the simulation repeatedly with varied npp and epp values from the interval $[0.0, 1.0]$ in 0.1 steps. Thus, we can compare all parameter combinations to derive reasonable parameter combinations.

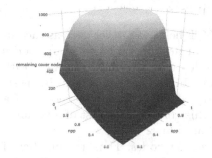
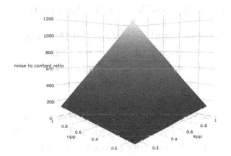

Fig. 3. Number of remaining covering nodes with randomized participation, varying npp and epp.

Fig. 4. The noise to content ratio with randomized participation, varying npp and epp.

The participation in introducing cover messages m_{cover} and the utilization of incident connections is visualized in Figs. 3 and 4. Figure 3 visualizes the impact of npp and epp on the number of remaining cover nodes, revealing that the number of remaining cover nodes stays stable for combinations down to $npp = 0.5$ and $epp = 0.4$, lower values result in a massive decrease in the number of remaining cover nodes. Figure 4 shows a near linear dependency of noise to content ratio and npp and epp respectively. We summarize key findings in Table 2 reporting the number of remaining cover nodes and noise to content ratio.

After fixing the epp to 0.3 which resembles a threshold for reasonable anonymity, we visualize the number of remaining covering nodes after each of the 19 communication messages in Fig. 5. With npp values between 1.0 and 0.6, the number of remaining cover nodes is kept at reasonable levels, with a npp of 0.5 the number of remaining cover nodes drops to below 50%; even lower npp values let the number of cover nodes even faster drop. Figure 5 suggests a threshold of npp at around 0.3–0.4. In this setup, the sender activity blends into the reasonable area between highly and averagely connected participants.

Table 2. Number of remaining cover nodes (RCN) and noise to content ratios (NCR) with varied *npp* and *epp* values

epp	npp	RCN	NCR	epp	npp	RCN	NCR	epp	npp	RCN	NCR	epp	npp	RCN	NCR
1.0	1.0	1000	1282	0.5	1.0	993	642	0.7	1.0	1000	898	0.2	1.0	718	257
	0.7	1000	898		0.7	921	449		0.7	991	629		0.7	510	180
	0.5	965	642		0.5	737	321		0.5	888	450		0.5	278	129
	0.2	67	257		0.2	26	129		0.2	42	180		0.2	6	52

The analysis of the 19 performed information dissemination processes also reveals that an adversary can perform an intersection attack [9] degrading the information sender's anonymity over time; the degradation speed depends on the parameters *npp* and *epp* but will remove covering nodes in the long run.

4.3 Time-Wise CT: Intervals and Requests

Adding timely-behavior to the generation of CT helps to further decrease accruing overhead due to cover messages m_{cover}. In an interval-based setup, nodes generate CT with pauses, assuming that nodes will not emit a message with every time step. Thus, we reduce the overhead by the interval-length. Request-based CT allows reducing the overhead further, as CT is only generated if a node wants to emit a message. Nonetheless, this comes at the cost of additional delay as the request for CT has to be distributed first.

Both settings reduce the activity of non-sender nodes. Thus, the number of remaining cover nodes decreases with each message being sent. We visualize this in Fig. 6 where the role of the *rp* is shown. The drop in anonymity, i.e., the drop in number of remaining cover nodes, is stronger than in the setting with randomized participation (visualized in Fig. 5).

For both interval- and request-based initialization, we perform our simulation. In addition to *npp* and *epp*, we also variate the *rp* parameter.

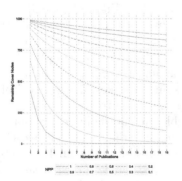

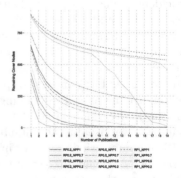

Fig. 5. The impact of *npp* on the number of remaining cover nodes in CT-applying communication with *epp* fixed to 0.3.

Fig. 6. The influence of varying relaying probability *rp* on preserving anonymity in timely delayed CT.

Interval-based Generation. The interval-size is set to 10 in our simulation. Thus, nodes are (depending on *npp* and *epp*) generating cover messages m_{cover} every 10th time step. When relaying all cover messages m_{cover} (i.e., setting $rp = 1.0$), the the results are similar to CT with randomized participation. Reducing *rp* increases the influence of *epp*'s setting: *rp* values ≥ 0.5 nearly remove the influence of *epp*, however, if $rp \leq 0.4$, the setting of *epp* gains importance as we have seen it in the setting of randomized participation.

In this interval-based setting, the parameters influencing anonymity and efficiency are *rp* and *epp*. *npp* loses importance as it is only evaluated in the first initialization step, after that, *rp* taking this role deciding whether cover messages m_{cover} are relayed or not.

Request-based Generation. The "extreme" setting of time-wise CT generation behavior avoids any generation of cover messages m_{cover} if not requested by a sender beforehand. Our simulations have shown that a waiting time of 23 time steps between the emission of CT-request and communication message is enough to spread the request far enough to generate a reasonable amount of CT. The results of this setting are then similar to those of the interval-based CT generation.

4.4 The Special Role of *rp*

Using the relaying probability *rp*, the probability of forwarding cover messages m_{cover} can be adjusted. As this is the important probability for covering the dissemination of communication messages, we also investigated the influence of *rp* on the number of remaining cover nodes and the ratio of noise to content.

As visualized in Fig. 6, lowering the relaying probability *rp* has a significant impact on the number of remaining cover nodes. The massive drop in the $rp = 1.0, npp = 0.2$ setting is known from the randomized setting: it is caused by falling below the threshold of $npp = 0.3$ where too few participants generate CT. While keeping three levels of *npp*, the same levels (1.0, 0.5, 0.2) on *rp* has a clear impact, forming three result-"bunches" in the plot.

4.5 Summary

Node participation is the most important parameter. Thus, anonymity and efficiency are mostly controlled by *npp* (and by *rp* in the time-depending scenarios).

Adjusting the node participation allows improving the efficiency by 50% while keeping 95% of cover nodes of. Another improvement of efficiency is yield by the usage of time-depending CT. Both interval-based and request-based generation reduce the overhead drastically at the cost of additional delay. Request-based CT requires additional time between request and message emission as requests have to be distributed upfront.

The randomization of participation enables an adversary to launch an intersection attack [3] diminishing anonymity on the long run—depending on the actual probabilities, the adversary can be able to remove 50% of cover nodes with around 3–5 messages emitted by the sender.

5   Conclusion

In this paper, we analyzed methods to reduce the overhead induced by CT. We identified four parameters controlling the generation of CT to protect anonymity; namely the participation and connection utilization probability, the time-wise behavior and the relaying probability.

We conducted an extensive parameter study, to understand the influence of the derived parameters on anonymity and efficiency. We identified that the node participation probability, which is comprised of the actual node participation probability and relaying probability in the case of time-dependent CT, is the most influencing parameter determining achievable anonymity and efficiency. The influence of connection utilization, i.e., the edge participation probability, is heavily depending on the setting of node participation probabilities. An efficiency improvement of 50% can be reached while maintaining the number of cover nodes at a level of about 95%. Time-depending CT generation is another possibility to reduce the messaging overhead that is imposed by covering communication. In time-depending settings, it is important to relay CT to ensure continuous protection. Additionally, if generating CT on request, the requests have to be distributed $\approx$23 time steps before the actual communication message is sent. Nonetheless, as we are randomizing the participation in CT, an adversary can launch an intersection attack diminishing anonymity in the long run.

In future work, we plan to utilize the findings of this paper to initialize CT in a controlled way to further reduce the overhead while keeping anonymity at a reasonable level.

Acknowledgements. This work has been co-funded by the DFG as part of projects B.2, D.4 within the RTG 2050 "Privacy and Trust for Mobile Users" and by the German Federal Ministry for Education and Research (BMBF, Software Campus project KomBi, grant no. 01IS12054).

References

1. Berthold, O., Federrath, H., Köpsell, S.: Web MIXes: a system for anonymous and unobservable internet access. In: Federrath, H. (ed.) Designing Privacy Enhancing Technologies. LNCS, vol. 2009, pp. 115–129. Springer, Heidelberg (2001). doi:10.1007/3-540-44702-4_7
2. Dai, W.: PipeNet (1998). https://cryptome.org/jya/pipenet.htm
3. Danezis, G., Serjantov, A.: Statistical disclosure or intersection attacks on anonymity systems. In: Fridrich, J. (ed.) IH 2004. LNCS, vol. 3200, pp. 293–308. Springer, Heidelberg (2004). doi:10.1007/978-3-540-30114-1_21
4. Dingledine, R., Mathewson, N., Syverson, P.: Tor: the second-generation onion router. In: SSYM 2004 (2004)
5. Freedman, M.J., Morris, R.: Tarzan: a peer-to-peer anonymizing network layer. In: CCS (2002)
6. Greenwald, G.: XKeyscore: NSA tool collects' nearly everything a user does on the internet' (2013). https://www.theguardian.com/world/2013/jul/31/nsa-top-secret-program-online-data

7. van den Hooff, J., Lazar, D., Zaharia, M., Zeldovich, N.: Vuvuzela: scalable private messaging resistant to traffic analysis. In: SOSP 2015 (2015)
8. MacAskill, E., Borger, J., Hopkins, N., Davies, N., Ball, J.: GCHQ taps fibre-optic cables for secret access to world's communications (2013). https://www.theguardian.com/uk/2013/jun/21/gchq-cables-secret-world-communications-nsa
9. Raymond, J.-F.: Traffic analysis: protocols, attacks, design issues, and open problems. In: Federrath, H. (ed.) Designing Privacy Enhancing Technologies. LNCS, vol. 2009, pp. 10–29. Springer, Heidelberg (2001). doi:10.1007/3-540-44702-4_2

Quantitative Analysis of DoS Attacks and Client Puzzles in IoT Systems

Luca Arnaboldi[✉] and Charles Morisset

School of Computing, Newcastle University, Newcastle upon Tyne, UK
{l.arnaboldi,charles.morisset}@ncl.ac.uk

Abstract. Denial of Service (DoS) attacks constitute a major security threat to today's Internet. This challenge is especially pertinent to the Internet of Things (IoT) as devices have less computing power, memory and security mechanisms to mitigate DoS attacks. This paper presents a model that mimics the unique characteristics of a network of IoT devices, including components of the system implementing 'Crypto Puzzles' - a DoS mitigation technique. We created an imitation of a DoS attack on the system, and conducted a quantitative analysis to simulate the impact such an attack may potentially exert upon the system, assessing the trade off between security and throughput in the IoT system. We model this through stochastic model checking in PRISM and provide evidence that supports this as a valuable method to compare the efficiency of different implementations of IoT systems, exemplified by a case study.

1 Introduction

A DoS attack targets the availability of a device or network [9], with the intent of disrupting system usability. The most common method is referred to as Flooding DoS [10], and may be used as an attempt to deplete the devices' resources including memory, bandwidth and/or battery. A DoS attack against an IoT network has the potential to be significantly more detrimental than one against a standard network. This increased vulnerability is due in part to the low computational power and battery power characteristic of IoT devices [13].

The extant literature has delineated several potential approaches that may be effective in the mitigation of a DoS attack [14]. This paper focuses on one such method, known as "Client Crypto Puzzles" [2], one of the most common mitigation techniques. We evaluate the probability of the system (or subsystem) being denied within a specific time frame in an IoT network. Using our proposed model we are able to assess properties such as: (i) At what point is the mitigation technique doing more harm than good? (ii) How does denial of a single device impact functionality of the entire system? (iii) Does it create a snowball effect?

Client puzzles take many forms, but the general purpose is to force the sender to perform a computationally intensive task prior to authentication, consequently reducing their ability to spam messages [2]. Client puzzles have been adapted in IoT systems [7] and have been shown to successfully decrease effectiveness of a DoS attack. It is however of high computational intensiveness.

© Springer International Publishing AG 2017
G. Livraga and C. Mitchell (Eds.): STM 2017, LNCS 10547, pp. 224–233, 2017.
DOI: 10.1007/978-3-319-68063-7_16

In the specific context of IoT, an additional consideration is that a client puzzle (especially one of high complexity) can place strain on the battery, causing high delays in throughput whilst a client is occupied with solving the client puzzles. If the puzzle drains battery at a rate equivalent (or more) than a flooding attack, the increased security may actually harm the system. In this paper we model the tradeoff between security and throughput in addition to the impact the increase in computation has on a device's battery life span. It is also the particular case where in the scope of the IoT one device being denied will not harm the system as one device may be performing an inconsequential or very small task. We model this through the connectivity of devices. We can observe the potential snowball effect of a system as the denial of one particular device will increase the probability that other devices are also going down. Through the model we can observe the scenario where DoS mitigation, throughput and decrease in battery are at optimal balance to obtain the best possible result in all three cases. From this, we may model the ideal setup given specific number of devices, connectivity of the devices and DoS strain. In particular we demonstrate that in some cases mitigation techniques can actually increase the likelihood of a DoS, due to drainage of battery.

The aim of this research is to quantify the potential impact of a DoS attack on a multi protocol network within the IoT and to gauge how a potential mitigation method affects performance. The key contributions include:

1. A model of two types of IoT device networks, one with DoS mitigation in place and one without.
2. Verification and simulation of these networks to investigate trade-off between security and throughput under a DoS attack.

The remainder of this paper is divided into the following sections; Sect. 2 - discusses other work concerned with quantifying impact of DoS and the IoT; Sect. 3 - describes our model; Sect. 4 - details our analysis technique; Sect. 5 - outlines the setup for our experiments; Sect. 6 - highlights findings and results; and Sect. 7 concludes the paper, summarising our contribution and ongoing work.

2   Related Work

Since their advent, systems security properties have been modeled and verified using a variety of tools including probabilistic model checking. Analysis of DoS mitigation techniques has been widely covered, Tritilanunt et al. [15] used colored petri net to verify the effectiveness of HiP client puzzles for DoS mitigation. They mainly used simulation under different scenarios of possible DoS attacks and proposed techniques to predict DoS attacks in advance.

Similarly Basagiannis et al. [5] also looked at HIP, making use of verification techniques. They used probabilistic model checker PRISM, introducing a probabilistic attacker model to analyze the effectiveness of HIP and created different attack paths to break the DoS mitigation technique. Their work focuses on a single complete exchange between an initiator and respondent, creating a Dolev-Yao-like attacker.

Several papers address modeling IoT, adopting various different approaches. Authors of [3,12] have worked on modeling a specific IoT protocol on the transport layer, looking at MQTT and CoAP respectively. Fruth [6] examines various properties of a Wireless Network protocol including connectivity and energy power through PRISM, and evaluates it on a Wireless Sensor Network System. The author evaluates the battery drainage of certain randomized protocols.

Throughput vs security is a common research question in analysis network. Abdelhakim et al. [1] present work on this particular topic in the context of wireless sensor networks. Their paper introduces a concept of security routing, optimized with throughput to present optimum routing.

An abundance of research exists on effectiveness of client puzzles and throughput vs security. However when we have devices actually going down due to battery strain we observe a phenomenon of snowball effect, and as a consequence the manner in which we implement the network needs to change. To the best of our knowledge we are the first to combine concepts of IoT Systems, restricted resources of IoT devices and DoS attacks in a probabilistic model checking environment.

3   Model for IoT Devices

To implement the model we made use of PRISM Model Checker [8] and Continuous Time Markov Chains (CTMC) to abstract systems of IoT devices. The PRISM tool also allows use of statistical model checking, a technique which is particularly effective since modeling multiple devices exacerbate the state space immensely. We ran a series of experiments using different parameters, including DoS attacks against different device setups and different parts of the network. The choice to use CTMC was due to their stochastic properties and the fact that events occur spontaneously, resulting in a wider range of scenarios. A DoS attack is unstoppable given enough time and resource sand as such we deemed time to be a key factor in our analysis. To calculate the likelihood of specific scenarios taking place we use the PRISM verification tools and Probabilistic Computational Tree (PCTL). PCTL is a probabilistic extension to Computational Tree Logic [4] and provides means to evaluate behavior of the system. The model abstracts an IoT network under DoS strain, and it is implemented as a system of *devices*.

A device is a sensor connected to the internet with its own power supply. A key aspect of the IoT is that different devices might have different battery lives and different security features (in this paper, we focus on whether a device is implementing a DoS mitigation technique). Hence, we consider the following device properties: a battery life, a message queue and connectivity (what other devices it can connect to). Battery life is a measure that is drained whenever a computationally intensive operation takes place such as sending a message and computing a client puzzle. A device can only hold a limited number of messages, and after the queue reaches capacity it cannot receive more until it has replied with acknowledgments. If a recipient device queue is full the initiator waits until it either frees up or timeouts and then resends. To model connectivity each device has a set of other devices it can communicate with and receive messages from. To implement the concept of processing time we implemented arbitrary delays when processing client puzzles.

We introduce the concept of "gentlemen devices" and "rude devices". A gentleman device will utilize "politeness", i.e. they will send a message and wait for an acknowledgment (or timeout if acknowledgment takes too long) from the recipient and conclude his current discussion with the device before initiating another message exchange with the same device. It can however simultaneously hold exchanges with other devices. Rude devices on the other hand may continue sending messages to devices within their connectivity before the full communication is over, replicating a flooding attack. The effects of these rude devices flooding spreads as even gentleman devices connected to the flooded device will not be able to commence an exchange if its message queue is full.

The attacker or rude device can have different rates of attack, mimicking different strengths of a DoS attack. We assume it sits outside the network and is not part of the connectivity so it can target any node, but gentleman devices cannot perform an exchange with it. To further simulate the attack strength, at each attack a proportional amount of battery is drained depending on the attack's intensity (rate). We use stochastic probabilities to target random parts of the system as we assume an attacker has no knowledge of the system setup. Due to the connectivity element an attack on one part of the system may exert a higher impact than an attack on another part e.g. If devices B and C only communicate with A, the denial of A stalls the whole system whilst the denial of B still allows the system to function.

Formally, a rude device R is a tuple $R = (S, s_{init}, A, R, L)$, where $S = \{idle, active\}$ is a set of states, $s_{init} = idle$ is the initial state, $A = \{msg, ack\}$ is a set of actions, R is a matrix containing the rates at which any of the actions are performed, e.g., $\left(\begin{smallmatrix} 0 & 1 \\ 1 & 0 \end{smallmatrix}\right)$ shows there is a rate of 0 to go from $idle$ to $idle$, a rate of 1 to go from $idle$ to $active$, a rate of 1 to go from $active$ to $idle$ and a rate of 0 to go from $active$ to $active$, finally L is an atomic proposition defined as guard ⟩ action where the guard must be true in order for the action to take place and take the attacker into the next state.

The behavior of a rude device is defined as follows: if the device is in state $idle$, there is a probability to move to the state $active$; if the device is in state $active$, the attacker chooses a random node in the network and starts flooding it. If that particular part of the network has mitigation technique in place at each message it has to solve the crypto hash before sending again. The attack continues until the devices battery has been drained. The attacker then goes back to idle. The guard is used to make sure the attacker behaves within the scope of the model. The first atomic proposition assures that the attacker does not target multiple parts of the network simultaneously and then switches to active and the second guard follows the steps to fill the message queue and drain the battery.

The other nodes in the network or gentleman devices may either have DoS mitigation techniques or not. A gentleman device G is formally defined as $G = (S, s_{init}, A, R, L)$, where $S = \{idle, sending, receiving\}$ is a set states, $s_{init} = idle$ is the initial state, $A = \{msg, ack, challenge\}$ is a set of actions, R is a matrix containing the rates at which any of the actions are performed, e.g., $\left(\begin{smallmatrix} 0 & 1 & 1 \\ 1 & 0 & 0 \\ 1 & 0 & 0 \end{smallmatrix}\right)$ shows there is a rate of 0 to go from $idle$ to $idle$, a rate of 1 to go from $idle$ to $sending$ as well as a rate of 1 to go to $receiving$, a rate of 1 to go from $receiving$ to $idle$ and a rate of 1 to go from $sending$ to $idle$, and L is an atomic proposition defined as guard → action, there are guards to enable the correct behavior of message exchange (e.g. $idle$, A to B, B to (ACK) A, $idle$).

The behavior of a gentleman device without mitigation technique is as follows: when $idle$, G is active and has a chance to begin a communication between any of his connected devices. From idle it can transition to any of two other states $sending$ and $receiving$. If $sending$, G sends a message to a connected device and the battery is drained, it then initiates a timer, if the acknowledgment is not received before the timer runs out the device goes back to $idle$ however the reset drains the battery, if it is received it finishes the exchange and also resets to $idle$. If $receiving$, the message is added to the queue and the initiator is noted as to direct the ACKs to the right initiator (multiple messages may be received at the same time). The acknowledgment is then sent and the device is reset to $idle$ and the queue is decreased. To implement a device with mitigation techniques, we add the following properties to a gentleman device; if in state $receiving$ before it can send the acknowledgment to a initiator with client puzzles there is a time delay to portray the time it would take to solve a puzzle. The time delay increases when the size of K increases, as it mimics how a harder puzzle is more difficult to resolve. We refer the reader to [2] for some examples of client puzzles.

4   Verification

To test our model we ran a variety of experiments with different systems and security setups. One of the key aspects of our experiment was how the impact of the DoS attacks scaled with different attack rates, different setups and how it effected the throughput and security to investigate the viability of these mitigation techniques in the context of the IoT. The ideal scenario is when the probability of being denied within time T is low and the throughput after T seconds is high. Observing these circumstances in finite systems where there is a set number of devices, we looked at all possible setups the system could take in terms of how many devices are protected and by what level of client puzzles, and then tested them under different DoS strains. Using the result we can tell which setup is the best suited to a particular rate of DoS and which setup will maximize throughput and security. We theorized that given the circumstances of the IoT and the relatively high processing times at certain levels of puzzle difficulty it would be the case that the lowering in chance of denial would not be as significant as the corresponding lowering in throughput caused by the processing delays, this is analyzed in the case study provided in Sect. 6.1.

We made use of statistical model checking when examining the larger models through PRISM's simulation engine. This approach is particularly useful on very large models when normal model checking is infeasible. Essentially, this is achieved by sampling: generating a large number of random paths through the model, evaluating the result of the given properties on each run, and using this information to generate an approximately correct result within a specific Confidence Interval (CI). Let X denote the true result of the query $P = ?[...]$ and Y the approximation generated. The confidence interval is $[Y - w, Y + w]$, i.e. w gives the half-width of the interval. The confidence level, which is usually stated as a percentage, is $100(1 - Confidence)\%$. This means that the actual value X should fall into the confidence interval $[Y - w, Y + w]100(1 - Confidence)\%$ of the time [11]. We tested for the following properties.

Throughput: The number of messages processed over a given time interval (cumulative messages sent/current time). By definition if a message takes longer to send the throughput will decrease, hence adding computationally intensive tasks that delay the transmittance of messages is going to decrease the systems throughput. However if they delay the likelihood of devices being taken down by an attacker the theory is that in the long run it will actually increase the throughput under DoS attacks. To calculate the throughput of the IoT system we make use of PCTL formula $R\{Msg\_sent\} = ?[C <= T]$ or what is the cumulative total messages sent by the system in time T and then divide the answer by the value T. The value Msg_sent is a reward structure that assigns one reward every time a successful message exchange is completed.

Likelihood of System being Denied: We defined the denial of a device, when either its battery has been completely drained or its connected devices have been drained and it therefore cannot transfer from the *idle* state. The whole system is down when all devices have been *denied*. This is once again monitored through PCTL over a restricted time, running different variables one can optimize the number of protected devices as well a what strength of protection to optimize the implementation least likely to be denied.

Snowball effect due to denial of further interest is the ability to recognize the *critical* sectors of a system. We defined a *critical* sector by examining the impact it's denial has on the rest of the system. Highly critical sectors are also the parts of the system which require more securing. We achieve this by measuring the *snowball effect* or rather after the denial of device A what is the new probability of the rest of the system being down. Theoretically highly *critical* devices will increase the probability substantially whilst non *critical* devices will make a small difference.

To observe the best case scenario of a particular setup, we define a setup as a particular spread and strength of mitigation techniques on a given configuration of devices. We observe the balance between security and throughput, the higher the ratio the better the setup for that particular DoS strength. To observe and test the initial hypothesis in Sect. 6.1 we create a case study on a specific scenario and evaluate the results for each possible implementation given specific assumptions.

5   Experiment Setup

We have used the model described above in PRISM Model Checker as well as PCTL to perform both quantitative verification and simulations, various properties where checked and the model was tested under different scenarios. For verification the full state space is explored whilst for simulation we use the following setup. **Number of Samples:** 100,000, **CI:** 0.001 and **Maximum Path Length:** 1,000,000. For the purpose of the model we were interested in evaluating two key properties: throughput and probability of denial.

We can also examine which part of the subnetwork has been denied first and specifically the time required for the denial to take place. The setup for each experiment was: **Client Puzzle Difficulties (K size):** 5 to 20 s, **Time of system (Seconds):** 20 to 200 s, **Devices in Network (All protected):** 9 and **Rude Devices:** 1. This differentiated from the case study where all the variables were tested in all possible setups (with some specifications explained in Sect. 6.1) to find the optimal setup.

Results from the initial setup highlight the key factors of our model (i) the way client puzzles drain battery (ii) the effectiveness of mitigation techniques to avoid denial of service and (iii) demonstrating that in finite time it can sometimes be useful to have a less intensive client puzzle as they can disrupt more than help.

6   Results

We demonstrated the potential strain that client puzzles place on a system and as can be seen in Fig. 1 at lower times (i.e. before any part of the systems are under DoS or haven't gone down yet), the higher client puzzles create such a strain that they increase the likelihood of going down rather than diminish it.

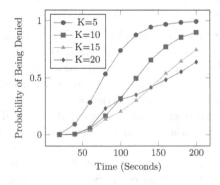 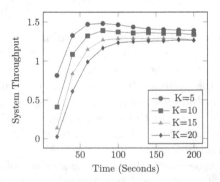

Fig. 1. The graphs represents a system being targeted by a DoS attack, the one on the left displays the probability of a DoS attack being successful over time (20 s to 200 s). The graph on the right represents the throughput of the system over time (20 s to 200 s).

It can be observed that the harder the puzzle, the lower the throughput, whilst the security is increased. Furthermore, due to the extra drainage in power of the more difficult puzzle, a smaller value of K performs better in earlier times (At time 80 s we observe that K = 20 has a higher denial probability than K = 15 this is due to the extra processing strain and battery drainage of the harder puzzle). As can be observed towards time 200 s the throughputs come to a stall as different parts of the system are denied. It is to be noted that as the lower puzzle difficulties are declining in throughput, K = 20 is on the rise, as the increase in security allows for some nodes to still output messages.

6.1 Case Study

We apply our model to a specific scenario to demonstrate its application. We assume a potential system engineer views their IoT network as under constant DoS attack. They wishes to know what would be the best way to optimize the balance between throughput of their system and the likelihood of being denied when implementing security mitigation for these DoS attacks. Furthermore, their IoT system is collecting very critical data in a short time frame so it is important for the system to work at its best for the initial 100 s. The setup is the following; A is connected to B, B is connected to A, C is connected to A, B and C, and D is connected to C. We also assume a rude device E, which is connected to all devices.

We ran every single scenario of setups (A protected, AB protected, B protected...) and for each scenario tried every single possible value of K. We set the value of Battery to be 50, a maximum message queue of 5, Time at 100 s, a single rude Device (E) with rate of attack the same as the rate of any gentleman device (ABCD) and the values of K from 5 to 15 tested on every protected device, the results can be observed in Table 1. If we use our formula of throughput/probability of denial, with the highest value being the most optimal result. We see that the scenario AD provided the best ratio at every different value of K, with scenarios including C being connected (the one with the most connectivity) not performing as well.

The results support our initial hypothesis that mitigation techniques actually increase the likelihood of denial through battery drainage alone. This is evidenced by the scenarios which had C protected that proved to be the most inefficient (throughput dropped significantly). The rude devices have an equal chance of attacking as the gentleman devices. As a consequence, since every single connection to a protected device will drain the battery and since there is equal chance a rude device will start an attack, the strain on the battery caused by normal message sending (and computing of puzzles) is more detrimental. However if we take ACD which theoretically protects the network on all levels and D which is not very connected and test both these two under a longer period of time (200 s) we can see the results are altered, as the attackers will continue until a device is denied. On the other hand, if it takes longer to take down a device, the overall system lasts longer and therefore the throughput is higher with the protected devices. We also show that identifying single *critical* devices

Table 1. Every scenarios for each setup of protected devices (PD) and unprotected devices (UD), each setup has a single rude device E targeting the other gentlemen devices

PD	UD	K = 5		K = 10		K = 15	
		Probability	Throughput	Probability	Throughput	Probability	Throughput
A	BCD	0.655	0.733353	0.712	0.713375	0.729	0.726894
AB	CD	0.624	0.654857	0.645	0.636341	0.829	0.646891
ABC	D	0.887	0.684555	0.963	0.580316	0.996	0.513519
ACD	B	0.956	0.547798	0.986	0.346246	0.997	0.241135
ADB	C	0.946	0.423408	0.951	0.309469	0.972	0.267136
AC	BD	0.964	0.772681	0.979	0.662404	0.98x8	0.582111
AD	CB	0.461	0.739893	0.415	0.690475	0.381	0.687251
B	ACD	0.496	0.741337	0.487	0.723239	0.465	0.717923
BC	AD	0.817	0.713618	0.899	0.617848	0.959	0.547188
BCD	A	0.938	0.520275	0.968	0.3279814	0.985	0.228197
BD	AC	0.927	0.454418	0.927	0.362362	0.954	0.313664
C	ABD	0.901	0.843735	0.91	0.72117	0.959	0.663217
CD	AB	0.897	0.555124	0.919	0.38078	0.939	0.279741
D	ABC	0.859	0.610293	0.878	0.536433	0.862	0.535952

and protecting them rather than the whole system can be a valuable technique. These results exemplify the potential application and benefit of these techniques.

As can be expected one simple solution to increase both the throughput and the security is to increase device battery or upgrade processing power. An alternative solution may be to replace the *critical* devices with more potent ones. However assuming the device specifications are constant and the only customization is the strength of the puzzles and which devices to protect, through our tool we are able to identify what produces the best results. The topic of battery adds a further layer to the common question of security vs output and creates several additional layers of complexity. What we have gathered from our analysis and results is in line with our initial hypothesis. Furthermore, this model enables the discovery of *critical* sections in an IoT system which might not be as easy to find compared to our simplified case study.

7   Conclusion

We have presented a model that provides means to quantify the effectiveness of a DoS threat on a potential IoT system. Our methodology enables for a potential user to make informed decisions regarding the potential implementation of their system. By using a combination of verification and simulation we confirmed the hypothesis that for the usage in IoT some mitigation techniques could potentially cause harm, however thanks to this tool, one can now make sure to maximize their systems effectiveness. Our future work will look into applying this model to a real world implementation to evaluate the effectiveness of the analysis. We also intend to evaluate different mitigation techniques and specific IoT protocols. Further experimentation could also assess different kinds of IoT devices. We have used the term IoT node to represent a low powered device. However further tests could also examine the best kind of device for balancing their processing power against effectiveness.

References

1. Abdelhakim, M., Ren, J., Li, T.: Throughput analysis and routing security discussions of mobile access coordinated wireless sensor networks. In: 2014 IEEE Global Communications Conference (GLOBECOM), pp. 4616 4621. IEEE (2014)
2. Aura, T., Nikander, P., Leiwo, J.: DOS-resistant authentication with client puzzles. In: Christianson, B., Malcolm, J.A., Crispo, B., Roe, M. (eds.) Security Protocols 2000. LNCS, vol. 2133, pp. 170–177. Springer, Heidelberg (2001). doi:10.1007/3-540-44810-1_22
3. Aziz, B.: A formal model and analysis of an IoT protocol. Ad Hoc Netw. **36**, 49–57 (2016)
4. Baier, C., Katoen, J.P., Larsen, K.G.: Principles of Model Checking. MIT press, Cambridge (2008)
5. Basagiannis, S., Katsaros, P., Pombortsis, A., Alexiou, N.: Probabilistic model checking for the quantification of DoS security threats. Comput. Secur. **28**(6), 450–465 (2009). http://www.sciencedirect.com/science/article/pii/S0167404809000042
6. Fruth, M.: Formal methods for the analysis of wireless network protocols. Oxford University (2011)
7. Hummen, R., Wirtz, H., Ziegeldorf, J.H., Hiller, J., Wehrle, K.: Tailoring end-to-end IP security protocols to the internet of things. In: 2013 21st IEEE International Conference on Network Protocols (ICNP), pp. 1 10, October 2013
8. Kwiatkowska, M., Norman, G., Parker, D.: PRISM: probabilistic symbolic model checker. In: Field, T., Harrison, P.G., Bradley, J., Harder, U. (eds.) TOOLS 2002. LNCS, vol. 2324, pp. 200–204. Springer, Heidelberg (2002). doi:10.1007/3-540-46029-2_13
9. Long, N., Thomas, R.: Trends in denial of service attack technology. CERT Coordination Center (2001)
10. Mirkovic, J., Dietrich, S., Dittrich, D., Reiher, P.: Internet Denial of Service: Attack and Defense Mechanisms (Radia Perlman Computer Networking and Security). Prentice Hall PTR, Upper Saddle River (2004)
11. Nimal, V.: Statistical approaches for probabilistic model checking. Ph.D. thesis, University of Oxford (2010)
12. Kumar, G.S.: Modelling and verification of CoAP over routing layer using spin model checker (2016)
13. Suo, H., Wan, J., Zou, C., Liu, J.: Security in the internet of things: a review. In: 2012 International Conference on Computer Science and Electronics Engineering (ICCSEE), vol. 3, pp. 648–651. IEEE (2012)
14. Talpade, R., Madhani, S., Mouchtaris, P., Wong, L.: Mitigating denial of service attacks. US Patent Ap. 10/353,527, 29 Jan 2003
15. Tritilanunt, S., Boyd, C., Foo, E., Nieto, J.M.G.: Examining the DoS resistance of HIP. In: Meersman, R., Tari, Z., Herrero, P. (eds.) OTM 2006. LNCS, vol. 4277, pp. 616–625. Springer, Heidelberg (2006). doi:10.1007/11915034_85

Author Index

Printed in the United States
By Bookmasters